D1594539

Pipeline Politics

Cornell Studies in Political Economy

EDITED BY PETER J. KATZENSTEIN

Pipeline Politics

THE COMPLEX POLITICAL ECONOMY
OF EAST–WEST ENERGY TRADE

BRUCE W. JENTLESON

CORNELL UNIVERSITY PRESS

Ithaca and London

Copyright © 1986 by Cornell University

First published 1986 by Cornell University Press.

International Standard Book Number 0-8014-1923-9
Library of Congress Catalog Card Number 86-47643
Printed in the United States of America
Librarians: Library of Congress cataloging information
appears on the last page of the book.

The paper in this book is acid-free and meets the guidelines for
permanence and durability of the Committee on Production Guidelines
for Book Longevity of the Council on Library Resources.

To my parents,
and to Barbara

Contents

Tables

9

Preface

This book has three principal objectives (and thus, I hope, three principal values to its readers). Its primary objective is to examine an important issue in American foreign policy: should the United States and its NATO allies trade with the Soviet Union, and if so, in which economic sectors and under what conditions? Since the mid-1950s, trade in the energy sector—that is, the West's imports of Soviet oil and natural gas and its exports of energy-related equipment and technology to the Soviet Union—has been especially controversial. The complexities of this issue were underlined rather dramatically by the controversy surrounding the Siberian natural gas pipeline of 1981–82. But as this book shows, by then the issue of East–West energy trade already had a long history. A similar dispute had simmered in the 1950s and surfaced in the 1960s. Then in the 1970s, as a function of both the world energy crisis and the rise and demise of détente, East–West energy trade took on even greater importance and became even more controversial. And while the Siberian gas pipeline issue itself subsided, the basic questions it posed are likely to continue to be of central importance to American foreign policy for the foreseeable future.

Second, and at a more analytic level, this book bears upon two of political science's most fundamental questions: What constitutes power? and How is influence achieved? Stripped to its basics, East–West trade in energy and its technology is a case of one nation-state attempting to wield its power to influence another. In this respect its implications proceed outward in a series of concentric circles, first to East–West trade in other sectors, then to other cases of international economic sanctions, and ultimately to a more general concern with power and influence in international relations. I do not at all claim that the lessons of this case are totally generalizable (a point discussed in more detail in Chapters 1 and 7), but I do believe that the findings presented here, and especially the framework I develop for analyzing the variables that affect the exercise of economic coercive power, have significance beyond the case of the Siberian pipeline.

Finally, this book attempts to fill a void in the body of literature now commonly categorized as international political economy. In my view the two most important developments in the scholarship of international relations in the 1970s were the rediscovery of the interrelationship of politics and economics ("political economy" is a nineteenth-century term) and the growing recognition of the interaction of the international and domestic levels of analysis. Most of the work that has been done along these lines, however, has focused on West–West or North–South relations. Almost by default East–West issues have remained largely the province of more traditional "realist" approaches. Yet East–West issues are sufficiently complex to require conceptualization in political economy terms. Such an exercise not only improves our understanding of East–West relations but also contributes to the development of more general theories of international political economy.

Chapter 1 sets forth the conceptual framework for my analysis of the politics of East–West energy trade. Chapter 2 examines East–West trade generally in the early Cold War period (1945–53), makes an initial application of the analytic framework developed in Chapter 1, and assesses the impact of sanctions on the Soviet Union during this period. Chapter 3 focuses on the first period of growing East–West energy trade in the mid-1950s. Chapter 4 analyzes the 1962–63 oil trade sanctions, their multidimensional politics, and their policy consequences. Chapter 5 discusses the development of East–West trade in oil and (increasingly) natural gas in the 1970s. Chapter 6 takes a detailed look at the Western alliance and American domestic politics of the Reagan administration's sanctions against the Siberian natural gas pipeline and the relationship between their intended and actual consequences. The concluding chapter reassesses the arguments put forward in Chapter 1 in light of the evidence provided in the intervening chapters and offers some final thoughts on the theoretical as well as the policy implications of the East–West energy trade issue.

Many people have contributed in many ways to my work on this book. I am privileged to have had the guidance of Theodore Lowi, Walter LaFeber, and Arch Dotson, whose criticism, ideas, and examples have been of immense value to me. I especially want to thank

Peter Katzenstein, who in so many ways has stimulated my intellectual growth and development. I also thank Ariel Levite for cheerfully serving as a sounding board for my ideas.

My work at Cornell University was supported by a fellowship from the Institute for the Study of World Politics. I have since received generous financial support from Junior Faculty Research Fellowships and Faculty Development Grants of the University of California, Davis, from the UC Davis Institute on Governmental Affairs, from the University of California Institute on Global Conflict and Cooperation, and from the American Council of Learned Societies. My department chairman, Randolph Siverson, has been especially supportive of my work. My colleagues Larry Berman, Alexander Groth, and Donald Rothchild offered useful critiques of parts of earlier versions of the manuscript, as have Gary Bertsch of the University of Georgia and three anonymous reviewers for Cornell University Press. At the Press, Walter Lippincott and Peter Agree were very helpful and supportive, and Barbara Salazar was a thoughtful and thorough editor.

Thanks also to my research assistants, Valerie Wiswell and Yu Yee, and to Paul Surovell, whose *Interflo* greatly facilitated our research. Jill Warner, Gertrude Fitzpatrick, Brenda Petersen, and Eunice Carlson all were conscientious typists and patient with my penchant for "one more" set of revisions. I also thank Charlyn Fishman, who assisted with the index, and Micki Eagle, who helped with the proofreading and in a number of other ways.

Finally, I am especially grateful to my son, Adam, who got to hear quite a bit about East–West energy trade on those cold nights in Ithaca; to my daughter, Kate, who has received her dosage more recently; and to my parents, Ted and Elaine, and my wife and friend, Barbara, whose roles in any success that I may achieve should not be underestimated and are never unappreciated, and to whom this book is dedicated.

Portions of this book have been adapted from three of my recent articles in *Will Europe Fight for Oil?*, edited by Robert J. Lieber (New York: Praeger, 1983); *International Organization* (Autumn 1984); and *Millennium: Journal of International Studies* (Spring 1986).

Bruce W. Jentleson

Davis, California

Abbreviations

bcf	billions of cubic feet
bcm	billions of cubic meters
CDU	Christian Democratic Party (West Germany)
CFP	Compagnie Française des Pétroles
CIA	Central Intelligence Agency
COCOM	Consultative Group–Coordinating Committee
COMECON	Council for Mutual Economic Assistance
EC	European Community
ECE	Economic Commission for Europe
EEC	European Economic Community
ENI	Ente Nazionale Idrocarburi
FDP	Free Democratic Party (West Germany)
FOP	Friendship Oil Pipeline
FRUS	*Foreign Relations of the United States* (Washington, D.C.: Government Printing Office, 1948–50)
IEA	International Energy Agency
IGP	Investment Guaranty Program
IL	International List
LNG	liquefied natural gas
mbd	millions of barrels per day
MFN	most favored nation
mmt	millions of metric tons
MNC	multinational corporation
NAM	National Association of Manufacturers
NATO	North Atlantic Treaty Organization
NPC	National Petroleum Council
NSC	National Security Council

OECD	Organization for Economic Cooperation and Development
OEEC	Organization for European Economic Cooperation
OPEC	Organization of Petroleum Exporting Countries
OTA	Office of Technology Assessment
PDC	Christian Democratic Party (Italy)
SNGP	Siberian natural gas pipeline
SONJ	Standard Oil of New Jersey
SPD	Social Democratic Party (West Germany)

Pipeline Politics

CHAPTER ONE

The Constraints on America's Economic Coercive Power

PIPELINE POLITICS: AN OVERVIEW

"We believe," Assistant Secretary of Defense Richard Perle stated in a November 1981 congressional hearing on the Siberian natural gas pipeline (SNGP),[1] "that the increasing dependence of our European allies on Soviet energy, and especially natural gas, will weaken the alliance politically and militarily." The estimated $10 billion to be spent by Western Europe to import Soviet natural gas "will finance . . . the modernization of the Soviet military and industrial establishment." Moreover, with Western Europe so heavily dependent on the Soviet Union for such a vital commodity, the Soviets will know that "in a crisis [they] might interrupt the flow of gas to achieve political purposes." Finally, and perhaps most threatening, "day to day influence . . . must flow like the gas itself. . . . Whether one calls it sensitivity or solicitousness or simply 'reality,' is there any doubt that our allies listen more carefully to kings and rulers who supply them with energy than to those who do not?"[2]

---

[1] This pipeline has been given many names. It originally was called the Yamburg pipeline, for the supergiant gasfield north of the Arctic Circle from which the gas was supposed to come. When problems delayed the development of this field, the already producing Urengoi field (150 miles to the south, and the world's largest gasfield) was tapped instead, and the pipeline began to be referred to as the Yamal pipeline, for the region in which the Urengoi field was located. It has also been called the Soviet–West European gas pipeline, the West Siberian natural gas pipeline, the Trans-Siberian natural gas pipeline, and undoubtedly numerous other names. For simplicity's sake I shall refer to it as the Siberian natural gas pipeline.

[2] Testimony before U.S. Congress, Senate, Committee on Banking, Housing, and Urban Affairs, *Proposed Trans-Siberian Natural Gas Pipeline: Hearings*, 97th Cong., 1st sess., 1981, pp. 113–17.

A month later, spurred by what he termed the Kremlin's "heavy and direct responsibility" for the imposition of martial law in Poland, President Ronald Reagan embargoed all American exports of energy equipment and technology to the Soviet Union.[3] For the next six months concerted efforts were made to persuade the European allies both to join the export embargo and to abandon their plans to increase their imports of Soviet gas. When these diplomatic efforts proved futile, the administration made the rather undiplomatic decision to try to force the allies to comply with its energy trade sanctions. On June 18, 1982, President Reagan announced that the United States was claiming extraterritorial application of its export controls to the European subsidiaries of American corporations, to those European companies producing under license from American firms, and to European companies using American-made parts. As he originally had done back in December, the president again stressed "our objective of reconciliation in Poland." Such rhetoric aside, it was quite clear that the American objectives ran much deeper than responding to events in Poland and were better reflected in Assistant Secretary Perle's earlier delineation of the political and strategic dangers considered inherent in East–West energy trade.

Western European leaders were no less blunt than Perle had been in expressing their disagreement with this analysis, its assumptions, and its implications. French Foreign Minister Claude Cheysson spoke of a "progressive divorce" within the alliance because "we no longer speak the same language." West German Chancellor Helmut Schmidt defiantly pledged that "the pipeline will be built." Even Conservative British Prime Minister Margaret Thatcher retorted that the real issue was "whether one very powerful nation can prevent existing contracts

---

[3]In July 1978, in response to the imprisonment of the Soviet dissidents Anatoly Shcharansky and Aleksandr Ginzburg, the Carter administration had imposed controls on exports of technology and equipment related to exploration for and production of oil and gas. Two months later it loosened the policy but kept the licensing requirement on the books. On December 29, 1981, the Reagan administration broadened the licensing requirement to include the export of equipment used in the refining and transmission of oil and gas (e.g., pipelayers, pipeline compressor stations). Even more to the point, while claiming that licensing applications would continue to be considered case by case, as a matter of policy the Reagan administration adopted a presumption of disapproval on all energy-related exports. The December 29 sanctions also banned the export of electronic equipment, computers, and other high technology to the Soviet Union; closed the Soviet Purchasing Commission; suspended Aeroflot service to U.S. airports; suspended negotiations for a new maritime agreement and strengthened controls governing access to ports; let exchange agreements lapse, including the agreements on energy and science and technology; and postponed negotiations for a new long-term grain agreement (this sanction later was the first to be lifted).

from being fulfilled."[4] Across the European political spectrum opposition parties sided with their partisan foes and against the American sanctions. This was one of the very few issues on which the conservative French leaders Raymond Barré and Valéry Giscard d'Estaing endorsed a policy of François Mitterrand. It also was a rare common ground for Labourites, Social Democrats, and Conservatives in Britain. And when Christian Democrat Helmut Kohl was elected the new West German chancellor, he immediately stated his intention to honor Social Democrat Schmidt's pledge that the pipeline would be built.[5]

The more the Reagan administration increased the pressure, the more steadfast the European governments became. On August 25 the French firms Dresser France and Creusot Loire went ahead and exported to the Soviet Union the first three turbine-powered compressor stations containing parts of American origin and made under license from American firms. Instantly the Reagan administration retaliated as it threatened to do by issuing an order prohibiting any and all American exports to these offending companies. A week later the Italian firm Nuovo Pignone sent its pipeline compressors on their way. The Reagan administration again retaliated with countersanctions. Next to ship was Britain's John Brown Engineering. American countersanctions again followed. Then the West German firms AEG-Kanis Turbinenfabrik and Mannesmann Anlagenbau; and again, as threatened, the punishment.[6]

Clearly, this was not the way allies were supposed to act toward one another. What made the intensity of this intra-alliance conflict over the SNGP even more striking was its contrast with the intra-alliance solidarity being exhibited at virtually the same moment on other major issues. Despite even more intense domestic opposition, for example, these same European governments stood firmly by their commitment to deploy a new generation of intermediate-range nuclear missiles on their soil. The same American president who was excori-

---

[4]*Newsweek*, August 2, 1982, p. 37; *Economist*, June 26, 1982, pp. 52–53; *New York Times*, July 2, 1982, pp. A1, A4.

[5]*Wall Street Journal*, July 23, 1982, p. 20; *New York Times*, October 5, 1982, p. 6.

[6]These sanctions were narrower in scope, limited to oil and gas equipment, services, and technology. The purpose, according to Commerce Secretary Malcolm Baldridge, was to avoid "unduly harming our allies and friends" while still "fully maintaining the goals laid out by the President." Baldridge also announced that the more comprehensive counterembargo against Dresser France and Creusot Loire was being reduced accordingly. The counterembargoes that followed against John Brown Engineering, AEG-Kanis, and Mannesmann also were limited to oil- and gas-related exports (Office of the Secretary, press releases of August 26, September 4, September 28, and October 5, 1982).

ated for his penchant for economic warfare was praised for his resolute leadership in reinvigorating the Western military posture. Similarly, there also was a great degree of alliance collaboration on the
even more closely related issue of firming up controls on East–West
high-technology trade. In January 1982 the first high-level review of
the COCOM embargo lists in twenty-four years was held (COCOM is
the acronym for Consultative Group-Coordinating Committee, the
multilateral organization created in 1949 as the basis for collective
Western trade controls). While not all the American proposals for
expanded high-technology controls ended up by being accepted, in
contrast to the dispute over energy trade, most were.[7] The accom-
panying rhetoric was like night and day; even a senior Pentagon
official remarked, "We're pleased with it [the new COCOM agree-
ment] . . . it gives us protection on the really critical items."[8]

Why, then, did the East–West energy trade issue prove so conten-
tious? The answer to this question begins with acknowledgment that
this issue historically has been a recurring source of intra-alliance
tensions. In fact, there are quite pointed parallels between the 1981–
82 SNGP dispute and the earlier 1962–63 controversy over the
"Friendship" oil pipeline (FOP).[9] Then the issues involved the increases in imports of Soviet oil, especially by Italy, where the Soviet
market share had gone over 20 percent, and in exports of wide-
diameter pipe, especially by West Germany, which had become the
source of 87 percent of the Soviet supply. The Kennedy administration's concerns then were analogous to those of the Reagan administration twenty years later. The FOP would make possible a signifi-
ciant increase in Soviet hard-currency earnings. It would increase the
risk that American allies might become too dependent on Soviet oil, as
Italy was already feared to be. And even more than the natural gas
pipeline, the FOP had military uses (e.g., logistical support for
forward-based troops) that could affect the already tenuous military
balance in Central Europe.

A second point, and a major difference between the two pipeline

[7]*American Metal Market*, April 16, 1984, p. 1; *Aviation Week and Space Technology*, July
23, 1984, p. 21. On this point see also Beverly Crawford and Stefanie Lenway, "Decision Modes and International Regime Change: Western Collaboration on East–West
Trade," *World Politics* 37 (April 1985): 375–402, and Michael Mastanduno, "Strategies
of Economic Containment: U.S. Trade Relations with the Soviet Union," *World Politics*
37 (July 1985): 503–31.

[8]*Wall Street Journal*, July 17, 1984, p. 35.

[9]For an earlier comparison of these two cases, see my "Khrushchev's Oil and Brezhnev's Natural Gas Pipelines," in *Will Europe Fight for Oil? Energy Relations in the Atlantic
Area*, ed. Robert J. Lieber (New York: Praeger, 1983), pp. 33–69.

cases, is that the United States was able to exert much more leverage over its allies' policies in the 1960s than in the 1980s. While not going to the extreme of boycotting Soviet oil, Italy did end up reducing its imports to 10 percent of total oil consumption, well below the level that could be considered politically precarious. West Germany, initially reluctant to join the pipe embargo, eventually went so far as to annul existing contracts on which delivery was pending. In 1982, however, it was the United States that was forced to give the most ground. As we shall see in more detail in Chapter 6, what the Reagan administration billed as a compromise agreement, under which the American countersanctions were lifted in exchange for European agreement to a series of joint studies of the issue, in reality was a major American concession. The Western Europeans not only fulfilled their original export contracts for the Siberian pipeline but went on to sign numerous new contracts totaling billions of dollars for this and other Soviet energy projects. And while actual Western European imports of Soviet gas increased less rapidly than had originally been planned, they nevertheless increased more than the United States wanted. Moreover, the factors limiting the gas import increases had more to do with falling world oil market conditions than with the politico-strategic imperatives being pushed by the United States.

Two interrelated questions therefore need to be addressed: What have been the sources of Western alliance conflict over East–West energy trade? And why has American leverage over its allies' policies weakened over time?

A second set of questions relates to the American domestic politics of the Soviet energy trade issue. For almost a quarter century following World War II there was solid consensual backing in the United States for anti-Soviet sanctions of any kind. It didn't seem to matter that passage of the Export Control Act of 1949 marked the first time in the history of the United States that export controls had been authorized in peacetime over anything more than munitions and weapons-manufacturing technology. Or that, as two legal scholars later concluded, "no single piece of legislation gives more power to the President to control American commerce."[10] In fact, the only significant congressional opposition in the 1950s and early 1960s came when presidents were deemed to be too lax in enforcing export controls. There even were instances (as Chapter 4 will show in regard

[10]Harold J. Berman and John R. Garson, "United States Export Controls: Past, Present, and Future," *Columbia Law Review* 67 (1967): 792.

to the role of Standard Oil of New Jersey and other major oil companies in the Friendship oil pipeline case) when private interest groups not only supported but abetted the sanctions policy.

The major shift in American policy came in 1971–72, when, as part of its overall détente strategy, the Nixon administration liberalized trade controls in the energy sector (as well as in other sectors, notably grain) as an inducement for Soviet political cooperation. The administration even went so far as to offer export credits and otherwise to promote two long-term, multibillion-dollar projects between American corporate consortiums and the Soviet government for the development of Siberian natural gas, its liquefaction, and its export to the United States. But whereas the old economic coercion policy could count on a supportive consensus, this new *economic inducement* strategy encountered strident and powerful opposition. Some of this conflict was fallout from the general "battle of the branches" incited by Vietnam and Watergate. Some pertained to the broader issue of linkage between any trade with the Soviets and their Jewish emigration policy. And some was specific to the energy trade issue itself. The cumulative result was a series of trade restrictions passed by Congress in 1974 which, while stopping short of the old economic coercion strategy, was enough to derail the Siberian gas ventures.

During the Carter administration, policy went through various phases, with energy trade first being permitted (January 1977–July 1978), then suspended (July–September 1978), then promoted (September 1978–December 1979), and finally restricted (December 1979–January 1981). When Ronald Reagan came to power, the reversion to energy trade sanctions was complete. And as with others of its anti-Soviet actions and entreaties, the Reagan administration expected the old Cold War consensus to be reenergized. With a steadier, more inspirational hand at the helm, the American people would shake off the paralysis that had set in as a result of the Vietnam complex, the false illusions of détente, and the malaise of the Carter presidency. With effective leadership, congressional bipartisanship and deference to the president's lead beyond the water's edge would be resurrected. Interest groups would set aside their own particularistic concerns and give precedence to the overriding national interest. The whole country would rally round the flag and meet the Soviet threat head on.

The reality, however, was quite different. Instead of mustering the old supportive consensus, the Reagan policy encountered substantial domestic opposition. One opinion poll showed even less support for the Reagan energy trade sanctions than the Carter grain embargo had initially received.[11] Business lobbyists, who on other policies gave Reagan wholehearted support, put export controls close to the top of the list of issues on which they worked against him. Congress, far from becoming more bipartisan or more deferential, challenged the SNGP sanctions and then weakened new legislation proposed by the administration to expand presidential authority to wield the embargo stick in the future. The executive branch itself was split by bureaucratic warfare that reached such intensity as to be one of the main factors precipitating Secretary of State Alexander Haig's resignation in June 1982.

Thus, as at the intra-alliance level, there is a need to explain the changes that have occurred in the American domestic politics of East–West trade. What were the bases of the old pro-sanctions consensus? And why did it erode in the 1980s?

Of course, if one were to believe the rhetoric of Soviet leaders, these questions really didn't matter very much. The Soviets' economy, they have repeatedly claimed, is not vulnerable to capitalist world trade sanctions. George Ball, under secretary of state during the FOP controversy, recounts that Soviet Ambassador Anatoly Dobrynin later "thanked" him for allegedly providing the impetus for the development of the Soviet wide-diameter pipe industry.[12] Similarly, the Soviet retort to the Reagan sanctions on the SNGP compressor stations was that their factories soon would "turn them out like blinis."[13]

It is true that the Soviet Union does have greater capacity than most nation-states to neutralize the costs that can be imposed on it through economic sanctions. First, this vast country, after all, is endowed with enormous economic resources, not the least of which are its virtually bottomless reserves of oil and natural gas. Second, as a command economy the state is able, at least in theory, to allocate and reallocate resources in accordance with political priorities and objectives. Third, its imperial dominance of Eastern Europe allows it to a great extent to redirect the resources and economic plans of six other countries as necessary to meet its own needs. And fourth, because its "normal" economic posture with respect to the West has been one of semi-autarky, it has been structurally less sensitive than more open economies to the denial effect of trade sanctions.

---

[11]Initially the Carter sanctions registered 76% support; initial support for the Reagan sanctions was only 46% (*Gallup Opinion Index*, Report no. 174 [January 1980], p. 8, and Report no. 203 [August 1982], p. 13).

[12]Personal interview, November 15, 1983, New York City.

[13]*New York Times*, July 20, 1982, p. D1.

But while these traits have made the Soviet Union less vulnerable to economic sanctions than democratic political systems—consumer economies, they have not made it inherently and totally invulnerable. Ultimately, even with its vast resources, command structure, and imperial dominance, the Soviet Union also must face the fundamental autarkic dilemma of limited endowments of at least some key factors of production. This has been particularly the case in the Soviet energy sector. Despite Dobrynin's boasts, the Soviet wide-diameter pipe industry never did develop fully. Today, more than twenty years after the FOP embargo, the Soviets still rely heavily on Western imports for the technologically sophisticated wide-diameter pipe needed for their major oil and natural gas pipelines. Nor have the compressor station "blinis" been turned out. In fact, as we shall see in later chapters, while their own industrial base generally has produced the bulk of the equipment needed, the Soviets repeatedly and consistently have had to rely on Western imports to break key technological bottlenecks in the oil and gas industry.[14]

In addition, while never more than a small share of their total oil and gas production, exports to the West have had a much greater relative value because of their importance as the Soviet Union's principal source of hard-currency earnings. By the early 1980s oil and gas exports were accounting for over 80 percent of the total hard currency earned by the Soviet Union. Consequently, unless their oil and gas exports to the West continued to grow—and given plummeting oil and gas prices on the one hand and the tightening of Western credits on the other, to grow even more rapidly—the purchasing power needed for such imports as Western grain and industrial machinery would suffer accordingly. It is for this reason in particular that the energy sector has been termed "not merely a part of the growing internationalization of the Soviet economy, . . . [but] the essential center of it."[15]

This is not to go so far as to accept the opposite presumption, as

[14]U.S. Congress, Office of Technology Assessment, *Technology and Soviet Energy Availability* (Washington, D.C.: Government Printing Office, 1981), pp. 35–37, 46–48, 53–55, 62–64, 67–70; Robert W. Campbell, *Soviet Energy Technologies* (Bloomington: Indiana University Press, 1981); Robert G. Jensen, Theodore Shabad, and Arthur W. Wright, eds., *Soviet Natural Resources in the World Economy* (Chicago: University of Chicago Press, 1983), pp. 316–23.

[15]Thane Gustafson, "Energy and U.S.–Soviet Relations: The Question of Eastern Europe," *Energy and National Security Proceedings from a Special Conference,* ed. Donald J. Goldstein (Washington, D.C.: National Defense University Press, 1981), p. 148. See also Gustafson, *Soviet Negotiating Strategy: The East-West Pipeline Deal, 1980–1984,* R-3220-FF (Santa Monica: Rand Corporation, 1985).

American leaders so often have done, that the Soviet economy is uniquely vulnerable to economic sanctions, and especially to energy trade sanctions. Whatever its problems and inefficiencies, the Soviet Union still is the world's leading producer of both oil and natural gas. In addition, we would do well to remember the old adage, attributed to the sixteenth-century theorist Jean Bodin, that "the best means for preserving a state, to prevent rebellion, sedition and civil war, and to maintain the good will of subjects, is to have an enemy."[16] Other authors have observed this pattern in other cases of trade sanctions.[17] In the case of the Soviet Union, as George Kennan first pointed out, Kremlin leaders always have been particularly adept at this kind of manipulation of external threats to enhance their own internal legitimation.[18] Thus, to the extent that American embargoes have functioned as reminders of the hostility of the rest of the world to the Soviet Motherland, they have not been entirely unwelcome.

The Soviet Union therefore has been neither inherently invulnerable nor uniquely vulnerable to energy trade or other American economic sanctions. This is precisely why the questions about the Western alliance and American domestic political economy do matter. For the extent of the economic coercive power that the United States has been able to bring to bear on the Soviet Union has been contingent on (a) the *multilateral constraint* of other countries, and particularly its Western European allies, acting as alternative trade partners, and (b) the *domestic constraint* of opposition at home sufficient to force a change of policy, to undermine the implementation of coercive measures, or to make them politically costly to sustain.

[16]Cited in Edward L. Morse, *Modernization and the Transformation of International Relations* (New York: Free Press, 1976), p. 32.

[17]George W. Baer argues, for example, that Mussolini manipulated the League of Nations sanctions against Italy "to intensify statism and to consolidate personal rule. . . . [The sanctions were] transformed by the Italian government into a case for rapid intensification of integral economic and political nationalism" ("Sanctions and Security: The League of Nations and the Italian–Ethiopian War, 1935–36," *International Organization* 27 [Spring 1973]: 178–79). In the case of Soviet sanctions against Yugoslavia, Tito's firm resistance made him even more "idolized by his closest associates in a way that was unique in Communist parties, whose leaders for the most part were creatures of Moscow" (Adam Ulam, *Expansion and Coexistence* [New York: Praeger, 1962], p. 462). Similarly, American sanctions against Cuba fed into "a Cuban self-image . . . that depicts Castro and his country as courageously marching forward and prevailing in spite of the economic aggression of the United States" (Donald L. Losman, *International Economic Sanctions: The Cases of Cuba, Israel, and Rhodesia* [Albuquerque: University of New Mexico Press, 1979], p. 129). See also Jerrold D. Green, "Strategies for Evading Economic Sanctions," in *Dilemmas of Economic Coercion: Sanctions in World Politics*, ed. Miroslav Nincic and Peter Wallensteen (New York: Praeger, 1983), pp. 61–85.

[18]Mr. X [George F. Kennan], "The Sources of Soviet Conduct," *Foreign Affairs* 27 (July 1947): 566–82.

To be sure, even with Western European collaboration and solid domestic support, there never has been any guarantee that sanctions would have maximal impact, either economically or politically. At least some degree of Soviet capacity to blunt or otherwise absorb the sanctions' impact also must be included in the analysis as a *unilateral constraint*. Beyond that consideration, though, *the likely impact of American economic sanctions can be expected to vary with the levels of the multilateral and domestic constraints*. The Soviet energy sector never has been, and is never likely to be, so weak that the United States acting alone could inflict major economic costs on it. Nor, however, has it ever been, nor will it ever be, so strong that it could painlessly withstand the economic impact of multilateral Western sanctions. Similarly, at the political level, the likelihood of influencing Soviet policy has depended greatly on whether the sanctions have been backed by the collective will of the Western alliance and by a strong American domestic consensus.

Pipeline politics therefore has had as much to do with intra-Western alliance and American domestic politics as with direct American–Soviet relations. For ultimately it has been the politics at these levels that has determined the constraints on American economic coercive power and, accordingly, the impact of economic sanctions on the Soviet Union.

CONCEPTUALIZATION AND MEASUREMENT OF SUCCESS

Before proceeding to develop this analytic framework, I must address two conceptual and methodological issues that relate to the central question of what constitutes "success" when one state uses economic sanctions against another. The first concerns the objectives pursued by the United States through its sanctions against the Soviet Union; the second concerns the problems involved in measuring the success or failure of sanctions in achieving these objectives.

American Objectives

My concern is principally with the *instrumental* objectives of American policy, as distinct from the *symbolic-expressive* objectives. This basic distinction was made by Johan Galtung in 1967, when he noted that there frequently are situations in which, irrespective of the actual impact sanctions may or may not have on their target state, leaders may feel that "something has to be done to express morality, something that at least serves as a clear signal to everyone that what the receiving [i.e., target] nation has done is disapproved of."[19] American leaders often have advanced this kind of argument to justify anti-Soviet sanctions. As leader of the Free World and in keeping with the Wilsonian tradition of its foreign policy, the United States has been said to have a unique responsibility to register its principled protest against Soviet transgressions.[20]

More often than not, however, America's foreign policy objectives have been more ambitious and more complex than just the affirmation of its idealism. Sanctions also have been invoked for more instrumental objectives, both economic and political. The economic instrumental objectives have involved what can be called, after Albert Hirschman, the "supply effect" of denying the Soviets the benefits of trade in order to impose costs on their economy.[21] Within this general category, the further distinction can be made between (1) *economic warfare* and (2) *economic defense* objectives. By "economic warfare" I mean sanctions close to comprehensive in scope and intended to inflict maximum costs and disruption on the Soviet economy: the imposition of sanctions is an offensive action. Sanctions imposed with the objective of economic defense, in contrast, have been limited in scope to those exports that have the greatest military significance; their intent is less to stunt overall Soviet economic growth than to avoid enhancing Soviet military capabilities.

The political instrumental objectives all have involved what Hirschman calls the "influence effect" of having a direct impact on Soviet policy or otherwise affecting the political balance of power.[22] The most blatant of such objectives has been (3) the *compellence* objective of forcing the Soviets to change a particular domestic or foreign policy. Linked to but distinct from the compellence objective has been (4) the

[19]Johan Galtung, "On the Effects of International Economic Sanctions, with Examples from the Case of Rhodesia," *World Politics* 19 (April 1967): 411.

[20]Take, for example, the statement by Adam Michnik, a leading Polish dissident, that the most important aspect of the Western sanctions were "as an act of solidarity with the Polish people. And if they were so conceived by Western leaders, then they have fulfilled their role" (Timothy Garton Ash, "A Talk with a Polish Orwell," *New York Times*, November 14, 1984, p. 29).

[21]Albert Hirschman, *National Power and the Structure of Foreign Trade*, rev. ed. (Berkeley: University of California Press, 1980), p. 14. Hirschman's book first appeared in 1945 and has long been considered one of the classic works on international economic coercion. Proceeding deductively from international trade theory and inductively from the case of Nazi Germany, Hirschman set his task as nothing less than "adding to Machiavelli's classic chapters, extensive new sections on the most efficient use of . . . instruments of economic warfare" (p. xv).

[22]Ibid., p. 15.

deterrence objective of discouraging any future Soviet aggressive intentions by signaling American will and resolve through sanctions. In this respect, as David Baldwin has emphasized, economic sanctions follow the more general precepts for deterrence and other bargaining strategies developed by Thomas Schelling.[23] Finally, and especially with regard to controls on imports from the Soviet Union, there also has been (5) the *containment* objective of limiting those imports that risk bringing the Soviets political influence over consuming countries, notably over America's Western European allies.[24]

All five of these instrumental objectives, in contrast to the symbolic-expressive objective, involve actual impact on the Soviet Union—disrupting its economy, limiting its military capabilities, influencing its current policy, influencing its future intentions, containing its political influence. By their very proclamation symbolic-expressive objectives can be presumed to have been achieved. The symbol is the substance, therefore the success is in the taking of the action in and of itself. The message of American idealism is sent, therefore it is received. American intentions are determinative. The efficacy of instrumental objectives, however, cannot be presumed so automatically. American intentions are not determinative because effects do not invariably follow from intentions. Other factors can and frequently do intervene to make the actual economic and political impact less than the United States had hoped.

It therefore is with the instrumental objectives that the most interesting research questions lie. In making this distinction I do not deny that, as Baldwin argues, in a certain sense even symbolic action is purposive behavior. But when he therefore drops Galtung's original distinction and reconceptualizes the coercer state's objectives as "symbolic instrumental," the objectives become confused with the instru-

[23]David A. Baldwin, *Economic Statecraft* (Princeton: Princeton University Press, 1985), esp. pp. 8–28 and 96–114. "The teacher who chooses to 'make an example' out of a misbehaving student," Baldwin points out, "is often more interested in the deterrent effects on the other children than in the effects on the particular recipient of the punishment" (p. 17). This example also is useful in regard to Schelling's compellence/deterrence distinction; for this original distinction, see Thomas C. Schelling, *Arms and Influence* (New Haven: Yale University Press, 1966), pp. 69–78.

[24]Other typologies of the objectives of international economic coercion have been proposed. See James Barber, "Economic Sanctions as a Policy Instrument," *International Affairs* (London) 55 (July 1979): 367–84; Sidney Weintraub, ed., *Economic Coercion and U.S. Foreign Policy: Implications of Case Studies from the Johnson Administration* (Boulder, Colo.: Westview Press, 1982), pp. 47–60; Angela Stent, *From Embargo to Ostpolitik: The Political Economy of West German–Soviet Relations, 1955–1980* (New York: Cambridge University Press, 1981), pp. 16–19; Gary C. Hufbauer and Jeffrey J. Schott, *Economic Sanctions Reconsidered: History and Current Policy* (Washington, D.C.: Institute for International Economics, 1985), pp. 29–30.

mentalities.[25] Both idealistic message-sending and deterrent signal-sending may be manifested in symbolic form. But the fundamental substantive differences remain between the affirmation of abstract ideals and the ultimately tangible objective of influencing another state's future policy intentions. Moreover, as follows from the preceding discussion of the success/failure dynamic, for the one the symbol is the substance while for the other it is but the medium.[26]

Measuring Success

A related concern involves the methodological problems surrounding the measurement of the success or failure of sanctions to achieve their objectives. Unlike wars, in which it usually is clear who won and who lost, economic sanctions never have clear-cut outcomes. Optimally, sanctions may impose substantial economic costs and bring significant political influence. But they never have caused a nation-state to surrender. Conversely, while they may fall well short of their instrumental objectives, they rarely have absolutely no impact on the target state. And the possibility remains that at least some of the coercer state's objectives will be achieved at the symbolic-expressive level.

A first step toward methodological clarity therefore is to think of degrees of success rather than in dichotomous yes/no terms.[27] One of the values of my disaggregation of American instrumental objectives into component subtypes is that it provides a conceptual basis for this more calibrated approach. Rather than stay at the crude level of statements about policy success or policy failure, within each case we can make more insightful assessments as to which objectives were achieved and which were not. Cross-case comparisons are similarly enriched, as cases can be compared both in the aggregate (were American sanctions more or less effective over time?) and also along particu-

---

[25]Baldwin, *Economic Statecraft*, p. 98.

[26]Take Baldwin's teacher–student example (n. 23). The moral message of "this is bad" inherent in the punishment given to the misbehaving student can be presumed to have been received by the rest of the students. But in terms of the deterrent effect of setting an example of what will happen to you if you misbehave, if the punishment imposed on the original bad student has little actual impact, the signal sent to the other students will be quite different from the one intended.

[27]The yes/no absolute notion of success or failure has been the basis for some of the rather poor historical scorecards that have been compiled. See Peter Wallensteen, "Characteristics of Economic Sanctions," *Journal of Peace Research* 3 (1968): 248–67; Klaus Knorr, *The Power of Nations: The Political Economy of International Relations* (New York: Basic Books, 1975), p. 152.

lar dimensions (e.g., did the deterrence value of sanctions change over time?).[28]

One of the problems that remains is to develop reliable empirical indicators of success. In theory, we are prepared to measure economic impact through such statistical conventions as trade turnover, GNP growth rates, industrial production indices, and inflation. But the data available on which to base these calculations are not always reliable. On the one hand, countries may not want to advertise their pain, and so their official economic statistics may understate the economic impact that sanctions actually may be having. Alternatively, they intentionally may overstate the economic impact so as not to blow the cover of covert alternative trade partners.[29]

Of the political influence objectives, only compellence can be measured confidently. The Soviet Union either did or did not change its policy. The containment issue of Soviet political influence in Western Europe as a result of expanded trade is more likely to involve subtleties of the relationship than to be manifested in blatant or otherwise easily recognizable and measurable forms. The question of successful political deterrence is even more problematic. Here we get into the realm of "nondecisions."[30] For if deterrence is successful, nothing happens.

These indicator reliability problems are linked to the problem of attributing causality. If, for example, American–Soviet deterrence does not break down (nothing happens, therefore a success), can it be established that American economic sanctions were a contributing factor? If they were, were they a necessary condition? A sufficient condition? It may even be that deterrence occurred in spite of, not because of, economic sanctions. The same causal permutations pose

[28]This approach owes much to the work of Alexander George on the "structured, focused" method for comparative case studies. See George and Richard Smoke, *Deterrence in American Foreign Policy: Theory and Practice* (New York: Columbia University Press, 1974), pp. 95–97, and George, "Case Studies and Theory Development: The Method of Structured, Focused Comparison," in *Diplomacy: New Approaches in History, Theory, and Policy*, ed. Paul Gordon Lauren (New York: Free Press, 1979), pp. 43–68.

[29]Following the embargo against Rhodesia, for example, a United Nations study concluded that Rhodesia's actual trade was 50% higher than the reported figure (Harry Strack, *Sanctions: The Case of Rhodesia* [Syracuse, N.Y.: Syracuse University Press, 1978], pp. 129–31).

[30]The classic statement of the general problem of nondecisions in politics at all levels is in two articles by Peter Bachrach and Morton Baratz, "Two Faces of Power," *American Political Science Review* 56 (December 1962): 947–52, and "Decisions and Nondecisions: An Analytical Framework," *American Political Science Review* 57 (September 1963): 632–42.

similar problems for the other objectives. Even if it can be determined that *B* followed *A*, it does not follow necessarily that *A* caused *B*.[31]

The "success score" scale developed in the recent study by Gary Hufbauer and Jeffrey Schott was an effort to resolve both the measurement and the causality problems.[32] But while their scale has the advantages of being explicit in its measurements and providing a standard for application to large numbers of cases, the coding procedures on which it rests raise their own reliability problems. The historical evidence rarely is so unambiguous as to allow for a "consensus view" of sanctions' impact, which is what they claim the scale is based on.[33] Even if the impact could be agreed upon, the causality issue would be likely to remain disputatious.

Further complicating matters is the relativity problem raised by Baldwin. He argues that the success or failure of economic sanctions ("economic statecraft") must be assessed in relation to the likely prospects or consequences of alternative policy options ("techniques of statecraft").

> Policy making involves making decisions, and decision making involves choosing among alternative courses of action. The advantages and disadvantages of various policy options acquire significance primarily by comparison with other options. Thus, in any decision-making situation, decision makers are always going to want comparative information about the costs and benefits of perceived alternatives.

Drawing on Schelling's theory of bargaining and credible commitments, Baldwin goes on to argue that the significance of the incurring of costs also is relative. Because self-imposed costs can communicate commitment and resolve, they "are not an unmitigated drawback but rather are often a blessing in disguise."[34]

These points are all too often missed when economic sanctions are analyzed without reference to the broader context of world politics in

---

[31]Here, too, there is a more general context for these problems. On the attribution of the causality of influence see Robert A. Dahl, "The Concept of Power," *Behavioral Science* 11 (July 1957): 201–15; J. David Singer, "Inter-Nation Influence: A Formal Model," *American Political Science Review* 57 (June 1963): 420–30; and David A. Baldwin, "Inter-Nation Influence Revisited," *Journal of Conflict Resolution* 15 (December 1971): 471–86.

[32]Hufbauer and Schott, *Economic Sanctions Reconsidered*, pp. 32–33 and passim.

[33]As an example, my assessment of the SNGP case can be contrasted with Baldwin's in *Economic Statecraft*, pp. 278–89.

[34]Ibid., pp. 15, 108.

which they occur.[35] If an American president's choice is between the embargo weapon and a nuclear weapon (or some other policy response with a high likelihood of escalation to nuclear war), then the relative worth of economic sanctions is obvious. We must keep this comparison at the level of a hypothesis, however, and not permit it to become a premise. American presidents may justify their actions in this way, but they rarely are confronted with a scenario that permits only two options. The relativity question definitely should be asked, but the answer should not be assumed a priori.

Similarly, while the Schellingesque deterrent value of incurring costs should be considered in any analysis, no presumption should be made. Incurring costs can deter, but it does not necessarily deter. This is, for example, one of the less ambiguous lessons of the 1980 grain embargo.[36] The domestic costs incurred were so severe as to cause President Ronald Reagan, who in virtually every other sphere was crafting a strong and strident Cold War foreign policy, to lift the grain embargo without the slightest Soviet quid pro quo—hardly a deterrence-enhancing action. The question of costs incurred by the coercer state therefore is relevant to assessments of success.

How, then, to deal with these methodological uncertainties and the analytical problems they spawn? Clearly, they preclude elegant theorizing. They also stop findings and explanations short of claims of certainty. But patterns and probabilities can be established. By identifying with a degree of generality sets of variables that can be shown to have a high probability of determining the success or failure of economic sanctions, we can speak about both patterns of causality and probabilities of outcomes. It is precisely for this purpose that my framework of the constraints on American economic coercive power is intended.

THE ALTERNATIVE TRADE PARTNER DILEMMA AND THE WESTERN ALLIANCE

Historically, the greatest obstacle to instrumental coercive success generally in cases of economic sanctions has been the multilateral constraint of other states acting as alternative trade partners for the target state. As Albert O. Hirschman has stated as a general proposi-

[35]On the basis of both his research and his experience in the Reagan administration, Henry Nau also emphasizes the importance of the broader strategic context. See his "International Technology Transfer," *Washington Quarterly* 8 (Winter 1985): 57–64.
[36]Robert L. Paarlberg, *Food Trade and Foreign Policy: India, the Soviet Union, and the United States* (Ithaca: Cornell University Press, 1985).

tion, "a country menaced with an interruption of trade with a given country has the alternative of diverting its trade to a third country; by so doing it evades more or less completely the damaging consequences of the stoppage of its trade with one particular country. The stoppage or the threat of it would thus lose all its force."[37]

There are two reasons why this to-trade-or-not-to-trade role played by alternative partners has been important. First is that even if a premium must be paid or some efficiency is lost, the ability to trade with an alternative partner substantially reduces the economic impact that sanctions can have. This has been true historically even in cases of extreme economic dominance, as when sanctions were imposed by the Soviet Union against Yugoslavia (1948) and by the United States against Cuba (1960). In both cases the immediate economic impact of the sanctions was highly disruptive, only to be assuaged by the intervention of alternative trade partners. For, consistent with another old adage, that the enemy of my enemy is my friend, the United States and its allies dramatically increased their trade and other economic relations with Yugoslavia.[38] The Soviet Union and its allies did the same for Cuba.[39] Similarly, in the two cases of "universal" sanctions, the League of Nations against Italy (1935–36) and the United Nations against Rhodesia (1965–78), the trade made available by alternative partners substantially reduced the economic costs of refusal to comply with international law.[40] Conversely, a case that has been called "the first success ever obtained at the highest level of politics by economic sanctions," the 1973 OPEC oil embargo, also was the one in which the targets were least able to find alternative trade partners.[41]

[37]Hirschman, *National Power*, p. 29.

[38]NATO nations, which in 1948 accounted for only 38.5% of Yugoslav imports and 30% of its exports, by 1954 had increased their shares to 78.5% and 71.5%. (The figures are derived from United Nations, Statistics Office, *Yearbook of International Trade*, various editions.) The West also granted additional aid, loans, technical assistance, and other special subsidies to Yugoslavia. For a detailed analysis, see Robert Owen Freedman, *Economic Warfare in the Communist Bloc* (New York: Praeger, 1970).

[39]The Soviet bloc's share of Cuban trade soared from 0.2% to 83.9% of imports and 2.0% to 77.4% of exports. See Losman, *International Economic Sanctions;* Anna P. Schreiber, "Economic Coercion as an Instrument of Foreign Policy: U.S. Economic Measures against Cuba and the Dominican Republic," *World Politics* 25 (April 1973): 387–413; and Gunnar Adler-Karlsson, *Western Economic Warfare, 1947–1967* (Stockholm: Almquist & Wiksell, 1968).

[40]On the Italian case see Baer, "Sanctions and Security"; Frederick W. Hartmann, *The Relations of Nations* (New York: Macmillan, 1973), p. 369; Margaret Doxey, *Economic Sanctions and International Enforcement* (New York: Oxford University Press, 1980); and Robin Renwick, *Economic Sanctions* (London: Croom Helm, 1981). On the Rhodesian case see Strack, *Sanctions;* Losman, *International Economic Sanctions;* Doxey, *Sanctions and Enforcement;* and Renwick, *Economic Sanctions.*

[41]International Institute for Strategic Studies, *Strategic Survey 1973* (London, 1973),

The second way that alternative trade partners undermine the co-ercive potential of economic sanctions is more political in nature. If, as in the Yugoslav and Cuban cases, the alternative trade is provided by states that are adversaries of the coercer, the target can feel it has the "safe haven" of a protector. From this more secure position there is less pressure to be compelled into submission or even to be deterred from future provocations. If, on the other hand, the alternative trade comes from the coercer's own allies, the threat to sustain the sanctions or escalate the level of confrontation loses much of its credibility.[42]

It is for both of these reasons that the collaboration of America's Western European allies has been critical to the instrumental success of its sanctions against the Soviet Union.[43] Even in the first two dec-ades of the postwar era, when Europe lagged technologically behind the United States, it still had the capacity to export military and indus-trial equipment and technology important to Soviet economic growth and military development. In addition, if the United States' own allies assumed the role of alternative trade partners, the political conse-quences could do even more to undermine American coercive objec-tives. The signal sent to the Soviet adversary is not a particularly compelling one if the process of sending it highlights a lack of alliance solidarity. Doubt also is likely to be cast on the credibility of American

---

pp. 1–2. See also Hans Maull, *Oil and Influence: The Oil Weapon Examined,* Adelphi Paper no. 117 (London: International Institute for Strategic Studies, 1975), and Young C. Kim, "The Interaction of Economics and Japanese Foreign Policy," in *The Interaction of Economics and Foreign Policy,* ed. Robert A. Bauer (Charlottesville: University Press of Virginia, 1975) pp. 98–101.

[42]In the Rhodesian case this was a ramification of the 1971 passage by the U.S. Congress of the Byrd amendment authorizing imports of Rhodesian chrome. As the *Rhodesian Herald* editorialized at the time, this defection by the world's leading defender of democratic values from the sanctions initiated by its closest ally and sponsored by the United Nations was "a wonderful boost for Rhodesian morale and a bitter setback for those who still seek the country's collapse. . . . [It] is at least a signal to the world that sanctions are not important enough to warrant serious sacrifice" (Strack, *Sanctions,* p. 164). Another example of this problem was the unwillingness of Britain and France to include oil, the one commodity most vital to Mussolini's Ethiopian expedition, in the sanctions imposed by the League of Nations. Not only was the economic impact of the sanctions diluted; more important, a message of weakness of will was communicated to Il Duce—and to observer Adolf Hitler. "Looking back," British Foreign Secretary Anthony Eden later wrote in his diary, "the thought comes again, should we not have shown more determination in pressing through with sanctions in 1935, and if we had could we not have called Mussolini's bluff and at least postponed this [second world] war? The answer, I am sure, is yes" (cited in Baer, "Sanctions and Security," p. 177).

[43]In recent years Japan also has been important as a potential alternative partner, especially for industrial equipment and technology. In other sectors other countries also are important, such as Argentina for grain. The focus here on Western Europe is based in part on a decision to delimit the study and in part on the longer historical perspective that it makes possible.

threats to sustain the sanctions or to reimpose them in the future and perhaps even on other Western commitments for collective action integral to a strong deterrence posture. Moreover, when such economically vital commodities as oil and natural gas are involved, it is not sufficient for the United States to abstain from excessive reliance on Soviet supplies. It is the amount of oil and gas the Europeans import that bears most directly on containment objectives.

The key question, then, is what factors determine whether or not Western Europe will play the role of alternative trade partner? Or, as posed at the outset, what have been the principal sources of West–West conflict over East–West energy trade?

I posit three factors as explaining both the recurring and the intensifying nature of this conflict. The first is that East–West trade in general and the energy issue in particular always have touched on a basic intra-alliance dispute over *foreign policy strategy*. In the broadest sense the dispute has been over whether détente and defense are complementary or contradictory strategies for relations with the Soviet Union. The Western allies always have agreed that the Soviet Union is a common adversary and that the core objective of their alliance is collective security; their differences have come over assessments of the nature of the Soviet threat and, accordingly, the best way to pursue the collective security objective.

Generally speaking, Europe has been more disposed to take the complementarity view. Initial European interest in developing détente can be traced all the way back to the thaw following the death of Stalin.[44] It also was European pressure that led to the 1967 NATO Harmel Report, with its statement that "military security and a policy of détente are not contradicatory, but rather mutually complement each other."[45] American policy was much slower to change. When in the 1970s the United States pursued its version of détente, these differences were lessened (although not totally removed).[46] But with the Reagan administration's reaffirmation of the view of détente and defense as contradictory, these differences have reemerged.

It is in this underlying context that the more specific disputes over East–West trade have occurred and therefore must be understood.

[44]Walter LaFeber, *America, Russia, and the Cold War, 1945–1984*, 5th ed. (New York: Knopf, 1984), p. 149; Richard W. Stevenson, *The Rise and Fall of Détente* (London: Macmillan, 1985), pp. 28–35.

[45]*Europa/Archiv*, vol. 3 (1968), p. D75.

[46]On the differences that remained see Henry A. Kissinger, *Years of Upheaval* (Boston: Little, Brown, 1982), pp. 128–94 and 700–746; and Raymond L. Garthoff, *Détente and Confrontation: American–Soviet Relations from Nixon to Reagan* (Washington, D.C.: Brookings Institution, 1985), pp. 106–26 and 473–501.

Only with regard to the need to embargo munitions, nuclear technology, and other exports that could directly and significantly enhance Soviet military capabilities have the allies consistently agreed on economic sanctions. Otherwise the United States has tended to favor a maximalist strategy, broadly construing the scope of trade on which controls should be imposed and being disposed to turn quickly to economic coercion in times of increased East–West tensions. The Europeans, in contrast, have been inclined toward a minimalist strategy, concentrating more narrowly on exports with direct military applications and giving greater weight to the possibility that the bonds of trade can help reduce political tensions.

Because of its inherent "strategic ambiguousness," energy trade has been precisely the kind of issue on which these two strategies have been most apt to clash. Whereas the strategic consequences of militarily relevant exports to the Soviet adversary are unambiguously negative, and while the strategic implications of consumer-type exports tend to be rather innocuous (other than in the extreme version of a full-scale economic warfare strategy), the strategic significance of energy trade never has been clear-cut. The United States has tended to stress the hard currency the Soviets stand to earn by exporting to Western markets, the dangers of dependence on the Soviets for commodities as vital as oil and natural gas, the military significance of pipelines, and the potential diversion of energy technologies to military uses. The Europeans have tended to stress the potential political and strategic benefits of developing trade in such an important sector. Economic relations are most likely to contribute to improved political relations, their reasoning has run, if they are promoted in those sectors of greatest mutual value.

A second source of the intra-alliance conflict over East–West energy trade has been the *divergent economic interests* at stake. It always has been the case (with the exception of grain exports) that Western Europe has stood to lose more business from anti-Soviet embargoes than the United States. While in the aggregate, even at their peak, exports to the Soviet Union still amounted to only a small share of total European exports, they have tended to be concentrated in such key sectors as the steel industry (e.g., wide-diameter pipe). Moreover, when recessions have hit, the marginal economic value and the absolute domestic political value of any lost markets (i.e., jobs) at all have been higher than most governments would like to risk.

In addition, and again of particular salience with respect to trade in the energy sector, American and European economic interests have diverged sharply with respect to the value of the goods being imported from the Soviet Union. This fundamental difference can be conceptualized as that between *energy producer* and *energy consumer* countries. The United States always has been in the position of being a producer country, able through a combination of indigenous resource endowments and corporate foreign holdings to meet much of its own energy demand and to profit from exporting to world markets. Consequently, the emergence of any new competitor for shares of the world market poses a threat to American economic interests. To the extent that such a competitor also adopts a price-cutting strategy, as the Soviet Union characteristically has done, there is a downward pressure on prices that can cut into profits no less substantially than lost market shares.

The strongest contrast is with Italy and West Germany, both energy consumer countries. As they have neither the national natural resources nor the foreign holdings to supply their own energy needs, their economic interest is in more, not less, competition among energy suppliers. What is the threat of lost market shares to producer countries is enhanced security through import diversification to consumer countries. What others see as unfair dumping they see as an attractive bargain.

Britain and France have had more ambiguous economic positions. Britain's Middle Eastern holdings and later its North Sea oil and gas discoveries have given it a producer identity vis-à-vis Soviet competition for domestic and world markets. But the export orientation of its industrial production and its long-standing and severe unemployment problems have given it something of an economically countervailing interest in the job-creation effects of energy equipment exports. French foreign holdings never were as substantial as British or American, but at least through the early 1960s they were enough to minimize interest in importing Soviet oil. However, between losses to host country nationalizations (Iraq, Algeria) and the effects of the OPEC crises, by the late 1970s France had been transformed from an energy producer to an energy consumer.

East–West energy trade, then, always has posed a problem for American–European relations because of both the basic dispute over foreign policy strategy and the structurally divergent economic interests that this issue raises. This is not to say that trade in the energy sector alone has raised these intra-alliance differences. My framework could be made to have more general applicability to East–West trade as an overall policy area. But the particular characteristics of the energy trade issue have made conflicts arising from these sources especially acute. The nature of the trade involved, on both the import

39

and export sides, is more strategically ambiguous than most, and therefore more prone to bring out broader and preexisting differences over foreign policy strategy. While in themselves these differences are far from irreconcilable, the problem is compounded by the higher and more inequitable economic opportunity costs that energy trade sanctions carry.

This is where the third factor, the economic and political resources of *American leverage,* comes in. As the largest and wealthiest member of the alliance, the United States has been in a position both to offer economic rewards as compensation for collaboration and to threaten punishments for noncollaboration. Economic compensation has taken various forms, including economic aid, substitute supplies of imports, and special purchases of exports originally destined for Soviet markets. Whatever the form, the intent has been to decrease the costs to Western Europe of collaborating with East–West trade controls. Economic punishments, such as the early 1950s linkage of Marshall Plan aid to collaboration with trade controls and the 1982 Reagan countersanctions, have been intended to increase the costs of noncollaboration. Either way the basic strategy has been, in effect, to make divergent economic interests converge.

Less tangible but potentially no less influential a source of leverage has been the political prestige of the United States as leader of the Western alliance. Prestige as it relates to influence in international relations can be conceived of as the authority to command as distinct from the power to compel. It is in part based on a state's military strength but more importantly related to what in a broader political and sociological context Harold Lasswell and Abraham Kaplan call the "deference values" of respect, rectitude, and affection.[47] While prestige is much more difficult to measure than more material sources of leverage, its importance has been stressed by numerous scholars, including Robert Gilpin, who terms it "the everyday currency of international relations."[48]

Prestige is of particular value in relations between allies. Overtly coercive leverage tactics tend to offend the sensibilities of junior partners and thus make collective action even more difficult to achieve.[49]

---

[47]Harold Lasswell and Abraham Kaplan, *Power and Society* (New Haven: Yale University Press, 1950), pp. 55–56.

[48]Robert Gilpin, *War and Change in International Politics* (New York: Cambridge University Press, 1981), p. 31. Two attempts to measure prestige quantitatively are Michael David Wallace, *War and Rank among Nations* (Lexington, Mass.: Heath, 1973), and Michael Haas, *International Conflict* (Indianapolis: Bobbs-Merrill, 1974).

[49]The same problem has been observed in other issues of intra-alliance relations.

To the extent that the alliance leader can draw on its own prestige as political capital for persuasion, it can avoid this potential boomerang effect. Allied governments in turn can then cast a policy unpopular because of its economic costs in terms of international responsibilities. Conversely, a backdrop of low American prestige can create a guilt-by-association context that adds to the disincentives working against collaboration.

We therefore should expect to find a relationship between the leverage that the United States can bring to bear through economic compensation, economic countersanctions, and prestige and the degree of European collaboration with the American-initiated sanctions. As I have already argued, the *recurring* nature of West–West tensions over East–West energy trade is a result of two inherent sources of conflict, the strategic ambiguity that brings out basic differences over foreign policy strategy and the divergent economic interests that are at stake. With the leverage variable added to the framework, it becomes possible to explain the variations observed over time in the intensity of the intra-alliance conflict. As we shall see, the imbroglio over the 1982 natural gas trade sanctions was far more severe and had an outcome far less favorable to American policy than the dispute over the 1962 oil trade sanctions, because *the sources of conflict had increased while the American resources of leverage had decreased.*

THE BLUFFER'S DILEMMA AND AMERICAN DOMESTIC CONSTRAINTS

To a much greater extent than other coercer states, the United States has had to cope with domestic constraints on its coercive power. This is not the kind of problem that authoritarian governments have had to worry much about, prone as they are to impose from above what they cannot evoke from below. But even in comparison with the foreign policies of other democratic political systems, America's has a history of being more acutely sensitive to domestic influences. Some authors have traced this general "weak state" pattern to the institutional structures that divide authority among the separate branches of

See, for example, John D. Steinbruner, *The Cybernetic Theory of Decision* (Princeton: Princeton University Press, 1974), chaps. 6–9; Henry A. Kissinger, *The Troubled Partnership* (New York: McGraw-Hill, 1965); Richard E. Neustadt, *Alliance Politics* (New York: Columbia University Press, 1970); and David P. Calleo and Benjamin M. Rowland, *America and the World Political Economy* (Bloomington: Indiana University Press, 1973).

41

government and fragment it within each branch.[50] Such structures create numerous access points for interest group and other pressures. They thus make more difficult the task of building the kind of supportive coalitions that are necessary for both the formulation and implementation of policy.

To the extent that efforts to impose economic sanctions on the Soviet Union have been so constrained, the result has been what may be called the "bluffer's dilemma." For when, as Bruce Russett and Harvey Starr argue in a more general context, domestic forces "prevent a government from pursuing certain policies or using certain capabilities, the credibility of that government declines in the eyes of other states. Its ability to influence them shrinks as its reputation as a 'bluffer' grows."[51] In the extreme case, domestic opposition actually may force an administration to lift its sanctions. Such an eventuality can be even more devastating in its effects than the intervention of alternative trade partners. Even if domestic opposition does not succeed in forcing an administration to lift the sanctions, it may raise the domestic political price of sustaining them sufficiently to undermine their credibility. Thus, while the sanctions still may have some economic impact, they are unlikely to communicate the kind of political message that is necessary to compel or deter an adversary.

My analysis focuses on *political ideology* and *group economic interests* as the two principal determinants of domestic constraints.[52] I use the term "ideology" in its generic sense, as a set of deeply rooted, intensely felt, and widely held values and beliefs that have a profound and pervasive influence on politics and policy.[53] This set of values and

---

[50]For the general weak state argument about the United States in comparison with other Western states, see Peter J. Katzenstein, "International Relations and Domestic Structures: Foreign Economic Policies of Advanced Industrial States," *International Organization* 30 (Winter 1976): 1–45; Stephen D. Krasner, "United States Commercial and Monetary Policy: Unravelling the Paradox of External Strength and Internal Weakness," in *Between Power and Plenty*, ed. Peter J. Katzenstein (Madison: University of Wisconsin Press, 1978), pp. 51–87; Andrew Shonfield, *Modern Capitalism: The Changing Balance of Public and Private Power* (New York: Oxford University Press, 1965), pp. 298–382.

[51]Bruce Russett and Harvey Starr, *World Politics: The Menu for Choice* (San Francisco: Freeman, 1981), pp. 237–38.

[52]For a fuller and more abstract discussion of this analytic framework, see my "From Consensus to Conflict: The Domestic Political Economy of East–West Energy Trade," *International Organization* 38 (Autumn 1984): esp. pp. 626–31. Ideology and group economic interests correspond to the macropolitical and microeconomic sources of conflict as defined and labeled in my article.

[53]Ideology in its broadest sense has been defined as "a way of thinking about man and society" (Theodore Adorno et al., *The Authoritarian Personality*, cited in Robert E. Lane, *Political Ideology* [New York: Free Press, 1962] p. 14). The anthropologist Clifford

beliefs does not necessarily have to be rooted in a formally developed doctrine—as, for example, is the case with Marxism-Leninism. What is important analytically, what distinguishes highly ideological politics, is the elevation of policy above politics. The substantive specifics tend to become less important than the ideological garb that, in the words of B. Thomas Trout, "equates them with societal purpose . . . gives them broad teleological meaning."[54] Alexander George refers to this process as the acquisition of "normative legitimacy," a close to irrefutable claim to being "consistent with fundamental national values and contributing to their enhancement."[55] The overwhelming effect is to make internal conflict (i.e., politics) less likely and, in extreme instances, by definition illegitimate.

It is the nature of foreign policy in general, as James Rosenau has written, to allow for "a degree of manipulation of symbols that is unmatched in any other political situation."[56] This has been especially true in the American weltanschauung. As Walter Lippmann observed fifty years ago, "in the great blooming, buzzing confusion of the outer world we pick out what our culture has already defined for us, and we tend to perceive that which we have picked out in the form stereotyped for us by our culture."[57] More recently, and in a sense even more revealingly, we find scholars as diverse in their perspectives as Franz Schurmann and Stephen Krasner disagreeing about the precise conceptualization and applications of ideology but agreeing on its centrality to American foreign policy.[58]

Geertz takes the next step toward a more political construct with his definition of ideology as "the authoritative concepts that render it [politics] meaningful, the successive images by means of which it can be sensibly grasped" ("Ideology as a Cultural System," in *Ideology and Discontent*, ed. David E. Apter [New York: Free Press, 1964], p. 63). See also Giovanni Sartori, "Politics, Ideology, and Belief Systems," *American Political Science Review* 63 (June 1969): 398–411.

[54]B. Thomas Trout, "Rhetoric Revisited: Political Legitimation and the Cold War," *International Studies Quarterly* 19 (September 1975): 254.

[55]Alexander, L. George, "Domestic Constraints on Regime Change in U.S. Foreign Policy: The Need for Policy Legitimacy," in *Change in the International System*, ed. Ole R. Holsti, Randolph M. Siverson, and A. L. George (Boulder, Colo.: Westview Press, 1980), p. 235.

[56]James M. Rosenau, "Comparative Foreign Policy: Fad, Fantasy, or Field?" *International Studies Quarterly* 12 (September 1968): 328.

[57]Walter Lippmann, *Public Opinion*, rev. ed. (New York: Free Press, 1960), p. 81. The context of Lippmann's observation was the rejection by the U.S. Congress of the League of Nations and the resurgence of American isolationism.

[58]Franz Schurmann, *The Logic of World Power* (New York: Pantheon, 1974), and Stephen D. Krasner, *Defending the National Interests: Raw Materials Investment and U.S. Foreign Policy* (Princeton: Princeton University Press, 1978). See also John S. Odell, *U.S. International Monetary Policy: Markets, Power, and Ideas as Sources of Change* (Princeton: Princeton University Press, 1982).

The construct I will use is the "Cold War ideology."[59] More specifically, I refer to two fundamental sets of values and beliefs that consistently have been invoked as the basis for elevating policy above the normal conflict and constraints of politics. First is the peculiarly American *anticommunist ethic*. American anticommunism, at home no less than abroad, always has had a certain crusade-like quality. In a general sense anticommunism can be seen as but the latest manifestation of the recurring historical syndrome that Richard Hofstadter has called "the paranoid style in American politics."[60] The reaction against communism has been particularly intense because to an even greater extent than earlier objects of American fears, communism has been seen, as Michael Parenti has observed, as "the diabolical antithesis of everything [Americans] have been taught to esteem. The communists are despotic, we are democratic; they are collectivistic, we are individualistic; they have a controlled economy, we have free enterprise; they are 'extreme,' we are moderate; they are godless, we are God's children; they are alien, we are Americans; they are evil, we are virtuous."[61]

Thus, when the Bolshevik Revolution actually brought Communists to power in the Soviet Union, that country came to be viewed as evil incarnate.[62] President Woodrow Wilson shared this moral outrage and feared that his vision of a new world order was endangered. "The world must be made safe for democracy" really translated into "democracy will make the world safe"—or, as Wilson put it, "peace must be planted on the tested foundations of political liberty."[63] It

[59]A similar formulation is William A. Gamson and André Modigliani, *Untangling the Cold War: A Strategy for Testing Rival Theories* (Boston: Little, Brown, 1971), pp. 26–57.

[60]Richard Hofstadter, *The Paranoid Style in American Politics and Other Essays* (New York, 1967). Louis Hartz makes a similar argument: "When a liberal community faces military and ideological pressure from without, it transforms eccentricity into sin, and the irritating figure of the bourgeois gossip flares into the fighting figure of an A. Mitchell Palmer or a Sen. McCarthy" (*The Liberal Tradition in America* [New York: Harcourt Brace Jovanovich, 1955], p. 12).

[61]Michael Parenti, *The Anti-Communist Impulse* (New York: Random House, 1969), p. 64.

[62]No less a source than the *New York Times* reported that eighteen-year-old girls were being forced to register at "bureaus of free love" and then were designated husbands without their consent. Also typical was the outraged outpouring of Senator Myers of Montana: "They utterly destroyed marriages, the home, the fireside, the family, the cornerstones of all civilization, all society. . . . They defy alike the will of God, the precepts of Christianity, the decrees of civilization, the customs of society." The influential *Literary Digest* reported "ceremonies in which effigies of Jesus, Moses and Mohammed were burned as youths danced around the bonfire." All of these instances are cited in James A. Nathan and James K. Oliver, *United States Foreign Policy and World Order*, 2d ed. (Boston: Little, Brown, 1981), p. 15.

[63]Cited in ibid., p. 12.

was on this basis that Wilson dispatched American troops in a joint anti-Bolshevik military intervention with the British and French. It also was on this basis that his attorney general, A. Mitchell Palmer, launched his Bill of Rights–trampling raids against the alleged communist threat on the home front. The very term "Red scare" is revealing of the emotionalism and paranoia that have been the essence of American anticommunism.

During World War II anti-Nazism superseded anticommunism.[64] But after the war the old anticommunist ethic resurfaced in the even more antagonistic form that Daniel Yergin has called the "Riga axioms."[65] In this view the Soviets were not adversaries with whom it was possible to cultivate mutual interests and to settle conflicts of interest peacefully, one great power to another. Rather they were international revolutionaries wholly committed to world conquest. They sought to impose their totalitarian order on free societies everywhere. They would not hesitate to use force to do so, and then to maintain their dominance through any repressive means they considered necessary.

All of this went beyond the normal antagonisms of power politics to evoke the image of a fundamental and profound moral conflict between the forces of good (us) and the forces of evil (them). It thus was ingrained in the American ideology that it was because of Soviet ideology that accommodation between the nations was impossible. Consequently, any policy that could be cast in these "ethical" terms of anticommunism/anti-Sovietism automatically became endowed with a righteousness that virtually made it the moral equivalent of war.

A second and related basis of the Cold War ideology has been the *national security imperative*, the redefinition of the traditional conception of providing for the national defense in the much broader terms

---

[64]Rep. Clinton Woodrum (D-Va.) made the classic statement of this position: "It is permitted in time of grave danger to walk with the devil until the bridge is crossed" (cited in George C. Herring, Jr., *Aid to Russia, 1941–1946* [New York: Columbia University Press, 1973], p. 22).

[65]The term is from Daniel Yergin, *Shattered Peace: The Origins of the Cold War and the National Security State* (Boston: Houghton Mifflin, 1977). Yergin dubs the alternate view of the Soviet Union as more of a traditional great power the "Yalta axioms." Another useful conceptualization differentiating the "essentialist" from the "mechanistic" and "cybernetic" views of the Soviet Union is Lawrence T. Caldwell and Alexander Dallin, "U.S. Policy toward the Soviet Union," in *Eagle Entangled: U.S. Foreign Policy in a Complex World*, ed. Kenneth A. Oye, Robert J. Lieber, and Donald Rothchild (New York: Longmans, 1979), esp. pp. 215–19. A third approach is William Welch's categories of the ultrahard "great beast," hard "mellowing tiger," and mixed "neurotic bear" views; see his *American Images of Soviet Foreign Policy* (New Haven: Yale University Press, 1970).

of safeguarding the national security. This is a much more encompassing concept of what has to be done to keep the nation secure and its interests well defended. In the past the basic American pattern had been to mobilize the defenses necessary to wage a war or otherwise meet a threat, and then to demobilize. But in a world in which both American interests and the principal threat to them were more global in scope than ever before, and in which the advent of nuclear weapons made deterrence of war more crucial than ever before, there could be no demobilization. There could be only constant vigilance.

Consequently, the requisites for security were much greater now than in the past. Since the threat was omnipresent, a constant level of readiness had to be maintained for deterrence to be effective. Such readiness meant in part permanently large armed forces, constantly improving weapons technology, a system of collective defense alliances, and an effective intelligence network. It also meant a comprehensive commitment of resources and the subordination of other national priorities to national security objectives. As the early and ardent advocate James Forrestal put it, "the question of national security is not merely a question of the Army and the Navy. We have to take into account . . . all the activities that go into normal civilian life."[66] An overriding authority was being claimed over any number of activities of "normal civilian life" (e.g., trade) traditionally outside the realm of foreign policy except in times of war. But while war may not have been declared, the danger was clear and present, nothing short of the functional equivalent of war.

Challenging a policy cloaked in the ideological garb of the anticommunist ethic and the national security imperative could be a risky political proposition. Even private sector groups whose interests were at stake had to think twice about opposing a policy equated with societal purpose. Accusations of trading with the enemy, for example, hardly were the kind of publicity American businesses wanted. As far as Congress was concerned, at least in the pre-Vietnam and pre-Watergate era, the Cold War ideology provided all the more reason, in Clinton Rossiter's words, to allow the president to be "a kind of magnificent lion who can roam widely and do great deeds." Checks and balances only needed to be kept tight enough to ensure that "he does not try to break loose from his broad reservation."[67] Congress,

---

[66]Cited in Yergin, *Shattered Peace*, p. 204.

[67]Clinton Rossiter, *The American Presidency*, rev. ed. (New York: New American Library, 1962), pp. 68–69. Thomas Cronin dubs this idealized notion "the cult of the presidency." For a discussion from the "cult" perspective, see Cronin, *The State of the Presidency* (Boston: Little, Brown, 1975), chap. 2. For a more historical approach, see

on the other hand, was held (and held itself) to be, in Robert Dahl's words, "remarkably ill-suited to exercise a wise control over the nation's foreign policy."[68] It was none other than Senator J. William Fulbright who, as late as 1961, wondered aloud whether because of "the dynamic forces of the twentieth century"—essentially, the demonic Soviet threat and the exigencies of safeguarding the national security—"the time has not arrived, or indeed already passed, when we must give the Executive a measure of power in the conduct of our foreign affairs that we have hitherto jealously withheld."[69]

By the early 1970s, though, the Cold War ideology had lost its irrefutability. The reasons are familiar and have been examined in the literature at great length.[70] The usual shorthand is Vietnam and Watergate. For some segments of the public and of the policy-making elite, these wrenching experiences only reinforced and confirmed the Cold War ideology. But far more people than ever before, at both the mass and the leadership levels, no longer subscribed to the demonic view of the Soviet Union. Nor, having experienced such serious abuses, were they so prepared to accept the infinite elasticity of the national security rationale or the blank checks of presidential prerogative. Consequently, foreign policy politics reflected not the con-

---

William E. Leuchtenberg, *In the Shadow of FDR: From Harry Truman to Ronald Reagan* (Ithaca: Cornell University Press, 1983).

[68]Robert A. Dahl, *Congress and Foreign Policy* (New York: Harcourt Brace, 1950), p. 3. See also Holbert N. Carroll, "The Congress and National Security Policy," and Samuel Huntington, "Congressional Responses to the Twentieth Century," both in *The Congress and America's Future*, ed. David B. Truman (Englewood Cliffs, N.J.: Prentice-Hall, 1965).

[69]J. William Fulbright, "American Foreign Policy in the 20th Century under an 18th-Century Constitution," *Cornell Law Quarterly* 47 (Fall 1961): 2. Fulbright may have had in mind something based on the 1936 Supreme Court *Curtiss-Wright* decision. At a time when the Court was striking down executive authority in domestic affairs, it ruled that in foreign affairs presidential authority was greater than those powers specifically delegated by legislative action. The Court opinion held the president to be "the sole organ of the Federal Government in the field of international relations—a power which does not require as a basis for its exercise an act of Congress, but which, of course, like any other governmental power, must be exercised in subordination to the applicable provisions of the Constitution" (Robert F. Cushman, ed., *Leading Constitutional Decisions* [Englewood Cliffs, N.J.: Prentice-Hall, 1977], pp. 135–40).

[70]Ole R. Holsti and James N. Rosenau, *American Leadership in World Affairs: Vietnam and the Breakdown of Consensus* (Boston: Allen & Unwin, 1984); William Schneider, "Conservatism, Not Interventionism: Trends in Foreign Policy Opinion, 1974–1982," in *Eagle Defiant: United States Foreign Policy in the 1980s*, ed. Kenneth A. Oye, Robert J. Lieber, and Donald Rothchild (Boston: Little, Brown, 1984), pp. 33–64; Joseph S. Nye, Jr., ed., *The Making of America's Soviet Policy* (New Haven: Yale University Press, 1984); George H. Quester, *American Foreign Policy: The Lost Consensus* (New York: Praeger, 1982); and I. M. Destler, Leslie Gelb, and Anthony Lake, *Our Own Worst Enemy: The Unmaking of American Foreign Policy* (New York: Simon & Schuster, 1984).

sensus bred by the unifying force of a single widely held ideology but the intense conflict and corresponding constraints that arise when one world view competes against another.[71]

One reason for the contrasts over time in the domestic politics of export controls involves this more general transformation of the political context. A second factor is the redefinition of the economic interests at stake in this issue area that resulted from the profound changes that were occurring in the American economy. Before the 1970s, trade with the Soviet Union had never really mattered very much in either macro- or microeconomic terms. While the business cycle had gone through periodic fluctuations, overall these were years of prosperity. As Table 1.1 shows, the general path of macroeconomic indicators was upward. Real GNP grew at an average rate of 2.7 percent. The trade balance was positive. Unemployment averaged 4.5 percent and inflation 3.0 percent.

At the micro level of group interests, no substantial losses were being incurred. American exporters had flirted briefly in the early postwar years with the lure of a vast pump-priming Soviet market, but this trade never developed. Even when, for example, in 1963 the Kennedy administration proposed the sale of $250 million in grain to the Soviet Union, the reaction in the farm belt was lukewarm at best. There was then no pressing need for new export markets. There was, though, a strong sentiment, as expressed by ten farm belt members of the House Agriculture Committee, that "the vast majority of American farmers, like the vast majority of all Americans, are unwilling to sell out a high moral principle, even for solid gold."[72] In other situations as well, as Chapters 3 and 4 will show, American business actually had an interest in excluding the Soviet Union from world markets. Thus a nation whose president had called upon it to bear any burden and pay any price was able to support anti-Soviet sanctions because the burden and price were basically affordable.

In the late 1970s, however, this economic context also began to change. As Table 1.1 shows, the trade account went out of balance, and both unemployment and inflation rates were up. Then in the early 1980s these indicators turned even more unfavorable. The combined toll of recurring recessions, mounting trade deficits, and spiraling inflation had snuffed out the old prosperity.

---

[71]As one analyst of public opinion polls put it, "as far as the public is concerned, we are neither in a period of détente nor in a cold war like the 1950s" (Tom W. Smith, "The Polls: American Attitudes toward the Soviet Union and Communism," *Public Opinion Quarterly* 47 [Summer 1983]: 279).

[72]Congressional Quarterly, *1963 Almanac* (Washington, D.C., 1964), p. 328.

Table 1.1. Macroeconomic indicators, United States, 1945–1983

Time period	Real GNP growth	Trade balance (imports/exports)[a]	Unemployment	Inflation
1945–69	2.7%	0.7	4.5%	3.0%
1970–79	3.2	1.1	6.2	7.1
1980–83	0.9	1.2	8.5	8.3

[a]A figure less than 1 indicates a positive balance of trade.
SOURCES: U.S. Bureau of the Census, *Statistical Abstract of the United States* (1984); Executive Office of the President, *Economic Report of the President* (1984); Federal Reserve Board of Governors, *Federal Reserve Bulletin* no. 9 (1984); United Nations, *Yearbook of International Trade Statistics* (1981).

The sanctions have increased the resulting pressures because the costs have to be borne disproportionately by particular groups within the society. Farmers have been the most salient example. Exports had come to account for an increasingly large share of output and the Soviet Union imported more American grain than any other customer in the world. But as the Siberian natural gas pipeline controversy showed, industrial exporting interests also have acquired strong enough stakes in the Soviet trade to mount a formidable lobbying campaign. Actual exports to the Soviet Union never have been very substantial, but in the midst of the worst recession since the Great Depression their relative importance far exceeded their absolute value. Under such economic conditions the burden to be borne and the price to be paid for anti-Soviet sanctions were much less affordable and therefore less readily dismissed from policy debates.

In sum, the central argument at the domestic level of analysis is that *the domestic politics of the Soviet trade issue have changed because the underlying domestic political economy has changed.* As long as anti-Soviet sanctions could be cast in strong ideological terms, and as long as prosperity minimized the motivations for economic gains from trade with the Soviet Union, consensus far outweighed constraints. Once these conditions no longer were met, the politics became more conflictual and constraining.

Perhaps if the old Cold War ideology had been totally discredited, a new consensus would have formed around a policy of promoting trade as an inducement to improved political relations. But while the old ideology has been weakened, it has not been totally discredited. It thus has acted as its own constraint on the alternative policy of promoting trade within an overall détente strategy as an inducement for

49

improved U.S.–Soviet relations. The result, as we shall see in more detail in Chapter 7, has been a worst-of-all-worlds scenario, in which both the old sanctions strategy and the new inducement strategy are constrained to the point of confronting American policy makers, no matter which way they turn, with the bluffer's dilemma.

In attempting economic coercion against the Soviet Union, then, the United States faces the following problem: On the one hand, anti-Soviet sanctions can have a certain symbolic value for American foreign policy irrespective of what the European allies do, what the domestic reaction is, and what the actual impact on the Soviet Union is. On the other hand, the Soviets may be able to resist even when the sanctions are joined by the Europeans and have strong support within the United States. Only if constraints are weak at home and abroad will American sanctions have any prospect of significantly weakening the Soviets' economy, limiting their military capabilities, influencing their policy, or achieving other instrumental coercive objectives. *Conflicts both with allies and with domestic constituencies therefore must be minimized if the United States is to achieve economic coercive power over the Soviet Union.*

CHAPTER TWO

The Onset of the Cold War and East–West Trade Controls, 1945–1953

LEAVING ONE WORLD BEHIND

As part of the World War II alliance against Adolf Hitler, the Soviet Union had been second only to Great Britain as a recipient of American lend-lease assistance. Shipments exceeded $9 billion in value and included aircraft, tanks, explosives, boots and shoes, industrial machinery, vehicles, oil refinery equipment and technology, food, and anything else needed to keep the Red Army going and the war-torn Soviet economy solvent.[1] In looking toward the postwar world, President Franklin D. Roosevelt reasoned that through continued economic relations with the Soviet Union and the new political mechanisms being constructed for conflict management and crisis resolution (e.g., the United Nations), the fatal flaws of the interwar period could be averted. In addition, what a wonderful pump primer for the domestic economy the vast Soviet market could be! As FDR's most trusted adviser, Harry Hopkins, enthusiastically forecast in 1944:

[1] A detailed inventory of American shipments to the Soviet Union under lend-lease can be found in U.S. War Department, Finance Department, *Quantities of Lend-Lease Shipments: A Summary of Important Items Furnished Foreign Governments by the War Department during World War II* (Washington, D.C.: Government Printing Office, 1946). Antony Sutton claims that this and other government sources systematically underestimate the assistance rendered and the technology transferred; see his *Western Technology and Soviet Economic Development, 1930–1945* (Stanford: Hoover Institution Press, 1970) and *Western Technology and Soviet Economic Development, 1945–1965* (Stanford: Hoover Institution Press, 1973).

Recently I've been talking with some Russians in this country. From what they told me I estimate that in the first year after the war they will want to buy as much as $750,000,000 worth of goods from us—electrical equipment, machine tools, power equipment, railroad equipment. They will have need to buy almost as much from us every year for the next ten years, perhaps longer. . . . The logical thing is to cooperate with Russia, make the maintenance of armaments by her and by us for defense against each other unnecessary.

The fears of American conservatives that the Soviets would use the benefits of trade to become a "destroying monster," Hopkins went on to say, would prove unfounded because "destroying monsters grow out of poverty. . . . Prosperous, healthy going countries have no need to attack others." While Russia had "a political philosophy different from our own," she, too, was eager to "return to her task of industrial expansion" and the "betterment of the lives of her people."[2]

The Rooseveltian One World view and strategy, however, quickly felt the strains of American–Soviet conflicts over the shape of the postwar order. In this context FDR tabled Treasury Secretary Henry Morgenthau's January 1945 proposal for a low-interest, long-term $10 billion loan to the Soviets. He was no more receptive to a formal application for a scaled-down $6 billion loan made by Soviet Foreign Minister V. M. Molotov. A few months later, on V-E day, the new American president, Harry S. Truman, abruptly terminated lend-lease assistance, going so far as to recall ships already at sea and laden with supplies. While Truman claimed that such action was compelled by the expiration of the statutory authority for lend-lease once hostilities had ceased, such an innocuous explanation, coming two weeks after his famed confrontation with Molotov over Poland, was not very credible.[3]

[2]Harry Hopkins, "What Victory Will Bring Us," *American Magazine* 137 (January 1944): 21. Hopkins was not alone in his anticipation of lucrative markets. The magazine *Industrial Marketing* called Russia "without doubt the richest potential export market for American industrial equipment and products in the immediate and future postwar period." New York financiers bandied about estimates of $1 to $2 billion in annual exports. See John Lewis Gaddis, *The United States and the Origins of the Cold War* (New York: Columbia University Press, 1972), pp. 187–88.

[3]The oft-quoted incident illustrative of this hardening of the American line is Truman's meeting with Molotov less than two weeks after his assumption of the presidency. Truman berated Molotov for Soviet intervention in the affairs of Poland in what Stephen Ambrose called "the language of a Missouri mule driver." When a shocked Molotov responded, "I have never been talked to like that in my life," Truman retorted, "Carry out your agreements and you won't get talked to like that." See Stephen E. Ambrose, *Rise to Globalism* (New York: Penguin, 1980), pp. 101–2, and Truman's speech of October 28, 1945, reprinted in *Department of State Bulletin* 13 (1945): 653–56.

Much more to the point was advice being cabled from Moscow. American Ambassador W. Averell Harriman, who as a financier and businessman back in the 1920s and early 1930s had been a leading proponent of normalized trade and diplomatic recognition, now urged that the Soviets be shown "that our willingness to cooperate in their vast reconstruction problems will depend upon their behavior in international matters."[4] George F. Kennan, the chargé d'affaires in Moscow, went even further, cautioning vigilance against any trade that might "again, as in the cases of Germany and Japan, be creating military strength which might some day be used to our disadvantage." For, Kennan continued, "the present Soviet economic program is one of military industrialization, designed to serve political purposes antagonistic to our interests. Our government has no reason to further this program."[5]

Initially, though, Truman pursued something of a mixed strategy. On the one hand, with economic defense objectives in mind, he embargoed aircraft, ammunition, munitions, army boots, and other exports with direct military applications. But $220 million worth of industrial machinery and other "nonlethal" supplies that had been in the lend-lease pipeline were freed up in October 1945. And machinery, vehicles, petroleum, energy technology, and other exports that could be argued to have indirect military significance still could be legally traded by the private sector. Thus in 1946 American exports to the Soviet Union still totaled $352 million—well below wartime lend-lease levels but higher than in the 1930s and than in any of the next twenty-five years. In 1947 total exports dropped 57.6 percent, but they still amounted to $149 million. Of that total, industrial machinery, agricultural equipment, and oil industry technology accounted for $119 million. As late as November 21, 1947, President Truman replied to a reporter's query about continuing Soviet purchases of American machinery, "I see no reason to stop it now."[6]

The nonchalance of such remarks belied the mounting foreign policy pressures of the emerging Cold War. Truman's own "doctrine," as laid out in his famous address to a joint session of Congress on March 12, 1947, had redefined the world in terms of a struggle

---

[4]Herbert Feis, *Churchill, Roosevelt, and Stalin* (Princeton: Princeton University Press, 1957), p. 646. See also Joan Hoff Wilson, *Ideology and Economics: U.S. Relations with the Soviet Union, 1919–1933* (Columbia: University of Missouri Press, 1974) and *American Business and Foreign Policy, 1920–1933* (Lexington: University of Kentucky Press, 1971).

[5]George F. Kennan, *Memoirs, 1925–1950* (Boston: Little, Brown, 1967), pp. 268–69.

[6]*Public Papers of the Presidents of the United States: Harry S. Truman, 1947* (Washington D.C.: Government Printing Office, 1963), p. 501.

between two blocs representing and propagating "alternative ways of life," one "distinguished by free institutions . . . and freedom from political oppression" and one that "relies upon terror and oppression . . . and the suppression of personal freedoms."[7] The Soviet Union had not been explicitly named as model and propagator of the second image, but that hardly was necessary. Any lingering doubts about the nature of the adversary were squarely addressed by George Kennan in his famous "Mr. X" article:

> There can never be on Moscow's side any sincere assumption of a community of aims between the Soviet Union and the powers which are regarded as capitalist. . . . If the Soviet Government occasionally sets its signature to documents which would indicate the contrary, this is to be regarded as a tactical manouevre permissible in dealing with the enemy (who is without honor) and should be taken in the spirt of *caveat emptor*. Basically, the antagonism remains. It is postulated.[8]

Domestic political pressures were increasing as well. The Soviet trade issue had come to a head in Congress for the first (but hardly the last) time during the summer of 1947 over continued American oil exports. How could we, protested one congressman, "with one hand send money abroad to prevent the extension of communism and with the other provide the mother country of communism with our goods?" With oil shortages and rationing in the Midwest, stormed another, "whom the gods would destroy they first make mad. . . . Think of it: rationing gas to American citizens and shipping 1,000,000 barrels per month to Russia."[9] A mandatory oil embargo bill was popular enough to pass the House. With the assistance of Arthur H. Vandenberg, chairman of the Senate Foreign Relations Committee, the administration succeeded in tying it up in the Senate. But with the presidential election little more than a year away, Truman could hardly be insensitive to the domestic political climate.

Declassified documents show that the key decision to tighten export controls beyond the economic defense objective was taken at a meeting of the National Security Council (NSC) on December 17, 1947. It was the determination of the NSC that "U.S. national security requires the immediate termination, for an indefinite period, of ship-

---

[7]"Special Message to the Congress on Greece and Turkey: The Truman Doctrine," March 12, 1947, in ibid., pp. 176–80.
[8]Mr. X, "The Sources of Soviet Conduct," *Foreign Affairs* 27 (July 1947): 572.
[9]*Congressional Record*, 80th Cong., 1st sess., vol. 93, pt. 6, June 20, 1947, pp. H7493, H7497.

ments from the United States to the USSR and its satellites which . . . would contribute to Soviet military potential."[10] This could have been interpreted as only a reaffirmation of the existing economic defense objective. But the new regulations announced the next month by Averell Harriman, who now was secretary of commerce, required "close scrutiny of all shipments of industrial materials and equipment which have direct or indirect military significance and which are destined for Eastern Europe."[11] The "or indirect" clause was the key. No longer was it considered sufficient to embargo only exports that would directly enhance Soviet military capabilities. Nonmilitary industrial machinery and equipment could not necessarily be shot back but they did strengthen the industrial base on which Soviet military capabilities depended. It therefore was no less imperative to control them.

At the same time that these new regulations were being promulgated publicly, a joint memorandum from Secretary of State George Marshall, Secretary of Defense James Forrestal, and Secretary of Commerce Harriman established an interdepartmental group with responsibility "for studying and formulating a statement on the means available for economic warfare." This memorandum made it clear that American policy now was geared to much more than the economic defense objective of limiting Soviet military capabilities, even so broadly redefined as to include industrial exports with only indirect military significance. The objective now was "to inflict the greatest economic injury to the USSR and its satellites," to apply the full economic squeeze in an effort to disrupt their economies more generally and stunt their economic growth—in short, not only to pursue economic defense but also to take the offensive and wage economic warfare.[12]

It also was at this time that trade controls came to have a third major objective, namely, to contribute to the more general American deterrence posture. The politico-strategic context of East–West relations had been changed dramatically by the Soviets' complicity in the February 1948 coup in Czechoslovakia and their June 1948 blockade

[10]Report by the National Security Council, "Control of Exports to the USSR and Eastern Europe," December 17, 1947, in *Foreign Relations of the United States: 1948* (hereafter *FRUS: year*), 4: 511–12.

[11]U.S. Department of Commerce, *Fourth Quarterly Report under the Export Control Act* (1948), p. 13. The details of the new regulations are laid out in George L. Bell, "New Export Licensing Policies of the Department of Commerce," *Foreign Commerce Weekly* 30 (March 6, 1948).

[12]Memorandum of conversation by the Acting Adviser to the Division of Occupied Areas Economic Affairs, March 16, 1948, in *FRUS: 1948* 4: 524–26.

of Berlin. Intensified trade controls provided the United States with another means of signaling its will to resist Soviet aggression. In this respect the broader export controls promulgated in March 1948 were a corollary to the Truman Doctrine and the Marshall Plan, the two other cornerstones of the new Cold War foreign policy already in place.

Accordingly, as Table 2.1 shows, American exports to the Soviet Union declined drastically in 1948 and 1949. Total exports fell from the 1947 quarterly average of $37.3 million to $20.8 million in the first quarter of 1948, $4.2 million in the second quarter, and $1.7 million in the third quarter. The figures for the first two quarters of 1949 would have been even lower were it not for a $4.3 million sale of

Table 2.1. Value of all American exports to the Soviet Union and exports of indirect military significance, 1945–1953 (thousands of dollars)

Year	All exports	Exports of indirect military significance[a]
1945	$1,838,292	n.a.
1946	357,792	n.a.
1947		
Quarterly average	37,344	$27,475
Total	149,377	109,906
1948		
1st quarter	20,829	19,169
2nd quarter	4,199	3,662
3rd quarter	1,678	292
4th quarter	1,173	624
Total	27,879	23,747
1949		
1st quarter	2,263[b]	233
2nd quarter	3,550[c]	101
3rd quarter	630	102
4th quarter	204	60
Total	6,647	496
1950	752	10
1951	55	0
1952	15	4
1953	18	4

[a]Includes the following product sectors: electrical machinery, engines and turbines, aircraft parts, petroleum, energy industry equipment, construction equipment, and vehicles.
[b]Includes $1,410,000 special sale of cotton; otherwise, $853,000.
[c]Includes $2,931,000 special sale of cotton; otherwise, $619,000.
Sources: U.S. Department of Commerce, Bureau of the Census, *United States Exports of Domestic and Foreign Merchandise: Country of Destination by Subgroup,* Report no. FT420, monthly editions, 1945–1953; *Summary of Foreign Commerce of the United States,* annual and monthly editions, 1945–1953.

cotton at the behest of powerful (and otherwise quite conservative) southern senators concerned with a glut in the cotton market. When exports with indirect military significance (such as industrial machinery, vehicles, oil, and oil industry equipment) are isolated, the policy shift is even more evident. As late as the first quarter of 1948 (when the new regulations had been announced but not yet implemented), these exports continued at relatively high levels. Thereafter, though, they fell to $3.7 million in the second quarter of 1948, to $0.3 million in the third quarter, and to $0.06 million by the fourth quarter of 1949.

DOMESTIC INSTITUTIONALIZATION OF PRESIDENTIAL AUTHORITY TO CONTROL EXPORTS

Up to this point exports had been controlled through temporary extensions of authority granted the president during World War II. Soon after his reelection President Truman submitted to Congress the Export Control Act of 1949, intended to institutionalize the embargo weapon against the Soviet Union and allow greater discretion in its use. Never before, except in times of war, had Congress granted a president the authority to control the export of anything but arms and munitions.[13] Even in extending the World War II authority, Congress had specified that it be exercised "to the minimum extent necessary."

But as Commerce Secretary Charles Sawyer stated in a message to Congress, "the need for control of exports is expected to continue for some time . . . to be essential to safeguard the security of the United States."[14] The new legislation empowered the president to embargo all exports to the Soviet Union and its allies and, if he deemed it necessary because of the possibility of transshipment to the Soviet bloc, to any other destination. The criteria governing the regulations were open-ended. They were to be "as he shall prescribe" and "to the extent necessary to achieve enforcement of this Act." Regulatory procedures were exempted from the Administrative Procedures Act because of their sensitive nature, yet violators still would be subjected to

---

[13]A summary history of export control law is provided in Harold J. Berman and John R. Garson, "United States Export Controls: Past, Present, and Future," *Columbia Law Review* 67 (1967): 791, n. 1.

[14]Commerce Department, *Sixth Quarterly Report* (1948), p. 2.

such severe administrative sanctions as loss of all export privileges and criminal penalties of fines up to $10,000 and a year in jail.

The rapid and overwhelming passage of the legislation clearly indicated that Congress concurred. The view of Congressman Clarence J. Brown (R-Ohio) that "this legislation is another step in conferring practically, well, let me say not dictatorial, but very broad powers on the Chief Executive" found little support among his colleagues. The dominant view and spirit of the times was better articulated by Eldon Spence (D-Ky.), House floor manager of the bill:

> Why should we not give the President these powers? We are not in normal times. Times have not been normal since 1940, when he was given these powers. I do not think it would be a good policy to put shackles on the President. . . . In these highly important international affairs, he ought to have the same powers . . . as the executives or dictators representing the enslaved peoples in totalitarian governments. We have got to trust these powers to somebody, and to limit them and restrict them by unnecessary conditions would weaken the very purpose for which they are given.[15]

The essence of this statement reveals the profound effect on policy of the Cold War ideology. It was not just some other adversary out there against whom export controls were being targeted. It was communists, the "dictators of enslaved peoples." Nor was this just the usual international rivalry or narrow defense concern. World War II may have ended, but the United States still was "not in normal times." The Congress already had seen fit to expand the executive's authority over foreign policy by creating a National Security Council, a Department of Defense, a Central Intelligence Agency, and a peacetime draft. It had authorized the president to negotiate the first peacetime military alliance in American history. It even had appropriated billions of dollars in economic aid to Western Europe. It thus was to be expected that it would readily pass the Export Control Act of 1949. Years later it would be said of this act that "no single piece of legislation gives greater power to the President to control American commerce."[16] But at the time the overriding consideration was that the end of

---

[15]*Congressional Record*, 81st Cong., 1st sess., vol. 95, pt. 1, February 17, 1949, pp. 1368, 1370, 1397. Committee hearings on the Export Control Act were characterized principally by affirmations of the need for this action. See U.S. Congress, Senate, Committee on Banking and Currency, *Extension of Export Controls: Hearings before a Subcommittee on S. 548*, 81st Cong., 1st sess., January–February 1949; and U.S. Congress, House, Committee on Banking and Currency, *Export Control Act of 1949: Hearings*, 81st Cong., 1st sess., February 1949.

safeguarding the national security against a demonic adversary justified extraordinary means. On such matters there would be no institutional constraints, only bipartisanship and deference.

However, if one rule of the game was that a president could have all the discretion he wanted for policies legitimized by the Cold War ideology, the second was that he had better use it. When, as we shall see, the Truman and Eisenhower administrations were willing to accept less stringent policies from the European allies, the American Congress became much less deferential. The first jousting on this issue had come in 1948 when Congressman Karl E. Mundt (R-S.D.) proposed an amendment to the Marshall Plan legislation requiring a cutoff of economic assistance to any country that traded with the Soviet bloc. With the bipartisan help of Congressmen Christian Herter (R-Mass.) and Jacob Javits (R-N.Y.) and Senator Arthur Vandenberg (R-Mich.), the Truman administration managed to water down the Mundt amendment. Instead of being automatic upon evidence of the existence of such trade, the termination of aid was made discretionary "whenever the Administrator determines that it is in the interest of national security." This language made it possible for the president to claim that the consequences of cutting off aid to an ally in need would more seriously endanger national security than nonmilitary exports to Russia could do.

In 1950–51, with American troops fighting Soviet-supplied North Korean communists and with, as Walter LaFeber puts it, McCarthyism playing "a starring role" in politics at home,[17] congressional pressure to punish other countries for trading with the Russians intensified. In his inimical fashion Senator Joseph McCarthy pointed the long finger and urged extreme action: "We should perhaps keep in mind the American boys and the few British boys, too, who had their hands wired behind their backs and their faces shot off with machine guns . . . supplied by those flag vessels of our allies. . . . Let us sink every accursed ship carrying materials to the enemy and resulting in the death of American boys, regardless of what flags those ships may fly. . . ."[18]

In September 1950 Senator Kenneth Wherry (R-Neb.) introduced a new bill requiring termination of aid to any allies who traded with the Soviets. Once again the Truman administration managed to di-

[17]Walter LaFeber, *America, Russia, and the Cold War, 1945–1971* (New York: Wiley, 1972), p. 107.
[18]Cited in Arthur M. Schlesinger, Jr., *Robert Kennedy and His Times* (Boston: Houghton Mifflin, 1978), 1: 105–6. One of McCarthy's key staff aides in his East–West trade investigations was the young lawyer Robert F. Kennedy.

lute the countersanctions by getting a clause added granting the executive the discretion to determine that there were overriding security reasons for continuing aid. But in mid-1951 the McCarthyite forces attacked again, and this time the dilution strategy failed. By unanimous votes both houses of Congress adopted the proposal by Senator James P. Kem (R-Mo.) making the termination of aid to any country conducting any trade with any communists nondiscretionary. Moreover, in a shrewd bit of parliamentary tactics the "Kem rider" was made veto-proof by its attachment to the supplemental appropriations bill that Truman vitally needed to support American forces then fighting in Korea.

Truman criticized the bill as self-defeating and unnecessary, arguing that "if we cut off our aid to a friendly country we might hurt ourselves more than we hurt the Soviet Union." He further contended that within the limits of realizing that "no one nation can successfully force its own system of controls upon every other nation . . . our experience thus far shows that effective controls can be accomplished by cooperation."[19] But since a veto of the entire appropriation bill was not possible without danger to the war effort in Korea, Truman had no immediate choice other than to sign the Kem rider into law.

The only recourse left was to support substitute legislation. What eventually passed Congress and was signed by the president was the Mutual Defense Assistance Control Act of 1951. Also called the Battle Act after its chief sponsor, Congressman Laurie C. Battle (D-Ala.), this law made termination of aid nondiscretionary only if a country exported items with direct military applications. With respect to all other exports, the president once again was left discretion not to punish if he found "that the cessation of aid would clearly be detrimental to the security of the United States." Reporting of any such exceptions to the foreign relations committees was required, and the State Department would submit a written report to Congress twice a year (later changed to once a year) on overall enforcement and compliance. But no provisions were made for legislative veto or other specific checks. It also was left to executive discretion to determine the line between direct and indirect military significance and to compile the corresponding 1-A (collaboration required) and 1-B (subject to presidential discretion) export control lists.[20]

[19]Statement by the President, "Rider in Third Deficiency Appropriation Bill Called Defective," *Department of State Bulletin* 24, no. 626 (June 25, 1951): 1028.

[20]Gunnar Adler-Karlsson, *Western Economic Warfare, 1947–1967* (Stockholm: Almquist & Wiksell, 1968), pp. 22–30.

This reinjection of discretionary clauses made it possible to avoid the termination of aid despite congressional protests. But the Battle Act also marked the outer limits of consensual politics. The Cold War ideology would not accommodate even a permissive attitude toward European–Soviet trade. Any further signs of "softness" therefore risked renewed attacks in Congress and, to mix terminology from two political scientists, arousal of the latent interest group of the inattentive public.[21] These were the voters who, while normally unconcerned about foreign policy, would be activated by the fears and emotions stirred up by the anticommunist ethic. Accusations of condoning European trade with the enemy definitely had this kind of activation potential, especially given the added context of all those tax dollars being "given" to the allies through the Marshall Plan.

Throughout this period, little or no countervailing pressure was being exerted by groups with an interest in trading with the Soviet Union. One reason was that at the time American exporters did not need the business. The pump priming that Harry Hopkins had envisioned as coming from the Soviet Union was coming from elsewhere. Between 1949 and 1953 total American exports grew at an average annual rate of 17.4 percent. Unemployment never was higher than 3.3 percent. In fact, during much of this period quotas had to be imposed to limit some exports irrespective of their destination because excess foreign demand was creating inflationary short supply situations at home.

A related factor was that past experiences had led American businessmen to feel that the Soviet market was risky.[22] There was a corporate if not personal memory that only a few years after Lenin declared that "we are emphatically in favor of economic arrangements with America, with all countries, but particularly with America," Stalin pulled in the welcome mat.[23] Additional claims over expropriations

[21]The concept of latent interest groups is central to the pluralist analysis of David B. Truman, *The Governmental Process* (New York: Knopf, 1951). The idea of the inattentive public is developed in Gabriel A. Almond, *The American People and Foreign Policy* (New York: Praeger, 1960).

[22]Wilson, *Ideology and Economics* and *American Business and Foreign Policy*. A less scholarly but fascinating account of the relations between American capitalists and the Soviet Union is Joseph Finder, *Red Carpet* (New York: Holt, Rinehart & Winston, 1983).

[23]Lenin is quoted in John Lewis Gaddis, *Russia, the Soviet Union, and the United States: An Interpretive History* (New York: Wiley, 1978), p. 91. Gaddis also cites (pp. 114–15) a 1930 report to the Politburo by Nikolai Krestinskii, deputy commissar for foreign affairs, which proposed that the Soviet Union increase pressure on the U.S. government to reconsider its policy of diplomatic nonrecognition by denying trade to American capitalists, who it was presumed would in turn lobby their government and who,

and renounced debts were added to those still outstanding from the Bolshevik Revolution, and exporters suffered as their sales plummeted from $114 million in 1930 to $13 million in 1932—at the very time that they needed all business possible. Thus, while there were exceptions such as Armand Hammer,[24] the historical reference of most American businessmen focused on the frequent gap between expected and actual rates of return and, worse, the ever-present risk that a communist state would resort to confiscation at a time and place of its own choosing.

Businessmen also felt a certain amount of concern over the consequences for the liberal international economic order if state trading economies were now to be allowed in.[25] What would happen to the systemic principle of governmental noninterference in the functioning of markets? Could the sanctity of contracts ever be assured? How would prices be determined? And what competitive advantages would the noncompetitive state trading monopolies have on world markets? For American businessmen these questions were partly ideological in nature, reflecting their commitment to the principles (albeit not always the practice) of laissez-faire at a time when all over the world national economic systems were being designed and redesigned. They also were in part a function of their own interest in preserving the status quo of an international economic order in which they were doing rather well. On an overall basis trade liberalization was functional to these interests because it created an expanding pie. But to invite in competitors who might disrupt the system or gain an advantage by their very unwillingness to abide by the rules of the economic game was a different matter indeed.

Finally, businessmen felt a fear of public wrath not unlike that which haunted politicians, only in their case it was the prospect of organized or even spontaneous boycotts by outraged consumers against those perceived as putting their private profits ahead of the security and welfare of the nation. The junior senator from Wisconsin was not averse to dragging businessmen in front of his Permanent

---

according to Marxist doctrine, should have no problem influencing the bourgeois executive. "The maximum contraction and eventual full cessation of our purchases will be our most important and convincing instrument for putting pressure on America," wrote Krestinskii. "The loss of Soviet markets, the importance of which has grown tremendously during the period of crisis [i.e., the Depression], will more quickly impel American business and political circles to reconsider their traditional position of not recognizing the USSR."

[24]A highly critical account of Hammer's dealings is in Finder, *Red Carpet*, pp. 135–39, 289–91. See also *Wall Street Journal*, August 30, 1984, pp. 1, 12.

[25]Samuel Pisar, *Coexistence and Commerce* (New York: McGraw-Hill, 1972).

Subcommittee on investigations and subjecting them to accusations of engaging in "traitor trade." However circumstantial the evidence, such an appearance could hardly be good for business.

Thus when President Eisenhower told America's young business leaders at the June 1953 convention of the Junior Chamber of Commerce that for the foreseeable future there would continue to be "one matter that overshadows all . . . one issue that effectively rules all others," his words were received with nary a blink. The president continued:

> It is—Our Nation's security.
> It engages every aspect of our lives. It arises in every arena in which a challenged civilization must fight to live.
> It is a military struggle. . . .
> It is an economic struggle. . . .
> It is a spiritual struggle. . . .
> For this whole struggle, in the deepest sense, is waged neither for land, nor for food, nor for power—but for the soul of man himself.[26]

Amidst such an apocalyptic struggle there clearly was no room for domestic constraints on American economic coercive power.

THE BASES FOR WESTERN EUROPEAN COLLABORATION

Gaining Western European collaboration, however, was not so easy. As Table 2.2 shows, before being disrupted by World War II, Western European trade with the Soviet Union and Eastern Europe had been more than 700 times the amount of comparable American trade. Moreover, the pattern of trade had been the highly complementary one detailed in Table 2.3: food, timber, fuels, and other raw materials flowed from east to west and manufactured goods, machinery, and vehicles from west to east. In the immediate aftermath of World War II, it appeared that this intra-European economic complementarity would be more important than ever. It was going to be difficult enough for Western European governments to feed their people without cutting off trade with the countries that traditionally supplied 25 percent of grain imports. How could bombed-out cities and villages be rebuilt without Soviet timber? Where would adequate fuel for heating homes and powering industry come from if the Polish

---

[26]Address by the President, Minneapolis, reprinted as "National Security and the Defense of Freedom," *Department of State Bulletin* 28, no. 730 (June 22, 1953): 863.

Table 2.2. Value of total trade, United States and Western Europe with the Soviet Union and Eastern Europe, 1938 (millions of dollars)

	United States	Western Europe[a]
Exports to:		
Soviet Union	$ 153.9	$ 75.3
Eastern Europe[b]	422.0	65.5
Imports from:		
Soviet Union	292.2	26.9
Eastern Europe	543.2	31.3
All exports and imports	$1,411.3	$199.0

[a]Western Europe includes all those countries that were later members of COCOM: Belgium, Denmark, France, Germany, Greece, Italy, Luxembourg, Netherlands, Norway, Turkey, and United Kingdom.

[b]Eastern Europe includes Albania, Bulgaria, Czechoslovakia, Hungary, Poland, Rumania, and the USSR (including Estonia, Latvia, and Lithuania).

SOURCES: Gunnar Adler-Karlsson, *Western Economic Warfare* (Stockholm: Almquist & Wiksell, 1968), p. 317, and Raymond F. Mikesell and Jack N. Behrman, *Financing Free World Trade with the Sino-Soviet Bloc* (Princeton: Princeton University Press, 1958), p. 5.

coal trade did not resume? According to the economist and *New York Times* correspondent Michael Hoffman, one of the principal motivations for the creation of the United Nations Economic Commission for Europe (ECE) in April 1947 was the promotion of intra-European trade as a stimulant to continent-wide economic recovery. Under the

Table 2.3. Commodity composition (selected) of Western European trade with the Soviet Union and Eastern Europe, 1938

Commodity group	Soviet Union	Eastern Europe
Imports:		
Food and beverages	38.2%	37.5%
Wood and paper products	32.8	22.8
Fuels	5.8	12.1
Subtotal, selected groups	76.8%	72.4%
Other	23.2	27.6
Total imports	100.0%	100.0%
Exports:		
Metals and manufactures	36.1	18.9
Machinery	23.2	17.1
Textiles and manufactures	9.0	15.6
Chemicals	6.4	8.6
Vehicles	7.7	5.5
Subtotal, selected groups	82.4%	65.7%
Other	17.6	34.3
Total exports	100.0%	100.0%

SOURCE: Derived from data in United Nations, Economic Commission for Europe, *Economic Survey of Europe in 1948* (Geneva, 1949), pp. 152–54.

stewardship of the Swedish diplomat Gunnar Myrdal, the ECE sought to redevelop trade to the point where by the early 1950s 19 percent of Western Europe's exports would go to Eastern Europe and 17 percent of its imports would come from there.[27]

The political legacy of two world wars on their soil within a generation also disposed Western European publics to balk almost instinctively at foreign policy strategies that ran the risk of leading once again down that slippery slope. As an American State Department official reported, the British ambassador "said we must bear in mind that the overwhelming public opinion of England still held to the view that war was not inevitable and that there was apprehension that steps of this type could be harmful in developing a situation which would make war more likely. He said this feeling led many in England to advocate the continuance of all possible relationships including economic in order to avert war."[28] Earlier in 1947 the British, who had been second only to Nazi Germany in total prewar trade with the East, had concluded a major sale to the Soviet Union of fifty-five gas turbines and an unspecified number of aircraft. Then on December 27 (only ten days after the NSC decision to move toward economic warfare) they signed a new major trade agreement with Stalin. This new agreement encroached even further on strategically sensitive areas by guaranteeing British exports of locomotives, generators, heavy machinery, and precision scientific and laboratory instruments.[29] An official government pronouncement hailed it as "not only the establishment of a short term programme but the development of Anglo-Soviet trade on a long term basis."[30]

By late 1949, however, the British as well as the other Europeans had changed course and become more (although not totally) willing to collaborate with a broader range of sanctions. According to State Department records, of the 202 export items on which the United States sought collective controls, agreement was reached to place 144 under total embargo (called International List I) and 6 under quota

[27]Michael C. Hoffman, "Problems of East–West Trade," *International Conciliation*, no. 511 (January 1957), pp. 275, 288–99. For similar hopeful estimates of a renewal of intra-European trade, see Organization for European Economic Cooperation, *Interim Report on the European Recovery Program*, vol. 1 (Paris, 1948), pp. 55 and 61.

[28]Memorandum of a conversation by the Assistant Secretary of State for European Affairs, "East–West Trade," June 5, 1951, in *FRUS: 1951*, 1: 1085–86.

[29]Adler-Karlsson, *Western Economic Warfare*, pp. 23, 143–44.

[30]*Board of Trade Journal*, January 3, 1948, p. 1. The *Times of London* went even further in its editorial, praising the trade agreement as expressing "the intention to develop relations eastward whenever possible as well as westward" (cited in Dudley Smith, *Harold Wilson* [London: Robert Hale, 1964], pp. 69–70).

restrictions (International List II), and to monitor but not control 27 others (International List III). Most of the items that were not placed on the international lists were industrial machinery and other exports whose military significance was not so direct or otherwise compelling. But the progress that had been made in gaining allied collaboration prompted one State Department official to report back to Washington that "it can now be stated that Western European trade security programs in general form an important adjunct to our own program."[31]

The next significant albeit partial step toward collaboration was the creation of COCOM (the Consultative Group–Coordinating Committee) in November 1949. The United States had pushed for the formation of some such adjunct to NATO because it believed that mutual consultation would result in "(a) . . . greater cooperation generally, (b) better implementation of controls, (c) the collective application of pressure against any country inclined to be recalcitrant, (d) the coordination of intelligence reports and prompt action . . . based upon mutual understanding of facts."[32] The allies, though willing to create a structure, balked at going too far toward its full and formal institutionalization. They agreed to consult and coordinate through COCOM. But they insisted that unlike NATO, COCOM should not be given a basis in treaty. Instead it existed only through the informal consent of the participating governments. Thus enforcement remained principally the responsibility of national authorities; no compliance measures were available to the multilateral organization other than diplomatic criticism. In addition, as rule-making authority was circumscribed by the unanimity principle, the scope of controls was likely to be defined by the least common denominator.

Secretary of State Dean Acheson instructed Harriman, the chief negotiator, that while "the United States was gratified in general at the results . . . and believes substantial progress has been made," it was necessary to begin the next step immediately and "raise specifically . . . [the] establishment of effective multilateral 1-B policy" (i.e., controls on exports with indirect military significance).[33] By late 1950 that further progress was forthcoming. British Foreign Secretary

[31]Policy paper approved by the Foreign Assistance Coordination Committee, "Existing East–West Trade Restrictions," July 1, 1949, in *FRUS: 1949*, 5: 130–33.

[32]Telegram, Special Representative in Europe for the Economic Cooperation Administration (Harriman) to the Administrator (Hoffman), March 19, 1949, in *FRUS: 1949*, 5: 99–100.

[33]Telegrams, Acheson to Harriman, December 7 and 15, 1949, in *FRUS: 1949*, 5: 177–81.

Aneurin Bevin and French Foreign Minister Robert Schuman issued a joint statement with Secretary of State Acheson affirming that "in addition to the embargo of exports of direct military significance . . . it is essential to restrict exports to the Soviet bloc of selected items which are required in key industrial sectors that contribute substantially to war potential."[34] Three days later a State Department memorandum concluded that our allies now recognized that "strategic considerations should be predominant in selecting items for control. . . . in principle at least, this should eliminate British opposition to controls where normal peacetime uses are said to predominate over strategic uses."[35]

Agreement in principle was quickly translated into implemented policy. On October 6 a long dispute between the United States and Britain was ended when the British imposed controls over all power-operated metal-working machine tools. The cost of these controls alone was estimated at almost $9 million. Controls also were increased in such sectors as chemicals, iron and steel, and vehicles. The *Board of Trade Journal,* an official government publication, stated that technical data also were now to be controlled more strictly because of the growing concern that "the object of the embargo or quantitative controls should not be defeated by the export of technical assistance, design data, manufacturing technique and special tools for making any controlled items."[36]

By the end of the London Tripartite Talks (October 17–November 20, 1950) the number of items under multilateral embargo had been increased from approximately 150 to 250, the quota list from approximately 50 to 123, and the monitoring list from approximately 30 to 100.[37] The same substantial degree of Western European collaboration continued through 1951–53. In November 1951 the *Board of Trade Journal* reported that Britain now was controlling "arms and ammunition and about 250 other items."[38] And the COCOM lists continued to grow. By August 1954, 320 items were under embargo, 92 controlled by quotas, and 102 monitored—a total of 514 items and an almost 200 percent increase over the initial scope of controls when COCOM was created in November 1949.

[34]Agreed Minute of the United States, British, and French Foreign Ministers, Tripartite Meetings of September 12–14 and 18–19, 1950, in *FRUS: 1950,* 4: 187–88.

[35]Telegram, Acting Secretary of State to U.S. Embassy, France, September 22, 1950, in *FRUS: 1950,* 4: 191–92.

[36]*Board of Trade Journal,* October 28, 1950, p. 670.

[37]Agreed Report of the London Tripartite Conversations on Security Export Controls, October 17–November 20, 1950, in *FRUS: 1950,* 4: 234–41.

[38]*Board of Trade Journal,* November 8, 1951, p. 789.

The effects of these stricter controls on European exports can be seen both in the aggregate and at the sectoral level. As the data in Table 2.4 show, after growing by 33 percent in the year before the formation of COCOM, Western European exports to the Soviet Union declined over the next two years by 39.4 percent. This decline may be compared with the 58.1 percent growth in total exports to all destinations during the same period. It also represents quite a short-fall from the $1.3 billion in Western European exports to the Soviet bloc originally projected by the Organization for European Economic Cooperation (OEEC) back when economic complementarity still appeared likely to be the principal determinant of trade patterns. The ECE attributed the decline "in general to the intensification of political tension and in particular to the more energetic application of licensing practices."[39]

Figures for individual nations conform to the same pattern. British exports to the Soviet Union, which had amounted to $54.7 million in 1938 and $49.4 million in 1947, dropped to a nadir of $10.4 million in 1951. France and West Germany registered only modest increases. Italian exports did increase in 1950–51, although at a fraction of the rate of increase of 1948–49, and they leveled off in 1952–53.

The exports that continued principally involved items with little even indirect military significance. Table 2.5 focuses on major commodity categories of general value to the Soviet industrial base: machinery, iron and steel, nonferrous metals, metal manufactures, chemicals, and precision instruments. From this angle as well, a major change in the pattern of trade is apparent. After an 85.8 percent

Table 2.4. Value of exports from European COCOM countries to the Soviet Union, 1948–1953 (millions of dollars)

Year	Value
1948	$ 88.7
1949[a]	118.0
1950	86.5
1951	71.5
1952	88.6
1953	134.2

[a]COCOM formed, November 1949.

SOURCE: United Nations, Economic Commission for Europe, *Economic Bulletin for Europe* 7 (August 1955): 52–53.

[39]United Nations, Economic Commission for Europe, *Economic Survey of Europe since the War* (Geneva, 1953), p. 60.

Table 2.5. Value of selected commodities exported from European COCOM countries to the Soviet Union, 1948–1953 (millions of dollars)

Year	Machinery	Iron and steel	Non-ferrous metals	Metal manufactures	Chemicals	Precision instruments	Total	Percent of total exports to Soviet Union
1948	$19.3	$6.7	$6.4	$1.6	$1.9	$2.3	$38.2	43.1%
1949	44.4	7.2	7.1	5.1	4.1	3.1	71.0	60.2
1950	52.1	3.1	5.3	4.0	0.7	1.1	66.3	76.6
1951	22.8	1.6	2.8	1.3	2.6	0.1	31.2	43.6
1952	10.2	7.6	2.0	0.6	3.4	0.1	23.9	27.0
1953	17.8	12.8	2.9	0.7	3.7	0.1	38.0	28.3

SOURCE: Derived from Gunnar Adler-Karlsson, *Western Economic Warfare, 1947–1967* (Stockholm: Almquist & Wiksell, 1968), Statistical Appendix C, pp. 269–314.

surge to $71 million in 1949, these important industrial exports fell to $66.3 million in 1950 and continued to decline through 1952 until they represented less than one-third the value of pre-COCOM levels. Moreover, the share of total Western European exports to the Soviet Union represented by these sectors dropped from a peak of 76.6 percent in 1950 to 27 percent in 1952. This percentage increased only slightly in 1953—an indication that any growth in exports that was then taking place was in such commodity groups as consumer manufactured goods.[40]

These were important lessons in how far the Europeans were and were not willing to go. As Chapter 1 has postulated, a first important factor contributing to collaboration on trade controls was the minimization of disputes over foreign policy strategy. The allies basically concurred with the more general deterrence objective of trade controls as an expression of collective will. While they stopped well short of inflicting on themselves a trauma akin to McCarthyism—as David Caute observes, the British managed to fight the Cold War without an "un-British affairs committee"[41]—the Europeans were no less alert than the United States to the Stalinist version of the Soviet threat. Especially for the British and French, still smarting from the wounds of failed diplomacy and ensuing war, the 1948 Czech coup, as Alexander George and Richard Smoke have observed, "evoked memories of the earlier fall of Czechoslovakia to Hitler" and thus "hardened

[40]Consumer manufactured goods as a share of total exports to the Soviet Union increased from 1.8% in 1949 to 14.5% in 1952.
[41]David Caute, *The Great Fear* (New York: Simon & Schuster, 1978), p. 20.

[their] image of Soviet leaders and their intentions."[42] A further reading of Soviet intentions (hostile) was taken from the Berlin crisis. Once the Soviets acquired the atomic bomb, the Europeans also reestimated their capabilities (formidable). Then came the Korean War, which, distant though it was, reinforced the need for a strong and credible deterrence posture. The cumulative effect was that to a greater extent than ever before—or since—the allies concurred with American estimations of the nature and severity of the Soviet threat.

A second important factor was that at this particular moment European economic motivations for trading with the Soviets were minimal. Exports had been growing rapidly without Soviet and Eastern European markets, averaging 30.1 percent annually between 1950 and 1954 in West Germany, for example. Unemployment was low (the British average was 1.7 percent) or falling (from 10.2 percent in 1950 to 7.0 percent in 1954 in West Germany). Moreover, even if the Europeans had wanted to trade, the Russians under Stalin did not. Table 2.6 shows the extent to which the Soviet Union turned itself and its satellites inward toward regional autarky. The trend was especially strong following the creation of the Council for Mutual Economic Assistance (COMECON) in 1949. By 1953 83 percent of the Soviet Union's trade was within its own bloc. Poland's 70.4 percent intrabloc trade, high as it was, was the lowest COMECON percentage. The pattern begins to change after Stalin's death, with first Georgi Malenkov and then Nikita Khrushchev turning more outward for trade. As Chapter 3 will show, this factor, along with others, contributed to shifts in Western European policy. But until then it made little economic sense to pursue trade with such an unwilling partner.

Thus European foreign policy interests were pointing toward trade controls, and their domestic economic interests did not seem to contravene this trend. It was reinforced by the extensive leverage the United States then possessed. American political prestige was rooted in the still fresh memories of World War II, an experience that more than anything else in the history of transatlantic relations was a tie that bound. The beneficence of the Marshall Plan added to the positive American image in quite tangible ways. And ultimately, the United States stood as Europe's protector at a time when self-defense was not yet again possible. All of these elements of prestige increased American influence in those immeasurable but potent ways discussed in general terms in Chapter 1. European leaders could invoke to their

[42]Alexander L. George and Richard Smoke, *Deterrence in American Foreign Policy: Theory and Practice* (New York: Columbia University Press, 1974), p. 110.

Table 2.6. Percentage of total international trade of seven Eastern bloc countries represnted by intrabloc trade, 1938, 1948, and 1953

Country	1938	1948	1953
USSR	5.2%	42.0%	83.0%
Bulgaria	31.0	78.0	87.0
Czechoslovakia	18.0	32.0	78.4
East Germany	—	75.0	86.0
Hungary	23.0	34.1	77.0
Poland	12.0	41.0	70.4
Rumania	27.0	70.6	84.4

SOURCE: U.S. Congress, House of Representatives, Joint Economic Committee, Subcommittee on Foreign Economic Policy, *A New Look at Trade Policy toward the Communist Bloc*, 87th Cong., 1st sess. 1961, p. 43.

publics the necessity and virtue of following the American lead as justification for any costs incurred in the process.

Besides being Europe's political protector, the United States was in the unusual position of being its economic provider. Between 1949 and 1953 a total of $15 billion in economic aid (87 percent of which was in outright grants) flowed from the United States to Western Europe through the Marshall Plan. As we saw earlier, the terms of the Battle Act tied Marshall Plan aid to collaboration with trade controls against the Soviet Union. Despite congressional pressures to do so, neither the Truman nor the Eisenhower administration ever actually invoked the Battle Act countersanctions. Nevertheless, the Battle Act remained in the background as a latent threat that Western European governments could not afford to ignore. The American president could always choose to invoke it if trade with the Soviet Union developed too far, or—an even more ominous possibility—the Congress might force him to do so. Thus, when Western European officials were asked by the Swedish author Gunnar Adler-Karlsson why they stuck to such strict controls in the early 1950s, "the answers invariably referred to the U.S. aid as the overridingly important reason."[43]

The United States also had other sticks at its disposal. At one point in August 1950, according to NSC records, the Truman administration threatened to counterembargo from export to Europe any industrial products with indirect military significance still being traded with the Soviet bloc.[44] Two months later came the joint statement by Bev-

[43]Adler-Karlsson, *Western Economic Warfare*, pp. 46, 47.
[44]Record of Actions by the National Security Council at its 66th Meeting (Action no. 347), August 24, 1950, in *FRUS: 1950*, 4: 179–80.

an, Schumann, and Acheson expanding controls to exports with indirect military significance. The U.S. Commerce Department compiled a blacklist of companies accused of transshipping goods of American origin or otherwise violating the embargo. Eventually 1,500 firms were denied U.S. government procurement contracts, business generated by Marshall Plan funds, and all trading privileges in the United States. The blacklist also was passed on to their home governments, which, if they chose, could add to the American measures.[45]

It is important to note that American economic leverage had positive sources as well. One such source was the special $100 million discretionary fund used in certain instances to compensate the allies for specific costs incurred by the control of trade.[46] "It is idle to demand of European countries a strict conformity," one American official reasoned, "unless some means is offered them which is compatible with their own economic possibilities."[47]

The United States also sought in less direct ways, as Harriman (now first administrator of the Battle Act) put it, to "remove the economic necessity" of trading with the Soviet bloc by developing both "new sources of supply for the goods imported from the bloc" and "new [export] markets in the free world so as to provide foreign exchange with which to pay for such imports."[48] This strategy acknowledged that while Europe's economic motives for trading with the Soviet bloc were dormant, they persisted. Inevitably, unless the United States could create other trade opportunities as alternatives (in essence, lure the potential alternative trade partners away from the target with alternative options of their own), the divisive factor of divergent economic interests would reemerge. Thus, while direct linkages never were drawn, such programs as the Offshore Procurement Policy, through which the Defense Department purchased $2.5 billion in European products at subsidized prices between 1951 and 1954, in a functional sense served the compensatory objective.

A similar argument can be made for American investment capital.

[45]Adler-Karlsson, *Western Economic Warfare*, pp. 55, 70.

[46]One example of the use of this compensatory fund was the $17 million in additional Marshall Plan aid granted France to cover the purchase of American coal as a substitute for Polish coal. See Theodore K. Osgood, "East–West Trade Controls and Economic Warfare," Ph.D. thesis, Yale University, 1957, p. 32.

[47]Memorandum, William Elliott, Director of Office of Defense Mobilization, to Brig. Gen. Robert W. Porter, Jr., Foreign Operations Administration, May 24, 1954, p. 7, in Clarence Francis Papers, Dwight D. Eisenhower Presidential Library.

[48]U.S. Department of State, *Second Semiannual Report to the Congress under the Mutual Defense Assistance Control Act of 1951* (hereafter referred to as Battle Act Report and no.), p. 43.

Even more than export markets, European reconstruction required massive infusions of capital. Through the Marshall Plan and such programs as the Investment Guaranty Program (IGP), which encouraged private investment in Europe by providing subsidies and risk insurance, the United States was transmitting such an infusion of capital.[49] While here, too, there was no direct link with collaboration in trade controls, with the McCarthyite Congress lurking in the background such programs provided a definite incentive to avoid actions that might endanger important economic benefits.

The United States' strategy thus was to draw on its own abundant economic resources as much as possible in order to make divergent economic interests converge. Combined with the political sources of American leverage, and in the context of a strong alliance consensus on basic foreign policy strategy, the strategy created conditions highly conducive to collective Western sanctions and, accordingly, to the minimization of the multilateral constraints on American economic coercive power.

SUMMARY: AMERICAN OBJECTIVES ASSESSED

Given, then, the low levels of both multilateral and domestic constraints in this early Cold War period, what success did the anti-Soviet sanctions register? Of the United States' principal instrumental objectives—economic defense, economic warfare, and deterrence—the second, with its vision of extreme disruption of the Soviet economy, was least furthered by the sanctions. The Soviets managed to rebuild their economy from the ravages of World War II despite them. They also made significant industrial advances, averaging 9 percent growth in industrial production between 1950 and 1953. Even the long-suffering Soviet consumer benefited from an 11.3 percent increase in the production of light manufactures and other consumer goods.[50]

The major reason for the limited impact of the sanctions as economic warfare may be traced to the unilateral constraint of the Soviets' capacity to substitute "domestic" production for what they could not import. The structure of their command economy was especially

---

[49]The best sources on the IGP are two books by Marina von Neumann Whitman: *The United States Investment Guaranty Program and Private Foreign Investment* (Princeton: Princeton University Press, 1959) and *Government Risk Sharing in Foreign Investment* (Princeton: Princeton University Press, 1965).

[50]G. Warner Nutter, *Growth of Industrial Production in the Soviet Union* (Princeton: Princeton University Press, 1962), pp. 198, 222.

useful for making the reallocations of resources necessary in such a situation. In addition (and this is why "domestic" is used loosely), their imperial strength conferred the added capacity to import goods in necessary quantities and on favorable terms from Eastern Europe.

Another limiting factor was the problem of policing the Western sanctions. As Averell Harriman stated with some concern in a report to Congress, the methods for getting around the enforcement of export controls were as "varied as the ingenuity of mankind."[51] There was espionage, military and industrial, both of which were productive investments for the Soviet Union in these years (how productive may never be fully known). There also was the transshipment gambit, the strategy of illegally routing and rerouting cargoes away from their ostensible destinations and to the Soviet Union. The high seas, free ports, the German border, the neutral countries—it was impossible to guard against all possible diversions. So while the governments of the COCOM members for the most part were being cooperative, the combination of enforcement problems within their boundaries and the availability of non-COCOM nations as alternative partners in themselves and as routes for illegal transshipments amounted to another (albeit lesser) type of multilateral constraint.

Sanctions were more successful in regard to the economic defense objective. Precisely how effective they were in limiting Soviet military technological capabilities cannot be known with certainty. Such speculations take us into the realm of the hypothetical. It is revealing, however, that even in these years of rapid overall growth the Soviets were experiencing major problems in the machinery and equipment sector. The domestic production rate for 1950–53 was -3.7 percent.[52] The Soviets tried looking elsewhere, increasing machinery and equipment imports from their satellites. By 1953 almost 30 percent of total Soviet imports, or $892.3 million, were in industrial machinery and equipment.[53] Yet only $17.8 million of this total came from the West (see Table 2.5), so that the Soviets had to turn to the less efficient suppliers of their own bloc. It seems reasonable to conclude that had the Soviets been able to import Western industrial machinery and technology, they could have substantially improved the industrial base on which their military capabilities rested. Consequently, while the sanctions were not crippling—after all, the Soviets did develop the atomic bomb and began to test the hydrogen bomb in

[51]State Department, Battle Act Report no. 2, p. 13.
[52]Nutter, *Industrial Production in the Soviet Union*, p. 222.
[53]Paul G. Marer, *Soviet and East European Foreign Trade* (Bloomington: Indiana University Press, 1972), p. 62.

these years—they did contribute to the maintenance of Western military technological superiority.[54]

Finally, and arguably most important, the sanctions did contribute to the political dimension of the Western alliance's deterrence posture. As another expression of the will to take collective action against the Soviet Union, economic sanctions reinforced the overall credibility of the Western alliance. Here again, what otherwise would have occurred can never be known for sure. But it seems reasonable to deduce that noncollaboration on the trade controls issue would have had serious credibility-eroding consequences for the overall Western deterrence posture.

Had the allies not collaborated as extensively as they did, even this limited coercive success would have been far more difficult, if not impossible. Consequently, when beginning in 1954 the Europeans showed increasing restiveness with the economic coercion strategy, the United States had cause for concern.

[54]Even though the Soviet Union tested a hydrogen bomb before the United States, its bomb was of much lower capability. Its yield was in the 200–400-kiloton range, whereas the American bomb tested three months later had a yield of 10 megatons. See David Holloway, *The Soviet Union and the Arms Race* (New Haven: Yale University Press, 1984), p. 24; Herbert York, *The Advisors: Oppenheimer, Teller, and the Bomb* (San Francisco: Freeman, 1976), pp. 75–110.

CHAPTER THREE

The Growth of East–West Oil Trade, 1954–1962

THE 1954 AND 1958 COCOM LIBERALIZATIONS

The first manifestations of Western European interest in increased trade with the Eastern bloc came in August 1954, when for the first time since its inception COCOM cut its embargo lists. As Table 3.1 shows, the number of exports under total embargo (International List 1) was scaled back from 320 to 226 items, the shortest it had been since the early days of the Korean War. The quota and monitoring (watch) lists, IL 2 and IL 3, were cut by even larger percentages. As a result, the total number of items under any form of multilateral control fell from 514 to 315.

The breakdown by major product category shown in Table 3.2 indicates that the extent of liberalization varied inversely with the

Table 3.1. Number of export items on COCOM lists before and after revisions of August 15, 1954

	List 1[a]	List 2[b]	List 3[c]	All lists
Before revision	320	92	102	514
After revision	226	26	63	315

[a]Items subject to total embargo.
[b]Items subject to quantitative restrictions.
[c]Items to be monitored.
SOURCE: Task Force on Economic Defense Policy to the Chairman, Council on Foreign Policy, "Draft Guidance Paper on East–West Trade," October 5, 1955, Annex 4, Attachment A, Box 1, Folder: CFEP-East-West Trade, Records of Clarence Francis, 1954–1961, Dwight D. Eisenhower Presidential Library, Abilene, Kans.

Table 3.2. Number of export items on COCOM lists before and after revisions of August 15, 1954, and percentage of items decontrolled, by product category

Product category	Before revisions	After revisions	Percentage of items decontrolled
General industrial equipment	41	14	65.8%
Chemical products	98	45	54.7
Chemical and petroleum equipment	49	25	49.0
Electronics and precision instruments	74	50	32.4
Metalworking machinery	78	53	32.0
Munitions and atomic energy	54	51	5.5

SOURCE: Task Force on Economic Defense Policy to the Chairman, Council on Foreign Economic Policy, "Draft Guidance Paper on East-West Trade," October 5, 1955, Annex 4, Attachment A, Box 1, Folder: CFEP-East-West Trade, Records of Clarence Francis, 1954–1961, Dwight D. Eisenhower Presidential Library, Abilene, Kans.

military significance of the export. The most extensive decontrol occurred in general industrial equipment (65.8 percent) and chemical products (54.7 percent), exports that were relatively insignificant militarily. Chemical and petroleum equipment, which (as we shall see) the United States argued were indirectly but nevertheless significantly related to the military balance, were decontrolled by 49 percent. In electronics and precision instruments and metalworking machinery, some of which had direct military applications (e.g., radar systems, aircraft, and tanks and their parts), the rates of decontrol were markedly lower (32.4 and 32.0 percent). And for the munitions and atomic energy lists, the military significance of which was considerable, the actual liberalization rate was even lower than the 5.5 percent indicated because the items removed from these lists were reclassified and still kept under embargo.[1]

The bulk of these actions were taken at European insistence and over American opposition. The basic American position still was that controls should encompass all those "industrial fields which serve to support the basic economy of a country and which therefore support

[1]Task Force on Economic Defense Policy to the Chairman, Council on Foreign Economic Policy, "Draft Guidance Paper on East–West Trade," October 5, 1955, Annex 4, Attachment A, p. 6. Box 1, Folder: CFEP-East-West Trade, Records of Clarence Francis, 1954–61, Dwight D. Eisenhower Presidential Library, Abilene, Kans.

Table 3.3. Number of export items on COCOM List 1 in four categories of action as recommended by the United States and as adopted by COCOM, 1954

Action	Recommended by U.S.A.	Adopted by COCOM
Retain or increase coverage	161	82
Retain with narrowed coverage	19	73
Downgrade to partial embargo or monitoring	11	32
Transfer to munitions or atomic energy lists	9	9

SOURCE: Task Force on Economic Defense Policy to the Chairman, Council on Foreign Economic Policy, "Draft Guidance Paper on East-West Trade," October 5, 1955, Annex 4, Attachment B, Box 1, Folder: CFEP-East-West Trade Records of Clarence Francis, 1954–1961, Dwight D. Eisenhower Presidential Library, Abilene, Kans.

either a peacetime or a wartime economy."[2] But of the 161 items for which the United States wanted controls to be kept the same or increased, 79 (49 percent) were decontrolled totally or partially (see Table 3.3). Coverage was retained but narrowed on 73 rather than 19 items. Another 32 (rather than the recommended 11) were downgraded to a less strict list. Only on those nine items recommended for transfer to the munitions and atomic energy lists were the American proposals acted upon fully. On these items, the State Department reported, "there was no debate."[3]

Part of the explanation for this reemergence of intra-alliance conflict over East–West trade was that in terms of general foreign policy strategy, European leaders were more inclined than the Eisenhower administration to respond to the "peaceful coexistence" overtures coming from the new post-Stalin Soviet leaders. No less a figure than Winston Churchill, the very man who seven years earlier had been one of the first to issue a clarion call for vigilance against threats from behind the "Iron Curtain" (a term he coined), now proposed that we begin trading through it. "There is one agency," Churchill argued,

> which everyone can see, through which helpful contacts and associations can be developed. The more trade there is through the Iron Curtain and between Great Britain and Soviet Russia and the Satellites, the better still

[2]Ibid., p. 4.
[3]State Department, Battle Act Report no. 5, pp. 20–21.

will be our chances of living together in increasing comfort. . . . The more the two great divisions of the world mingle in the healthy and fertile activities of commerce, the greater is the counterpoise to purely military calculations. Other thoughts take up their places in the minds of men.

Churchill's point was not that the Soviets were no longer a threat. Military equipment should remain under embargo. But "it must be remembered," he continued, that the decisions to extend controls to exports with only indirect military significance had been taken "three or four years ago in circumstances which we can all feel were different from those which now prevail."[4]

An even more important factor was the rekindling of European economic incentives for trade with the Soviet Union. For one thing, the post-Stalin Soviets not only were interested in trade with the noncommunist world but were actively courting it. A month after Stalin's death the Soviets ended their boycott of the ECE transbloc trade talks and sat down to negotiate, as Michael Hoffman noted, with a " 'business is business' attitude."[5] Their commercial missions, in the words of a later researcher, started "trotting the globe like energetic salesmen."[6] They became regular entrants in noncommunist trade fairs, increasing from 8 exhibits in 6 countries in 1951 to 58 exhibits in 26 countries in 1953 and 149 exhibits in 41 countries in 1955. London, Lyon, Milan, Brussels, Amsterdam, and Salonika all were included in the Soviet itinerary.[7]

The prosperity that Europe had been enjoying in the early 1950s was fading. The combined average economic growth rate of Britain, France, Italy, and West Germany in 1953–54 was about 50 percent less than the 1949–52 rate. A key factor in this slackening of overall economic growth was the slowdown in the growth of export markets. France saw its exports stop growing in 1953. Italy managed an 8.7 percent increase, but its exports were still equal to only 62 percent of its imports. West German exports grew 9.5 percent, but this figure

[4]*Parliamentary Debates*, House of Commons, 5th ser., vol. 524 (February 25, 1954), cols. 587–88. For empirical confirmation of the lessening of tensions as perceived by European leaders following Stalin's death, see Kjell Goldman, "East–West Tension in Europe, 1946–1970: A Conceptual Analysis and a Quantitative Description," *World Politics* 26 (October 1973): 108–25.

[5]Michael C. Hoffman, "Problems of East–West Trade," *International Conciliation*, no. 511 (January 1957), p. 296.

[6]Suchati Chuthasmit, "The Experience of the United States and Its Allies in Controlling Trade with the Red Bloc," Ph.D. dissertation, Fletcher School of Law and Diplomacy, 1961, p. 380.

[7]State Department, Battle Act Report no. 8, p. 15, and no. 6, p. 8.

was well below the spectacular 77 percent average annual growth in its exports during 1948–52. What was growing more rapidly, however, was the unemployment rate—27 percent above the 1950 rate in France, 25 percent higher in Great Britain, 15 percent higher in Italy. And while unemployment had declined in West Germany, its rate still was the highest in Western Europe.[8]

At the same time that European economic interest in trade with the Soviet Union (and, by extension, Eastern Europe) had increased, the economic resources on which the United States could draw for leverage had decreased. Marshall Plan aid had begun to dry up: from a peak of $6.3 billion it was down to $637 million. The American economy was suffering its own recession, which in turn had set off a surge in American protectionism. As one European report concluded, the United States could no longer offer compensation for East–West trade controls when "formidable barriers to the expansion of sales" were being erected in its market.[9] European exports to the United States actually fell off 12 percent in 1954. Congress had even been reluctant to renew the Reciprocal Trade Acts Agreement, granting only a one-year extension and sending a signal that was interpreted as portending more protectionism in the future. All this was reinforced by such additional actions as the replacement of the preferential Offshore Procurement Policy by the discriminatory Buy American Act.[10]

Thus the driving force for this initial growth in European–Soviet trade was economic in nature. While American prestige remained high, it did not counter Europe's economic motivations for increasing its trade with the Soviet Union. The Eisenhower administration still perhaps could have resorted to more punitive forms of leverage. It was reluctant to do so, though, for fear of further exacerbating intra-alliance tensions. Thus when further liberalization of COCOM controls was proposed in 1958, the Eisenhower administration took the position that "the best interests of the United States would be served by liberalizing the multilateral controls on trade . . . thereby facilitating accord with our allies."[11] Strict unilateral American controls were

[8]Economic growth rates calculated on the basis of national income statistics, United Nations, Statistical Office, *Monthly Bulletin of Statistics* 10 (July 1956): 148–50; export growth rates from United Nations, Statistical Office, *Yearbook of International Trade, 1955*, pp. 311, 327, 421, 677; unemployment rates from *Monthly Bulletin*, July 1956, pp. 18–20.

[9]United Nations, Economic Commission for Europe, *Economic Survey of Europe since the War* (Geneva, 1953), p. 107.

[10]Robert A. Pastor, *Congress and the Politics of U.S. Foreign Economic Policy, 1929–1976* (Berkeley: University of California Press, 1980), pp. 101–2.

[11]Executive Office of the President, National Security Council, "Basic National Security Policy," NSC 5810, April 3, 1958, p. 18, Modern Military Section, U.S. National Archives, Washington, D.C.

continued, but the COCOM embargo list (IL 1) was cut an additional 35 percent.[12]

While there was a certain logic to this attempt to straddle the objectives of intra-alliance harmony and economic coercion, some basic tensions remained unresolved. The issue on which they came to a head was East–West oil trade. For beginning in 1956 the new Soviet premier, Nikita Khrushchev, launched what a later author would call his "rather spectacular oil offensive in the Capitalist World."[13]

THE SOVIET OIL OFFENSIVE

Back at the turn of the century Russia had been the world's leading producer of oil.[14] Since then, however, decades of revolution and war had taken their toll on the Soviet oil industry. At the end of World War II oil production was at its lowest point since 1930. Postwar reconstruction made for some increases in production. Stalin also resorted to such measures as seizing drilling equipment from occupied territories and "negotiating" concessionary agreements with oil-rich Rumania.[15] But at the time of Stalin's death the Soviet Union still was a net importer of oil.[16]

The COCOM embargo covering "all basic specialized equipment for the exploration, production and refining of oil petroleum and natural gas" was intended to keep the Soviets in this predicament.[17] A 1950 study by the CIA had concluded that without Western supplies "the Soviets cannot be expected to make any spectacular improve-

---

[12]*Economist*, August 16, 1958, p. 556; *Board of Trade Journal*, August 15, 1958, pp. 314–21, and August 22, 1958, p. 378.

[13]Josef Wilczynski, *The Economics and Politics of East–West Trade* (New York: Praeger, 1969), p. 259.

[14]Russia produced 10.43 million metric tons in 1900, or 50.8% of total world production; the United States was second with 8.6 million metric tons (Heinrich Hassmann, *Oil in the Soviet Union* [Princeton: Princeton University Press, 1953], Table 37, pp. 147–49).

[15]Two examples: first, the occupying Soviet army reportedly removed 80% of Austria's oil-drilling and field-maintenance equipment. While still holding the region of Matzen (between Vienna and Zistersdorf) they also pumped out oil at an annual rate of 65,000 metric tons. Second, they took advantage of Rumania's rich oil resources by demanding that 40% of the $300 million in reparations payments be made in the form of petroleum products. In addition, they "negotiated" tax, tariff, and profit exemptions for the Sovromgas and Sovrompetrol joint ventures (incoming airgrams, American Legation Vienna to Secretary of State, March 22, 1949, and American Legation Bucharest to Secretary of State, March 18, 1949, Box 223, Science, Economics, and Natural Resources Division, National Archives).

[16]Marshall I. Goldman, *The Enigma of Soviet Petroleum: Half-Full or Half-Empty?* (London: George Allen & Unwin, 1980), pp. 74–75.

[17]State Department, Battle Act Report no. 1, p. 43.

ments in the near future."[18] The public evidence coming from the Soviet Union was sporadic but corroborative. In an April 1949 speech, Minister of the Oil Industry Nikolai K. Baibakov criticized the industry for its "unsatisfactory" progress and announced plans for a major reorganization. Later that year the *New York Times* reported that oil equipment was "number one on Russia's priority list of goods wanted from the United States." The following year the *Times* reported an open letter to the Kremlin from oil workers self-critically acknowledging production shortfalls but also requesting help in obtaining more and better drill bits.[19]

The problems in the refining sector were even more severe. The CIA estimated a 40 percent shortfall for general consumption of refined products and 50 percent for more sophisticated military requirements, such as high-octane jet fuels. One American economist calculated that the Soviet refining industry lagged forty-nine "technological years" behind the West.[20] It was with such pervasive problems in mind that an NSC study in December 1952 reconfirmed the earlier CIA findings. The United States needed to be wary: the Soviet oil industry's weaknesses might feed its appetite for "the vast petroleum reserves of the Middle East." But any notion that the Soviets could lift their own industry up by its bootstraps was dismissed out of hand. "The story of world exploration and discovery of crude oil reserves," the NSC proclaimed, remained "largely the story of American ingenuity, technological advancement and the financial incentives of private enterprise under our form of government."[21]

All of this makes the Soviet oil industry's achievements beginning in the mid-1950s even more impressive. The declining rates of growth were quickly reversed, and by 1958 total production was 100 percent greater than it had been at Stalin's death. When production reached 147.8 million metric tons in 1960 (3 million barrels a day), the Soviet Union displaced Venezuela as the world's second leading producer of

[18]Central Intelligence Agency, Office of Reports and Estimates, "The USSR Petroleum Industry," ORE 24-49, January 5, 1950, p. 6, Papers of Harry S Truman, PSF, Harry S Truman Presidential Library, Independence, Mo.

[19]*New York Times*, January 17, 1949, p. 3; September 23, 1949, p. 3; June 23, 1950, p. 16.

[20]G. Warren Nutter, *Growth of Industrial Production in the Soviet Union* (Princeton: Princeton University Press, 1962), p. 273. See also D. M. Duff, "Refining in Russia," *Oil and Gas Journal*, March 17, 1952, p. 181; Antony Sutton, *Western Technology and Soviet Economic Development, 1945 to 1965* (Stanford: Hoover Institution Press, 1973), pp. 133–37.

[21]Report of the Secretary of the Interior and Petroleum Administrator for Defense to the National Security Council, "National Security Problems Concerning Free World Petroleum Demand and Potential Supplies," December 8, 1952, p. 16, Papers of Harry S Truman, PSF, Truman Presidential Library.

oil (behind the United States). Khrushchev's Seven-Year Plan forecast for even more rapid growth of production, to 240 million metric tons by 1965, was disputed by American government and industry analysts only to the extent that they anticipated that the plan's goal would be exceeded.[22]

One reason for this sudden reversal of Soviet fortunes was the higher priority now being given by Soviet planners to the energy sector. Capital investment increased from an average annual rate of 5.55 billion rubles (1946–53) to 9.02 billion rubles (1954–58). Endorsement of this priority in January 1959 by the 21st Party Congress led to even larger investments of 16.1 billion and 17.1 billion rubles during the next two years.[23] As a result, exploratory as well as production activity was stepped up. The number of geophysical crews searching for new oil reserves increased from 286 in 1950 to 600 in 1957 and 1,186 in 1961. Exploratory drilling increased by 81 percent between 1955 and 1960, and by another 149 percent between 1960 and 1965. Estimates of proven oil reserves grew from 1.4 billion metric tons in 1955 to 2.96 billion in 1960 and 3.8 billion in 1965.[24]

Nor did present production seem to be constrained technologically. The relatively shallow, easily reachable deposits of the Urals-Volga region accounted for over 70 percent of total oil production. The Soviet turbodrill was less efficient than Western rotary drills, but it was adequate for the soft, shallow Urals-Volga reserves. A price would be paid later for inefficient drilling methods, but for the present, oil production grew rapidly.[25]

If anything was vaster than Soviet oil reserves, it was Soviet natural gas reserves. The Seven-Year Plan mandated more than 300 percent increases in both proven reserves and annual production. This target was achievable because the production of natural gas, like that of oil, benefited from the central location and relatively undemanding geology of major deposits. Over 50 percent of the production and 47 percent of the proven reserves were in the Russian Republic, with an additional 31 percent of production and 21 percent of reserves in the Ukraine. The newly discovered Gazli deposits in Uzbekistan were less

[22]The most detailed account of technical and economic developments in the Soviet oil industry is the two-volume study by the National Petroleum Council (NPC), *Impact of Oil Exports from the Soviet Bloc* (Washington, D.C., 1962). See also the report of an American business-government delegation to the Soviet Union in 1960, Robert E. Ebel, *The Petroleum Industry of the Soviet Union* (Arlington, Va: Royer & Royer, 1961).

[23]Ebel, *Soviet Petroleum Industry,* pp. 20–24.

[24]NPC, *Impact of Soviet Oil Exports,* 2: 106.

[25]Ebel, *Soviet Petroleum Industry,* pp. 52–56; NPC, *Impact of Soviet Oil Exports,* 2: 83–85; and esp. Robert C. Campbell, *The Economics of Soviet Oil and Gas* (Baltimore: Johns Hopkins University Press, 1968), pp. 108–20.

central but had the advantage of providing a principal fuel source for the planned new industrial centers in Sverdlovsk, Chelyabinsk, and other points in the Urals.[26]

While virtually all of the natural gas was for domestic consumption (the one exception being some small exports from deposits located near the Polish border), one of the purposes of the increased production was to allow domestic conversion to gas and thus to free more oil for export. The combination of gas conversion and the strides made in increasing oil production did create a rather substantial surplus of oil for export. In 1955 only 3.7 million metric tons were exported, equivalent to 5.2 percent of total oil production; by 1960 oil exports totaled 29.8 million metric tons, or 20.2 percent of production.[27]

The Soviets gave high priority to increases in oil exports at this time for three principal reasons. First, oil helped maintain Soviet dominance in Eastern Europe. The East German uprising of 1953 and the Polish and Hungarian uprisings of 1956 drove home the lesson that more rapid economic growth and improvements in the standard of living would help maintain political stability within the Soviet sphere of influence. Because Polish coal, Rumanian oil, and other, smaller indigenous fuel supplies could provide only a part of Eastern Europe's growing energy needs, the Soviet Union also had to fuel Eastern Europe's economic development. In this light it is particularly interesting to note the 77 percent increase in Soviet oil exports to Eastern Europe in 1957, the year following the Polish and Hungarian revolts, after only a 35 percent increase in 1956.[28]

Second, and for related foreign policy reasons, the demand for oil in other communist countries needed to be met. Beginning in 1950 the addition of the People's Republic of China to the communist world cost the Soviets over 1 million metric tons of oil annually. By 1959 China was receiving more than 3 million tons of Soviet oil. With Cuba also added to the list of communist world customers, total oil exports to ideological brethren amounted to 20.7 metric tons in 1962.[29]

A third priority was penetration of Western European oil markets. Here there were important economic as well as political objectives that related back to Khrushchev's peaceful coexistence strategy.[30] Oil was

[26]NPC, *Impact of Soviet Oil Exports*, 2: 111–24.
[27]Ebel, *Soviet Petroleum Industry*, p. 56; Campbell, *Economics of Soviet Oil*, p. 4.
[28]Derived from NPC, *Impact of Soviet Oil Exports*, 2: 251.
[29]Robert E. Ebel, *Communist Trade in Oil and Gas* (New York: Praeger, 1970), p. 44.
[30]Nikita Khrushchev, "On Peaceful Coexistence," *Foreign Affairs* 38 (October 1959):

the only Soviet export capable of generating the hard-currency earnings necessary for the Seven-Year Plan's long shopping list of consumer and capital goods. Agricultural products, a major export to Western Europe in earlier years, were no longer in surplus.[31] Soviet manufactured goods had a reputation for shoddy quality and unappealing packaging. Oil, on the other hand, was something with which the Soviets were well endowed and which Western European economies needed in large quantities.

The political gains the Soviet Union sought through oil exports to Western Europe were precisely what the containment objective was intended to avert. A central aim of Khrushchev's peaceful coexistence strategy was to weaken the unity of the Western alliance by improving Soviet–West European relations. Oil trade especially fitted this strategy because it involved such an economically strategic commodity that, in a reversal of the Western coercive influence strategy, a large volume of trade might bring the Soviet supplier influence over its European customers. Moreover, even short of forging actual dependencies, the oil trade could demonstrate the benefits of improved relations and thus, in Walter LaFeber's words, "influence Western policies by playing upon the peace hopes of the European middle class."[32]

With these ends in mind, the Soviets began in 1956 to increase their sales to Western Europe by cutting prices. The average price per barrel charged "free world" customers was about a third less than the costs to fellow communist countries.[33] As of 1958 the Soviet price also

---

1–18; Adam B. Ulam, *Expansion and Coexistence* (New York: Praeger, 1968), pp. 572–628.

[31]By the late 1950s the Soviets were able to maintain a positive food trade balance with hard-currency countries only by cutting back on food exports to other communist countries. But the $37.8 million (net) earned from food exports to hard-currency countries in 1959 and the $42.5 million (net) in 1960 could hardly finance major purchases of capital goods. By 1963 food trade with hard-currency countries was negative, in large part because of the first major American grain sale. For data on the 1959–65 period see Oleg Hoeffding, "Recent Structural Changes and Balance of Payments Adjustments in Soviet Trade," in *International Trade and Central Planning*, ed. Alan A. Brown and Egon Neuberger (Berkeley: University of California Press, 1968), p. 319. For an early analysis of the trends in Soviet agriculture see the report by the Central Intelligence Agency, "The Soviet Grain Problem," Report no. 00616/6313, November 1, 1963, Box 518, National Security Files, John F. Kennedy Presidential Library, Boston.

[32]Walter LaFeber, *America, Russia, and the Cold War* (New York: Wiley, 1971), pp. 148–49.

[33]The major oil companies cried dumping, and the director of Soyuzrefteksport responded that the posted price mechanism itself was artificial. The American econo-

moved under the posted price for Arabian crude. When prices were cut again in 1960, the gap with Arabian crude widened and the Western price dropped to about half the intrabloc price.[34] Pricing for refined petroleum products followed a similar pattern. In 1958 prices were cut 22.5 percent for Western European customers (only 6 percent for Eastern European satellites). Prices continued to decline over the next four years until in 1962 they were 55.7 percent below 1957 levels (only 8.3 percent for Eastern Europe).[35] When the oil was bartered for manufactured and capital goods, real prices were even lower.

As expected, exports to Western Europe rose as prices fell. Between 1955 and 1957, when Soviet oil was more expensive than Persian Gulf oil, Soviet exports to Western Europe grew by 2.49 million metric tons. In the two years after the price differential had been established, the growth was 4.05 million tons. By 1960 the total volume of oil being exported to European COCOM countries was more than four times the volume of 1956.

By 1960 the key to the continued growth of oil exports to both Western and Eastern Europe, and also one of the centerpieces of Khrushchev's Seven-Year Plan, was the "Pipeline of Friendship." This 7,500-kilometer pipeline would begin in the rich Urals-Volga fields and branch off into Poland, East Germany, Czechoslovakia, Hungary, and Soviet ports on the Black and Baltic seas. Some of the oil would supply these Eastern European countries, and some would be sent on to Western Europe. The trunk line was to be built with 40-inch-diameter pipe so that the carrying capacity could be increased to 862,000 barrels a day. Thus the export price would be kept down, as the costs of transport by wide-diameter pipe were 39 percent less than for 24-inch pipe and 72 percent less than for railroad transport.[36]

The problem, though, was that throughout the 1950s the production of oil pipe had been a glaring exception to the pattern of progress in the Soviet oil industry. Only 84 percent of the pipeline planned

---

mist M. E. Adelman dismisses the dumping charge as unwarranted. He contends that the Soviets were behaving as rational monopolists in Eastern Europe and as rational market entrants in Western Europe. They made prices competitive when and if necessary and then set them "low enough to make the sale and no lower" (*The World Petroleum Market* [Baltimore: Johns Hopkins University Press, 1972], p. 201).

[34] See the curves of average Soviet prices to satellites and to free world customers and of Arabian crude in NPC, *Impact of Soviet Oil Exports*, 2: 258.

[35] Ibid., p. 251; Campbell, *Economics of Soviet Oil*, p. 234.

[36] Calculations based on data in NPC, *Impact of Soviet Oil Exports*, 2: 190. Pipe of 24 inches also had a much inferior carrying capacity of 260,000 barrels a day.

under the Sixth Five-Year Plan had been laid. If the Seven-Year Plan's target was to be fulfilled, pipeline construction would have to increase 500 percent over the 1951–58 period. The emphasis on wide-diameter (40-inch) pipe made the problem of meeting Plan targets even more difficult.[37] Western estimates were that at the time the Soviets had only "token amounts" of domestic production capacity for wide-diameter pipe, and were not likely to achieve additional capacity much before 1963.[38] Even then a problem would remain: how could the steel industry, already strained by the demands of rapid industrialization and military buildup, produce enough tonnage?

At this point, then, both parts of the oil offensive strategy came together. In order to increase oil exports to Western Europe the Soviets needed to import the equipment necessary to build their new export pipeline. Consequently, of all the exports decontrolled by COCOM at its 1958 meetings, the most important action from the Soviet perspective was the lifting of controls on "oil drilling, production, refining and *distribution* equipment."[39] The latter category included wide-diameter oil pipe.

PIPE FROM WEST GERMANY AND OIL TO ITALY

Given the information available on the Soviet oil offensive strategy, the Eisenhower administration's willingness to allow wide-diameter pipe to be included in the 1958 COCOM liberalizations seems curious. The explanation may lie in a Commerce Department memorandum dated June 10, 1959. Figures presented in this document purport to show that the United States still had a 77 percent share of total world production capacity for all pipe greater than 24 inches in diameter. Moreover, the Swedish, West German, Italian, and French producers who constituted the non-American 23 percent were believed to have much of their capacity filled with the demands of the Rotterdam–Rhine, North–West, and southern European pipeline projects. Therefore, the Commerce Department concluded, even if alternative

---

[37]Some 13% of total Plan requirements, or 2.4 million tons for 8,068 kilometers of pipeline, was scheduled to consist of 40-inch pipe. Most of this pipe (about 2 million tons) actually was intended to transport domestic natural gas, as part of the domestic gas conversion aspect of the oil export strategy. But since end use could not be determined, any Western embargo had to be total. Moreover, the greater the Soviet capacity to convert domestic consumption to natural gas, the greater its capacity to export oil. See NPC, *Impact of Soviet Oil Exports*, 2: 190, 198, 211–20.

[38]Ibid., p. 46.

[39]*Board of Trade Journal*, August 22, 1958, p. 378 (emphasis added).

Table 3.4. Volume of wide-diameter pipe imported by the Soviet Union from principal suppliers, 1958–1962 (metric tons)

Country	Volume imported	Volume contracted[a]	Total volume
West Germany	695,000	172,000	867,000
Italy	140,000	100,000	240,000
Sweden	35,000	100,000	135,000
Japan	—	25,000	25,000
All principal suppliers	870,000	397,000	1,267,000

[a]As of October 1962.

SOURCES: Research Memorandum RES-13, "Western Efforts to Prevent Large-Diameter Linepipe Exports to the Soviet Bloc," Bureau of Intelligence and Research (Thomas L. Hughes) to the Secretary of State, April 3, 1963, NSF, Box 223, File: NATO Pipe Embargo, John F. Kennedy Presidential Library, Boston; and National Petroleum Council, *Impact of Oil Exports from the Soviet Bloc* (Washington, D.C., 1962), 2:214, 216.

suppliers were "to ship their entire annual output, the small quantity still would retard Russia's gas and oil pipeline program in its current Seven Year Plan."[40]

How seriously Commerce had miscalculated the extent of non-American production capacity soon became apparent. Between the COCOM decontrol in late 1958 and late 1962, the Soviet Union was able to import some 870,000 metric tons of pipe from the West. Table 3.4 shows the principal sources of this pipe: West Germany, Italy, Sweden, and Japan. West Germany alone accounted for 80 percent. The first contract for 3,200 tons had been signed almost immediately after the 1958 COCOM liberalization. From there the increases were to 159,000 tons in 1959, 179,500 tons in 1960, and 207,500 tons in 1961.[41] The culmination, as Chapter 4 will show, was a new contract announced on October 5, 1962, for an additional 163,000 tons, which if honored would bring the Friendship Oil Pipeline (FOP) close to completion at maximum carrying capacity and on schedule.

West Germany had become interested in trade with the Soviet Union later than most other Western European nations. One reason was that its export control regulations were more heavily influenced by the United States. Until April 1952 West German exporters had to comply with the U.S. unilateral embargo list rather than with the less restrictive COCOM lists.[42] The government of Chancellor Konrad

[40]Memorandum for the Record, Department of Commerce, "East–West Trade," June 10, 1959, in Joseph Rand Records, 1954–61, Eisenhower Presidential Library.

[41]Angela Stent, *From Embargo to Ostpolitik: The Political Economy of West German–Soviet Relations, 1955–1980* (New York: Cambridge University Press, 1981), p. 101.

[42]Gunnar Adler-Karlsson, *Western Economic Warfare, 1947–1967* (Stockholm: Almquist & Wiksell, 1968), p. 72.

Adenauer also had its own political agenda, to which it linked East–West trade relations. While beginning in the mid-1960s the *Ostpolitik* of the Social Democratic Party (SPD) cast trade as a means to better political relations, the Christian Democratic (CDU) governments of the 1950s and early 1960s placed greater emphasis on resolving outstanding political issues as a precondition to economic relations.[43]

Total trade between West Germany and the Soviet Union grew 110 percent over the two years following the signing of a first trade agreement in April 1958. The Germans supplanted the British as the Soviets' leading Western trading partner. Their principal motivations for doing so were economic. The Adenauer government made some foreign policy linkages but did not push them particularly forcefully. During the early stages of the 1958–59 Berlin crisis, for example, it suspended trade with East Germany but continued to trade with the Soviet Union. The official logic was that "precisely because the present political situation is not favorable, we feel we should do our best to maintain good relations with the Soviet Union in other fields, such as trade."[44] Ultimately the Adenauer government settled for minimal political concessions and, consistent with West German economic interests, soon signed a new agreement for expanded trade.

West Germany's economic interest in trade with the Soviet Union was nowhere greater than in the steel industry. Through most of the 1950s continued growth of steel production had been made possible by the growth of export markets. The 12.5 percent average annual growth between 1953 and 1957 was fueled by a 47.5 percent growth rate in exports. In 1958 exports declined 15.3 percent and total production was pushed down 7 percent. Export-led growth required expanding markets, a role the Soviet Union was willing and able to play.[45] By 1960 steel exports to the Soviets had increased from $13.9 million to $83.5 million, accounting for a major part of the renewed growth in production (22.5 percent annually) and total exports (25 percent).[46]

By 1962 the only segment of the German steel industry that was

---

[43]Stent, *From Embargo to Ostpolitik*, pp. 20–67, and Robert W. Dean, *West German Trade with the East: The Political Dimension* (New York: Praeger, 1974), pp. 109–21.

[44]Dean, *West German Trade with the East*, p. 122.

[45]For a discussion of the export-led growth strategy, see Michael Kreile, "West Germany: The Dynamics of Expansion," in *Between Power and Plenty: Foreign Economic Policies of Advanced Industrial States*, ed. Peter J. Katzenstein (Madison: University of Wisconsin Press, 1978), pp. 191–224.

[46]Based on data from United Nations, *Monthly Bulletin of Statistics* and *Yearbook of International Trade*, and Organization for European Economic Cooperation/Organization for Economic Cooperation and Development (OEEC/OECD), *Foreign Trade*, ser. B, Exports by Commodity Group and Destination.

expanding was pipe production. All of Europe was beginning to suffer from excess steel capacity. Total European consumption of steel
had slowed to a 3 percent annual growth rate, while production continued to grow at a 6 percent clip. On the financial markets, steel
stocks slumped in early 1963 to 23 percent below their levels of the
previous year and 32 percent below their 1961 peak. The *New York
Times* reported that the European steel industry was engaged in "the
fiercest competition—largely international—that Europe has known
for years."[47]

In this context of economic stagnation of a key sector of the economy—only exports of machinery and motor vehicles exceeded those of
steel—there was little prospect that West Germany would forgo one
of its few growth markets. Robert Dean claims that the Soviets had
become the largest purchaser of German steel pipe in the world. In
fact, one reason why the American Commerce Department's estimates of world production had been so far off was that they did not
consider that large and guaranteed orders from the Soviets would
stimulate new investment by German firms.[48]

On the oil import side the principal American concern was with
Italy. On an overall basis COCOM imports of Soviet oil had increased
400 percent since 1956. But as Table 3.5 shows, far and away the
principal importer was Italy. In fact, by 1959 Italy had passed Finland
as the largest noncommunist importer of Soviet oil by volume. By
1960 it had surpassed China as the best customer for Soviet oil in all
the world. Under the terms of a series of trade agreements signed in
October 1960 and March 1961, Italian imports reached 4.8 million
tons in 1960 and 6.3 million in 1961. This figure translated into a 22
percent Soviet share of the Italian oil market, which in Washington
translated into a dangerously high level of dependence.[49]

The oil import data also show a significant but smaller increase in
West German oil imports while little to no oil was being imported by
France, Great Britain, and the United States. This selective attraction
to Soviet oil is curious because it differs from the overall pattern of
East–West trade, in which Italy ranked fourth among COCOM na-

[47]March 27, 1963, p. 9. The steel industry of the European Economic Community as a
whole was operating at only 83% of capacity in 1962, compared to 93% in 1961.

[48]In March 1963 the State Department offered a more sober estimate of the American
share of world production at 50%. See Memorandum, Ambassador Timberlake to
Secretary Rusk, "Large Diameter Pipe Shipments to USSR," March 21, 1963, Box 223,
National Security Files, Kennedy Presidential Library.

[49]NPC, *Impact of Soviet Oil Exports*, 2: 467–68. On the Italian–Soviet oil trade agreement see also *Economist*, November 5, 1960, p. 572; *Christian Science Monitor*, November
25, 1960, p. 21, and March 16, 1961, p. 12.

Table 3.5. Volume of Soviet crude oil imported by five COCOM nations, 1950–1962 (thousands of metric tons)

Year	Italy	West Germany	France	Great Britain	United States
1950	6	0	0	0	0
1956	290	0	260	0	0
1958	1,030	260	180	0	0
1960	3,920	1,240	130	0	0
1962	6,180	1,920	90	0	0

SOURCE: United Nations Statistical Office, *World Energy Supplies*, 1955–58, 1958–61, 1961–64, Table 10, "World Movement of Crude Petroleum."

tions, Britain and France second and third. Yet when French President Charles de Gaulle signed a major trade agreement with the Soviets in 1960, he rebuffed offers to include oil import quotas. By 1962 French imports of Soviet oil had fallen to minimal amounts. British Prime Minister Harold Macmillan also rejected a Soviet offer to include an oil quota in the five-year Anglo–Soviet trade agreement signed in March 1959. Reginald Maulding, president of the Board of Trade, informed the House of Commons in June 1961 that a new offer of 2 million metric tons a year with guaranteed annual increments also was turned down. The Board of Trade continued its restrictive policy of issuing import licenses only to meet the limited need for a particular type of heavy fuel oil.[50]

This selective attraction to Soviet oil imports has its explanation in what essentially were intra-European divergences of economic interests on the specific issue of East–West oil trade. These divergences were based on the differential positions in the international energy economy of Italy and West Germany as *oil consumer* nations and of Great Britain and France (and the United States) as *oil producer* nations.[51] Oil consumer nations, as defined back in Chapter 1, are those that lack the capacity to satisfy a substantial share of their domestic demand for oil through either indigenous production or international consortia in control of the oil resources of foreign nations. For

[50]*Board of Trade Journal*, April 17, 1959, p. 918; December 16, 1960, p. 1431; June 16, 1961, p. 1411.
[51]While French Middle Eastern holdings were not so extensive as American or British, the Compagnie Française des Petroles (CFP) did hold a 23.75% interest in the Iraq Petroleum Company and a 6% interest in the Iranian Oil Consortium. It also at that time controlled the rich oil fields of Algeria (independence was not achieved until 1962) and the French Sahara. In addition, the CFP was granted favored access for exploration and development in most franc-zone countries.

them the Soviets' oil provided a means of bringing prices down through increased competition for their markets. Oil producer nations, in contrast, are those that are able to fulfill much of their national demand for oil through domestic production and/or foreign ownership. With at least some control over their own oil supply, oil producer nations felt less compelled to diversify their supplier portfolios. In addition, for them any gains from lower import prices were more than offset by the direct costs to their own corporate interests and the general disruption of the closed, integrated, and orderly marketing practices from which their own oil exporters benefited so greatly.

A closer look at Italian policy illustrates this intra-European divergence of economic interests. Italy imported nearly all of its oil, 95 percent of it from the Middle East. The predicted "Texas-sized deposits" in its own Po Valley never materialized, and the oil deposits finally discovered in the Gela region of Sicily were small and expensive to refine. Yet Italy was converting to oil at an even faster rate than other European countries. Its 56 percent share of total energy consumption represented by oil was well above the continental average of 30 percent. Consequently, between 1956 and 1960 Italian oil imports increased 70 percent from 17 million to 29 million metric tons. By 1963, oil represented 63.8 percent of Italian energy consumption, and imports were pushed up another 62 percent to 46.6 million metric tons.

Soviet oil's relative inexpensiveness was a major source of its appeal to an importing nation with such rapidly increasing demand for oil. By purchasing large volumes, Italy got the discounted price of $1.08 per barrel, $0.30 below even the average price charged other Western European customers.[52] These purchases of Soviet oil had a doubly favorable impact on Italy's balance of payments. Scarce hard currency was preserved when Italy could reduce its purchases of Middle Eastern oil (an estimated $25 million saved in 1961), while the 235 percent increase in Italian exports to the Soviet Union helped the other side of the balance-of-payments ledger. Some of these exports—for example, 240,000 tons of wide-diameter pipe—were directly bartered for the oil. Others represented part of the overall improvement in commercial relations facilitated by the oil trade. For a nation with a $1 billion trade deficit, these were important economic gains.

Less salient but also important was the calculation following the

---

[52]NPC, *Impact of Soviet Oil Exports*, 2: 469; Dow Votaw, *The Six-Legged Dog* (Berkeley: University of California Press, 1964), p. 36.

Suez crisis that by reducing dependence on Middle East oil supplies, Soviet oil enhanced an importing country's security of supply. A 1958 report of the Organization for European Economic Cooperation (OEEC) had stressed the urgency of achieving "a reasonable dispersal of our commitments" in the wake of Suez.[53] The OEEC did not propose that Europe turn to the Soviets for this reasonable dispersal, but the inference was one that Italian leaders (and, to a lesser extent, other oil consumer governments) drew for themselves.

A final factor in the Italian case was the role played by Enrico Mattei, the dynamic president of the state-owned energy company Ente Nazionale Idrocarburi (ENI).[54] Since the mid-1950s Mattei had been pursuing a source of oil supply outside the "seven sisters" network. His basic objective was to gain for ENI (and through it, the Italian state) control over production and pricing decisions as well as a larger share of the profits. Mattei repeatedly had sought to gain access to Middle Eastern supplies. In return for production concessions he offered to build refineries in Morocco, Libya, Tunisia, and other North African countries just beginning to produce oil. But for the most part these ventures proved expensive and yielded only nominal amounts of oil.

The much larger volumes and cut-rate prices that Moscow then was eager to offer fitted perfectly into Mattei's strategy. ENI would not own its own supplies, but it still would have a source independent of the major international oil companies. Interestingly, Mattei appeared to have been even more enthusiastic about this strategy than the government of Prime Minister Amitore Fanfani. It was Mattei who traveled to Moscow to negotiate the oil trade agreements signed in October 1960 and March 1961. According to one of his biographers, the level of imports Mattei agreed to was much higher than Prime Minister Fanfani originally wanted.[55]

Yet Mattei had such a strong political base that, as another biographer put it, he could "adopt the policy of acting first and getting sanction later."[56] He was one of postwar Italy's true *condottieri*, a for-

---

[53]Organization for European Economic Cooperation, *Europe's Need for Oil: Implications and Lessons of the Suez Crisis* (Paris, 1958), p. 43.

[54]One can get a sense of Mattei and his impact on Italian politics and economic policy from Votaw, *Six-Legged Dog*, and P. H. Frankel, *Mattei: Oil and Power Politics* (New York: Praeger, 1966).

[55]According to Votaw (*Six-Legged Dog*, pp. 5, 22, 159), Fanfani's lukewarm initial support for the Soviet oil deal had as much to do with his concern not to offend Arab governments by turning to a new source of oil as it did with the political influence issues raised by the United States. See also *Christian Science Monitor*, December 12, 1961, p. 12.

[56]Frankel, *Mattei*, p. 140.

mer resistance fighter, member of Parliament, leader of the Christian Democratic Party (PDC), and aggressive builder of ENI into the largest industrial enterprise in Italy. His personal following was such that any prime minister who might have tried to rein him in, Dow Votaw has noted, would have risked "major political upheaval" within the PDC and at the polls.[57]

Under Mattei the total assets of ENI had grown from 43.9 billion lire to 292.6 billion. It owned wholly or in part sixty-eight companies spanning numerous sectors of the economy. The AGIP chain of service stations, famous for its symbol of a six-legged dog, had a 25 percent share of gasoline sales. Five refineries were owned jointly by ENI and such major oil companies as Standard Oil of New Jersey (SONJ). ENI also counted as part of its empire a manufacturer of heavy machinery and wide-diameter steel pipe, an engineering services firm, a uranium exploration company, a synthetic rubber company, a bank, and its own newspaper, *Il Giorno*.[58]

Thus it was with great concern that the United States looked upon the burgeoning Italian–Soviet oil trade. To Washington a breaching of the structure of containment, not economic benefits, was the dominant dimension of such a large volume of trade in such a vital commodity. A January 1962 State Department policy paper stressed the need "to prevent future growth of Italian dependence on trade with the Soviet bloc, particularly in strategic imports such as oil." Secretary of State Dean Rusk went even further, calling a reversion by Italy to at least a partial boycott of Soviet oil the number one issue in Italian–American relations.[59]

THE POLITICAL ECONOMY OF AMERICAN OPPOSITION

As part of the Soviet–American "spirit of Camp David," the Eisenhower administration had allowed some liberalization of trade in consumer-goods sectors: a $17 million textile mill, $5.3 million

---

[57]Votaw, *Six-Legged Dog*, p. 5. Alan Posner argues that the PDC was constrained from interfering with ENI's operations by its vested interest in the firm's success and popularity. The public enterprise was an alternative model for economic organization distinct from pure capitalism, Marxism, and the discredited fascism ("Italy: Dependence and Political Fragmentation," in *Between Power and Plenty*, ed. Katzenstein, pp. 231–32). Norman Kogan makes a similar point, arguing that ENI was less dependent on the PDC than the reverse because its quasi-socialistic nature brought it some support from parties of the left (*The Politics of Italian Foreign Policy* [New York: Praeger, 1963], p. 97).

[58]Votaw, *Six-Legged Dog*, pp. 42, 85.

[59]State Department, "Italy: Guidelines for Policy and Operations," January 1962, NSF, Countries: Italy, Box 120, Kennedy Presidential Library.

worth of automobile engine-making equipment, and approximately $1 million worth of agricultural machinery for such projects as a 1,000-cow dairy farm and an "American-style" broiler industry.[60] Thus the economic warfare objective was relaxed somewhat. No longer was it American policy to seek total disruption of the Soviet economy. Now the Eisenhower administration was willing to permit some trade, at least in consumer goods sectors. The result was a rapid increase in American exports to the Soviet Union, from $3.4 million in 1958 to $60 million in 1960.

Oil industry equipment and technology, however, were not included in the limited liberalization. Here the old economic warfare objective of disrupting Soviet growth and development still held. Accordingly, a review of the relevant SITC categories in the Comprehensive Export Schedule reveals the approval of only one export with any relevance to the oil industry, a $29,412 sale of drilling equipment in 1960. American manufacturers' requests for licenses to export other oil drilling equipment, seismographic equipment with possible applications to oil exploration, and compressors for natural gas pipelines were denied.[61] In one of the more prominent cases an application for a license to export $2.5 million worth of wide-diameter pipe was rejected on three separate occasions. The Commerce Department reported that extensive interagency consultations had affirmed that "approval of the application would not be in the national interest."[62]

John F. Kennedy came to office, according to his secretary of commerce, Luther H. Hodges, with a feeling that "generally we ought to have more trade between the Soviets and us."[63] But he, too, took only limited steps in this direction. He lifted the ban on imports of Soviet crabmeat, a control considered particularly noxious by the Soviets because it originally had been imposed in the early 1950s on the grounds that the canning was done by slave labor. Secretary of State Dean Rusk urged this basically symbolic gesture (crabmeat imports were not exactly a major source of hard-currency earnings) as a "tangible demonstration of our desire to improve U.S.–Soviet relations."[64]

[60]U.S. Department of Commerce, *50th Quarterly Report under the Export Control Act of 1949*, p. 8; *51st Quarterly Report*, p. 13; *52nd Quarterly Report*, pp. 10–11. On U.S.–Soviet trade in this period, see Dan Caldwell, *American–Soviet Relations from 1947 to the Nixon-Kissinger Grand Design* (Westport, Conn.: Greenwood Press, 1981), pp. 181–87.

[61]Commerce Department, *36th Quarterly Report*, pp. 8–9; *53rd Quarterly Report*, p. 3; *54th Quarterly Report*, p. 3.

[62]Commerce Department, *47th Quarterly Report*, pp. 5–6.

[63]Interview with Luther H. Hodges, Oral History Collection, Kennedy Presidential Library.

[64]Memorandum, Rusk to President, "Soviet Crab Meat," February 26, 1961, NSF, Countries: USSR, Box 176, Kennedy Presidential Library.

Kennedy would not, however, go so far as a transition-period task force recommended. The task force, chaired by the future under secretary of state George W. Ball, reportedly recommended "a virtual scrapping of the existing embargo" in favor of "a new policy that would acknowledge the mutual advantages of expanding East–West trade and that would invite the Soviet Union to join in a code of fair practices for international trade."[65] The new, politically cautious president was dubious of the reception that liberalizing legislation would receive in Congress. His foreign policy advisers also preferred to reserve such actions for possible later use as an inducement requiring reciprocation by the Soviets. Accordingly, at the Vienna summit in June 1961 Khrushchev was offered trade liberalization but only in the context of "progress in reaching solutions on unresolved issues."[66] Such progress did not necessarily have to precede the liberalization, but political and economic relations did have to be linked in some way.

Not only did Khrushchev reject the linkage, contending that better political relations were possible only as a result of the normalization of trade and other relations; his positions on the other issues and general comportment so discouraged Kennedy that after the summit he confided to Theodore Sorensen: "I did not come away with any feeling that an understanding so that we do not go over the brink would be easy to reach." In a speech to the nation, Kennedy referred to the summit as "a very sober two days." Soon thereafter, tensions over Berlin again reached crisis proportions. On August 4 the administration threatened to reconsider all aspects of U.S.–Soviet relations, including the economic, unless the crisis were resolved. Less than two weeks later the Berlin Wall was under construction. Kennedy told the nation that Berlin was "the great testing place of Western courage and will, a focal point where our solemn commitments . . . and Soviet ambitions now meet in basic confrontation."[67] Before the month was out, American intelligence reported that the Soviets had resumed

[65]The full text of the Ball report was never released. This characterization appeared in the *New York Times* on January 8, 1962. It was never confirmed by the administration, but when Paul Kitchin, chairman of the House Select Committee on Export Control and a leading critic of any and all trade with the communists, requested a copy, Ball turned him down. See Kitchin's statement and the exchange of letters in *Congressional Record*, 87th Cong., 2d sess., vol. 108, pt. 1, February 1, 1962, pp. 1400–1401.

[66]State Department, "Position Paper for the President's Meeting with Khrushchev, Vienna, June 3–4, 1961," May 25, 1961, p. 2, President's Office Files (POF), Countries: USSR, Box 126, Kennedy Presidential Library.

[67]Theodore C. Sorenson, *Kennedy* (New York: Harper & Row, 1965), pp. 618–20, 667.

nuclear testing. Cold War tensions, far from diminishing, were being heightened.

Shortly after the Vienna summit the CIA prepared an assessment of the potential impact of stricter economic sanctions against the Soviet Union. This report acknowledged that the Soviets had shown over the past decade that they could achieve substantial economic growth and military sophistication despite Western trade controls. In the long run, the CIA concluded, the United States should not expect sanctions to have more than a "minimal" effect. In the short run, however, the prognosis was more impressive: "disruption would be significant, particularly to the attainment of some key industrial goals of the USSR's current Seven Year Plan." Singled out as a sector most vulnerable to short-run disruption was that of wide-diameter pipe; Soviet shortfalls in its production were predicted to last at least through 1963 and possibly through 1965.[68]

A State Department memorandum declared that completion of the Friendship oil pipeline would threaten U.S. interests because it would:

(1) facilitate and improve relative military, strategic and economic strength of USSR, (2) provide additional and less vulnerable means to supply petroleum to armed forces in Eastern Europe while permitting undetected build-up of petroleum stockpiles, (3) sharply reduce burden on overloaded transport, freeing facilities for carrying other critical logistical requirements, and (4) permit Soviets to intensify oil offensive to non-bloc countries.[69]

Stopping the FOP would serve the American objectives of deterrence (point 1), economic defense (points 2 and 3), and containment (point 4). The deterrence and economic defense objectives were considered especially pressing, according to Sorenson, because in the immediate context of the Berlin crisis, "the imbalance of ground forces that the two sides could rapidly deploy in the area was an excessive temptation to Khrushchev to cut off access to Berlin."[70] Ultimate completion of the FOP might not be stoppable, Rusk admitted, but an embargo that

[68]Central Intelligence Agency, Office of Research and Reports, "Estimated Impact of Western Economic Sanctions against the Sino-Soviet Bloc," RR EP 61-47, July 16, 1961, pp. 2, 4–5, accessed through *Declassified Documents Quarterly Catalog* (Washington, D.C.: Carrollton Press), microfiche.

[69]Telegram, Rusk to American embassies in Western Europe, Sweden, Soviet Union, and Japan, December 18, 1962, NSF, Box 223, File: NATO, Pipe Embargo, Kennedy Presidential Library.

[70]Sorenson, *Kennedy*, p. 662.

could cause a delay of "eight months to two years" might get past the immediate crisis.[71] The most pressing threat to containment was in Italy, where imports of Soviet oil already had reached the danger point at which manipulation for political influence seemed feasible. If the FOP were completed, West Germany might approach a similar threshold soon.[72]

Finally, and in the longer view, the State Department was wary of the FOP's potential as a source of hard-currency earnings. In 1960 oil exports to Western Europe had brought in $263.2 million, or 31.5 percent of total Soviet hard-currency earnings. Oil exports were the single most important element in the Soviets' ability to import industrial machinery, wide-diameter pipe, and other machinery, equipment, and technology from the West.[73] Thus, while not articulated in this particular State Department memorandum, the economic warfare objective of generally disrupting the Soviet economy also was a key part of American policy.

By the summer of 1962 the Kennedy administration was under increasing domestic pressure to do something about the FOP and about European–Soviet trade in general. The previous September the House of Representatives had established a Select Committee on Export Control to conduct a comprehensive policy review. But the direction of this policy review was quite different from what the Ball task force had in mind when it originally proposed such an overhaul. The House committee was chaired by Paul Kitchin (D-N.C.), who, in his own words, "definitely [leaned] toward the extreme of a total embargo to all Communist-dominated countries." Otherwise, Kitchin warned his colleagues, there would be an ever-increasing risk that "the free world countries [would] sink deeper into the quicksands of a world dominated by international communism as expressed by Marx and Lenin."[74]

The Kitchin Committee's recommendations became the basis for the Export Control Act of 1962, which tightened trade restrictions in two principal respects. First, it reduced the discretion available to the president to permit trade even in consumer goods. The old legislation had implied but had not explicitly stated that "economic significance" was grounds for embargo. It had been through this loophole that

[71]Telegram, Rusk to American embassies, December 18, 1962, NSF, Box 223, File: NATO, Pipe Embargo, Kennedy Presidential Library.

[72]"We value trade," Khrushchev was quoted as saying, "least for economic reasons and most for political reasons" (cited in NPC, *Impact of Soviet Oil Exports*, 2: 417).

[73]Derived from Ebel, *Communist Trade in Oil and Gas*, p. 70, and Hoeffding, "Recent Structural Changes," p. 316.

[74]*Congressional Record*, 87th Cong., 2d sess., vol. 108, pt. 1, February 1, 1962, p. 1400.

Eisenhower and Kennedy had moved away from the total economic warfare of the early 1950s and had allowed American exports to the Soviet Union to increase from $3 million in 1958 to $43 million in 1961.[75] By the new law, which passed by votes of 339 to 0 and 57 to 2, Congress closed this discretionary loophole on the grounds that the reintensification of the Cold War made any and all trade inimical to American interests.[76]

The 1962 Export Control Act also mandated that efforts to get the allies to comply with these tougher standards be stepped up. One of the methods recommended in the Kitchin Committee report was to claim extraterritorial application of American export controls to the foreign subsidiaries of American-controlled corporations. This claim had been made in some past cases, and in each instance it engendered a major dispute on both policy and legal grounds with the countries where the subsidiaries were located.[77] Senators Kenneth Keating (R-N.Y.) and Thomas Dodd (D-Conn.) were sent to Europe to assess the allies' export controls. Upon their return they issued a scathing report on the laxness of Europe's commitment to trade controls and on the Kennedy administration's avoidance of enforcing the Battle Act sanctions.[78]

Using the forum of the Senate Judiciary Subcommittee to Investigate the Administration of the Internal Security Act, of which he was ranking minority member, Senator Keating conducted a series of hearings to expose "the dangers in the situation . . . so that effective action can be taken to deal with the Communist oil war."[79]

> Khrushchev has threatened to bury us on more than one occasion. It is now becoming increasingly evident that he would also like to drown us in a sea of oil if we let him get away with it. . . . If these tactics continue to succeed, there is danger that Western countries will become increasingly dependent on Soviet oil supplies for vital defense as well as industrial activities. The danger such a situation would pose to the security of the free world cannot be overstated.[80]

[75]UN, *Yearbook of International Trade Statistics, 1962*, p. 720.

[76]Congressional Quarterly, *1962 Almanac*, pp. 295–300, 350–52, 618, 666–67.

[77]For a rundown of the instances through 1970 in which extraterritoriality was claimed in export control cases, see Jack N. Behrman, *National Interests and the Multinational Enterprise* (Englewood Cliffs, N.J.: Prentice-Hall, 1970).

[78]U.S. Congress, Senate, Committee on the Judiciary, Subcommittee on Internal Security, *Report on Export Controls in the United Kingdom, France, Italy, Federal Republic of Germany, Belgium and the Netherlands*, 87th Cong., 2d sess., 1962.

[79]U.S. Congress, Senate, Committee on the Judiciary, Subcommittee to Investigate the Administration of the Internal Security Act and Other Internal Security Laws, *Export of Strategic Materials to the USSR and Other Soviet Bloc Countries: Hearings*, 87th Cong., 2d sess., October 26, 1962, pt. 3, p. 370.

[80]U.S. Congress, Senate, Committee on the Judiciary, Subcommittee to Investigate the

Keating's warnings were seconded by no less liberal a Democrat than Senator Hubert H. Humphrey (Minn.). Soviet oil exports, Humphrey argued on the Senate floor, are "one of the major threats that face us . . . perhaps even more dangerous than the military offensive threat."[81] The old Cold War consensus still was very much intact. Congress still was bipartisan in its support for anti-Soviet policies. Its only objection was to the Kennedy administration's reluctance or inability to implement fully the economic coercion strategy. As with Truman in 1951 when the Wherry Resolution and Battle Act were passed, Congress asserted itself more to get the president to act than to constrain him.

Revealing of the heavily ideological sentiment prevalent among the public at large were the activities of a group called the Committee to Warn of the Arrival of Communist Merchandise on the Local Business Scene. Operating in forty-seven states, these committees harassed merchants who dared to sell products imported from communist countries. Activists would canvass the city with handbills saying: "Always buy your Communist products at ——." They defended consumer boycotts as "doing what we can to fight Communism on the local scene." This was not high-powered, sophisticated Washington lobbying, but such localisms do constrain the political readings taken by elected officials (presidents as well as congressmen and senators).[82]

There was a second, more economic ground on which the Kennedy administration was being pressured specifically on the oil trade issue. To go back to the distinction drawn earlier between European oil producer nations (Britain, France) and oil consumer nations (Italy, West Germany), the United States was the quintessential oil producer nation. It both possessed extensive domestic production and took the lead role in the international consortiums that controlled the world's richest oil reserves outside the Soviet Union. The American Big Five—SONJ, Socal, Socony Mobil, Gulf, Texaco—controlled 64 percent of Middle Eastern proven reserves, had $2 billion invested in the region in fixed assets, and were accustomed to the larger profit margins gained by selling oil in the price range of $1.75 to $2.00 a barrel. When challenged by host governments, consumer governments, or

---

Administration of the Internal Security Act and Other Internal Security Laws, *Soviet Oil in East–West Trade: Hearings,* 87th Cong., 2d sess., July 3, 1962, p. 1.

[81]*Congressional Record,* 87th Cong., 2d sess., vol. 108, pt. 9, June 23, 1962, p. 11489.

[82]In addition to memos discussing these vigilante groups, the files of the Kennedy Presidential Library include some extraordinary letters received at the White House from members. See White House Central Files, Box 240, "Boycotts–Embargoes." The *New York Times* ran a series of stories on these groups on November 4, 13, and 14, 1962.

competing producer nations, this classically ologopolistic industry characteristically presented a united front.[83]

The major oil corporations were especially sensitive to the Soviet competition for markets and price-cutting tactics because at this time their profits already were being squeezed. World oil markets were glutted (and access to the world's largest market, the United States, was inhibited by its oil import quotas). With oil suppliers coming on line more rapidly than world consumption was growing, the pressure on prices was downward. At the same time host governments were escalating their demands for shares of the profits and control over production and investment decisions.

The entry of the Soviet Union into world markets exacerbated both of these trends. In 1959 and again in 1960, the majors cut their Persian Gulf posted price in order better to compete with Soviet oil for European markets. They made this decision in haste and without consulting the host governments, for whom it was something of a final straw. Ironically, it was within a month of the Soviet-prompted price cut of August 1960 that the oil ministers of Iraq, Saudi Arabia, Kuwait, Iran, and Venezuela met in Baghdad to form a new group called the Organization of Petroleum Exporting Countries (OPEC).[84]

This squeeze from excess supply, Soviet oil, and restive host governments was straining the basic organizational pattern of the oil firms. Oil companies traditionally have relied more heavily than other firms on internal financing of investment. J. E. Hartshorn claims that 94 percent of investment capital between 1951 and 1960 came from internal resources.[85] This pattern of financing made high rates of return and continuous expansion essential to the firm's economic health. Yet the 1951 average rate of return of 17 percent had fallen to 11 percent by 1960. SONJ's 22 percent drop in profits between 1956 and 1959 exemplified the industry's problems.[86]

---

[83]Robert Engler, *The Brotherhood of Oil* (Chicago: University of Chicago Press, 1961), pp. 67–69.

[84]The stated purpose of OPEC at its inception was to facilitate "regular consultation amongst its members with a view to coordinating and unifying the policies of the members." With the oil companies' strategy for competing with the Soviets through price cuts very much in mind, the first resolution passed by OPEC stated "that members shall demand that Oil Companies maintain their prices steady and free from all unnecessary fluctuations: that members shall endeavor, by all means available to them, to restore present prices to the levels prevailing before the reductions" (cited in J. E. Hartshorn, *Politics and World Oil Economics* [New York: Praeger, 1967], pp. 18–19).

[85]Ibid., p. 96; see also Christopher Tugendhat, *Oil: The Biggest Business* (New York: Putnam, 1968), pp. 258–60.

[86]Hartshorn, *Politics and World Oil Economics*, p. 97; Engler, *Brotherhood of Oil*, pp. 38–39.

A less immediately measurable trend to which Soviet oil exports
were contributing, but one that in the long run was even more significant, was the strain on the basic vertically integrated structure of the
worldwide industry. The majors were used to controlling the flow of
oil from wellhead to gasoline pump, profiting at each stage of the
process. As with other raw materials, the profit margins were larger in
extraction and refining than in retail sales. It was for this reason that
Mattei's ENI in Italy and private as well as state enterprises in other
oil consumer nations were seeking nonintegrated suppliers of crude
and building their own refineries.[87] American industry sources estimated that 81 percent of Soviet crude exports to noncommunist
countries in 1961 were sold to nonintegrated marketers and
government-owned companies.[88]

It also is worth bearing in mind the historical enmity between
American oil companies, especially Standard Oil of New Jersey, and
past Soviet governments. When the Bolsheviks first came to power,
they nationalized all foreign oil interests.[89] In response, even when
Lenin reissued the invitation to invest in Russian oil, SONJ and fifteen other companies holding unsettled claims agreed in the "London
memo" of July 4, 1922, to form a united front (*"front uni"*) in refusing
to deal with the Bolsheviks.[90] A few years later, when the major oil
companies tried to organize their markets and set prices through the
Achnacarry agreement, the cartelistic arrangements were undermined by Russia's oil export policy. By 1932 Stalin was exporting 6.1

[87]Mattei had become a veritable bête noire as far as the major international oil
companies were concerned. He had been determined for a long time either to break into
the Middle Eastern consortiums or to break them up. His tactics often were unorthodox
(he tried, for example, to arrange a marriage between the daughter of Italy's ex-king and
the shah of Iran). His rhetoric was as vituperative as that of any nationalist leader; e.g.,
"The people of Islam are weary of being exploited by foreigners. The big oil companies
must offer them more than they are getting" (Votaw, *Six-Legged Dog*, pp. 17–18). It was
Mattei who first violated the 75/25 partnerships by offering the shah a 50–50 split
(Tugendhat, *Oil*, pp. 151–53).

[88]NPC, *Impact of Soviet Oil Exports*, 2: 457.

[89]Under the tsars, foreigners controlled over 60% of the Russian oil industry. The
leading foreign investors were the Swedish brothers Robert and Ludwig Nobel and the
Rothschilds (Hassmann, *Oil in the Soviet Union*, pp. 26–28).

[90]Speculating against the fall of the Bolshevik regime, SONJ had purchased a half
interest in the Nobel brothers' Russian General Oil Corporation. The price was low
enough, given a certain set of political assumptions, to invite speculative investment.
When the Bolsheviks did not fall, SONJ was left with the proverbial worthless pieces of
paper (Joan Hoff Wilson, *Ideology and Economics: U.S. Relations with the Soviet Union*
[Columbia: University of Missouri Press, 1974], pp. 164–68). On the failure of the *front
uni* because of "Western greed and Russian negotiating skill," see Goldman, *Enigma of
Soviet Petroleum*, p. 24.

million metric tons, almost double 1930 levels and 28 percent of total Soviet production, to Western European customers.[91]

Of course, the oil industry strove to point out the threat of Soviet oil to American foreign policy interests as well as its own. Markets lost to the Soviets reduced the contribution that the oil companies made to the American balance of payments at a time when the deficit was threatening America's capacity to maintain a global military and political presence. In a memorandum prepared for Assistant Secretary of Commerce Jack N. Behrman, SONJ estimated direct losses at $638 million in 1962.[92] Industry sources also estimated that host governments friendly to the United States lost $350 million between 1954 and 1960 and an additional $145 million in 1961 in direct revenues, plus much larger indirect losses from unemployment and lower local procurement. And if economic consequences were not sufficient cause for concern, "the ultimate goal of the Soviet bloc is to extend its political control, destroy freedom and communize the world, and it uses its monopoly of foreign trade to further these objectives. This, in short, is the problem the free world faces when trading with the Soviet Bloc."[93]

The oil industry's direct pressure on the Kennedy administration increased. George F. Getty II, president of Tidewater Oil, proposed an antitrust exemption to allow the oil companies to work together to make their prices competitive with the Russians'. "We are now faced with a situation," Getty stated, "where oil companies either act in concert or watch the Soviets disrupt and dominate major international oil markets." Senator Mike Monroney, Democrat from the oil state of Oklahoma, sponsored legislation to provide such an antitrust exemption. Congress also held hearings on a proposal by Gordon Reed, the chairman of Gulf, for a multilateral boycott of Soviet oil— an idea that would be embodied a few months later in a NATO resolution.[94]

In November 1961 the administration responded by commissioning the National Petroleum Council (NPC) to conduct a study of the Soviet oil threat and to make "such comments and conclusions as are

[91]Hassmann, *Oil in the Soviet Union*, pp. 54–55.

[92]Memorandum, Emilio G. Collado, Vice President of Standard Oil of New Jersey, to Jack N. Behrman, Assistant Secretary of Commerce, "Scale of Oil Industry Equipment Exports to the Soviet Bloc," July 7, 1964, Box 6, Papers of Jack N. Behrman, Kennedy Presidential Library.

[93]NPC, *Impact of Soviet Oil Exports*, 2: 482–84, 1:xiii.

[94]Getty in *Journal of Commerce*, June 5, 1961; Monroney in ibid., July 11, 1961, and November 16, 1961; Reed in *World Petroleum*, September 1961, pp. 54–56.

deemed appropriate."[95] The NPC study group was headed by George T. Piercy, vice-president of SONJ, and included officials of Socal, Socony Mobil, Texaco, Gulf, Marathon, Tidewater, and Phillips. Its two-volume study became the most complete collection of data in English on the Soviet oil industry. Its recommendations for a Western boycott of Soviet oil and embargo of wide-diameter pipe exports received a wide hearing.[96]

It was in this domestic context of the still potent Cold War ideology and of economic interests threatened by Soviet trade that the Kennedy administration decided to step up pressure on the West Germans and Italians. At an NSC meeting on July 17, 1962, Secretary of State Dean Rusk spoke against the pipe embargo–oil boycott proposals. Export controls, he stated, "should concentrate on the denial of commodities or technology which would *directly* increase the net military strength of the bloc, *narrowly defined.*" Other forms of trade, conducted by our allies as well as by us, could "influence them [the Soviets] over the long run to become more responsible and peaceful members of the community of nations."[97]

Interestingly, the principal proponent of the trade controls in the cabinet was Commerce Secretary Luther Hodges. He questioned whether the analysis of political gains from trade was "a reasonable possibility" or "a mere expression of hope on our part."[98] He also stressed that the messages being sent from Capitol Hill could not be ignored. "The recent changes in the [Export Control] Act reflect a congressional intent that export controls should be administered in a more restrictive manner than has been the case for the last few months. . . . [It would be] unwise to adopt a policy of export control which will almost assuredly subject the Administration in the coming months to time consuming and harassing investigations."[99] He did not mention congressional elections, but few in the room were unaware that they were only a few months away.

Hodges' final point was that he, as the official in the executive branch with direct responsibility for promoting the interests of the American business community, was not yet convinced that the bene-

[95]John M. Kelly, Assistant Secretary of the Interior, to Walter S. Hallaman, Chairman of NPC, cited in NPC, *Impact of Soviet Oil Exports,* 1: 1.

[96]Senator Keating devoted an entire subcommittee hearing to the presentation of the NPC findings and policy recommendations. See n. 79, above.

[97]State Department, Memorandum for the NSC, "Review of Export Control Policy," July 10, 1962, NSF, Box 313, Meetings and Memoranda, Papers of President Kennedy, Kennedy Presidential Library (emphasis added).

[98]Hodges to Kennedy, reply to Rusk memo, July 16, 1962, in ibid.

[99]Hodges to Kennedy, July 10, 1962, in ibid.

fits of trade with the Soviets outweighed its risks and costs. Old debts still had to be resolved, and most businessmen were wary of entering communist markets without prior bilateral treaties regulating such commercial matters as patent rights, credit terms, and fair trade practices. While he did not explicitly mention the immediate interests at stake for the oil companies, the administration's association with the NPC study suggests that this clearly was a consideration.

The NSC ruled in favor of Hodges' antitrade position. It adopted a definition of military significance broad enough to encompass exports that make "a significant contribution to Soviet bloc activities or which disrupt essential Free World economic arrangements." Moreover, this definition was specifically said to imply actions "to deny pipe and pipeline equipment in an attempt to limit the Soviet potential for disrupting the pattern of Free World oil supply."[100] The NSC records also showed that the decision was made at this meeting to step up pressures on the allies to cooperate with the pipe embargo.

Thus domestic political forces were aligned squarely in favor of a tough policy to boycott oil and to embargo wide-diameter pipe. Such a policy was in the economic interests of a key pressure group and had deeply rooted ideological support within Congress as well as the general public.

SUMMARY: EARLY SIGNS OF THE ALTERNATIVE TRADE PARTNER DILEMMA

The Kennedy administration clearly did not have to worry about domestic constraints on its anti-Soviet sanctions. To a certain extent the Soviet Union's own economic capabilities did provide it with some built-in protection against sanctions (a unilateral constraint, in the terms introduced in Chapter 1). Since 1956 the Soviets had demonstrated their ability to develop their energy resources and rapidly increase their oil production. However, they still lacked the technological capacity to produce their own wide-diameter pipe. Thus, while cutting off their pipe supply would not be economically incapacitating, it could delay completion of the pipeline and perhaps even force them to fall back on their own less efficient pipe of smaller diameter. The limiting of the pipeline's export capacity would potentially serve both the United States' containment objective of limiting its Western European allies' imports of Soviet oil and its economic

100National Security Council, Record of Actions, no. 2455, July 17, 1962, in ibid.

warfare objective of disrupting the Soviet economy. It also would have the economic defense value of limiting the pipeline's utility for Warsaw Pact military logistical functions. And perhaps most important, the collective action of a Western pipe embargo and oil boycott would serve as the kind of forceful demonstration of alliance solidarity that amidst the heightened tensions of 1961–62 would reinforce the overall Western deterrence posture.

The key to achieving all of these objectives, however, was overcoming the principal multilateral constraints of West German pipe exports and Italian oil imports. For as long as the Soviet Union had those alternative trade partners, these key American policy objectives would be threatened—and more seriously if those trade relationships continued to grow. The problem faced by the Kennedy administration therefore was how to secure the collaboration of nations whose economic interests, at least according to their own sovereign calculations, led them to trade rather than sanction.

Chapter Four

The Oil Trade Sanctions of 1962–1963

Italy and the Economic Sources of American Leverage

American efforts to do something about Enrico Mattei's thirst for Soviet oil had begun in the last weeks of the Eisenhower administration. Following the announcement of the October 1960 Italian–Soviet oil trade agreement, the National Security Council decided to take the issue to NATO. Some basis for involving NATO could be derived from Article II of the North Atlantic Treaty, which established as one of the organization's purposes the effort "to eliminate conflict in [members'] international economic policies and . . . encourage economic collaboration between any or all of them."

The original intent of this treaty provision had more to do with bringing down trade barriers than putting them up. But it was to the American advantage to stretch the letter of the treaty. Drawing in NATO would accent the politico-strategic dimension of the oil trade issue. A more favorable hearing of the American case was considered likely because the defense ministries of member nations had more influence in NATO than in COCOM or the OECD. Reaching a decision also would be easier because, unlike COCOM, NATO was not bound by the unanimity rule. In addition, there was a certain moral force attached to NATO decisions which could reinforce the will of European governments to stand up to domestic pressures.

In March 1961 the NATO Committee of Economic Advisers issued a preliminary study that conformed with the basic American position that all energy trade should be more strictly controlled. NATO took no further action, however, until June 1962, when it voted a partial boycott resolution. This resolution called on member nations to restrict their imports of Soviet oil to a 10 percent market share, a level that was partly the result of compromise and partly a strategic calculation of the point at which an oil supplier stood to gain political influence over an oil importer.

The problem was that the one dissenting vote was from the one country at which the resolution was aimed: Italy. And while there was no formal veto power under NATO rules, ultimately it was up to each individual nation to enforce the resolution.

Italy also resisted pressures brought directly by France and Great Britain. Within weeks of the October 1960 oil agreement the French delegates in the parliament of the European Economic Community (EEC) unleashed a torrent of criticism. In July 1961 France pushed a resolution through the EEC Council of Ministers calling on member nations voluntarily to restrict their imports of Soviet oil to the market share that had obtained in 1960. This was a more lenient measure than the American NATO resolution, but it also was rejected by Italy. An even more loosely worded resolution passed by the EEC parliament in March 1962 met the same fate.[1] At the same time *The Economist* excoriated Mattei as "Italy's Cromwell" and condemned Prime Minister Amitore Fanfani for allowing Mattei to run "a state within a state."[2]

It bears repeating that France and Britain were not usually supporters of American trade controls. They resisted the initial efforts to create COCOM in 1949, and agreed to join only after its regulatory powers had been scaled back. They led the 1954 and 1958 COCOM liberalizations over American opposition. And at the time of the oil dispute their overall trade with the Soviet Union was growing by 18 and 12 percent, respectively.

Their positions in the international economy as oil producer nations, however, led them to side with their "sister" on oil and oppose the Soviet competition. British Petroleum, for example, had seen its net returns decline by almost a third in four years as a result of the oil

---

[1] In June 1962 the EEC issued an official statement "to define the principles of a common energy policy such as will best meet the general needs of the European economy." While general policy was "to turn down no prospective supplier and to do business with all comers," a Community-wide quota on Soviet oil was proposed. The stated reason was that "the Community cannot afford to ignore the danger which a suspension of these imports would represent." See High Commission of the European Economic and European Coal and Steel Community, *Memorandum on Energy Policy* (Brussels, 1962), pp. 7, 13, 16.

[2] *Economist*, November 5, 1960, p. 575.

glut and Russian price competition.[3] The French were further motivated by the repeated encroachments on their de facto sphere of
control in North Africa by Mattei's refinery and joint production
ventures. Even more flagrant, especially in the eyes of Charles de
Gaulle, were Mattei's alleged dealings with the Algerian FLN, to
which he had been accused of providing financial assistance in return
for oil concessions in an independent Algeria.

Nevertheless, by mid-1962 it was becoming apparent to Kennedy
administration officials and oil company executives that the strategy
of pursuing leverage through the structured channels of existing
multilateral institutions was not getting anywhere. Before the NATO
resolution was brought to a vote, William Reinhardt, the American
ambassador to Italy, cabled Washington that it would be "interpreted
by Italians mainly as an effort to defend the interests of the 'petroleum cartel' and to limit Mattei's bargaining power with Western
companies."[4] Reinhardt's analysis was confirmed by a scathing attack
on the NATO resolution delivered in early July by Foreign Minister
Attilio Piccioni in the Italian Senate.[5] While the Fanfani government
may not have been totally supportive of Mattei's original initiative, it
had to avoid being perceived as giving in to the United States at the
expense of Italian economic interests and national pride. Mattei was
boastful but accurate when he told a *Washington Post* reporter two
months after the Soviet oil deal that attacks on him by the oil companies and the State Department "only build me up as a national
hero."[6] For, as P. H. Frankel has observed, more than any Italian
leader of his time he appealed to "the traditional predilection of the
Italians for limiting their identification with their allies of the day and
for cultivating a certain degree of independence."[7]

What began to take shape at this point was a classic example of
leverage through economic compensation. It involved the State Department and major American international oil companies in their
own effort to get Italy to collaborate with oil import controls. The
basis for this partnership was the convergence of the State Department's political interest and the oil companies' economic interest in

[3]*Economist*, May 19, 1962, p. 698.
[4]Telegram, Reinhardt to Rusk, April 25, 1965, National Security Files (NSF), Box
223, John F. Kennedy Presidential Library, Boston.
[5]Norman Kogan, *The Politics of Italian Foreign Policy* (New York: Praeger, 1963), p.
95.
[6]*Washington Post*, December 25, 1960, p. C5.
[7]P. H. Frankel, *Mattei: Oil and Power Politics* (New York: Praeger, 1966), p. 140.

rolling back the Soviet share of Italian oil markets. In April 1962 Under Secretary of State George McGhee met with W. R. Stott, director and executive vice-president of Standard Oil of New Jersey, in what Secretary of State Rusk reported was "a detailed exploration of an accommodation with Mattei." Stott stated that SONJ "would be agreeable to try to accommodate ENI's need for an assured supply of cheap crude oil."[8] The question of whether or not to deal directly with Mattei or to go through the Fanfani government was debated. The agreement was that Stott would meet with Mattei while the State Department would pressure the Italian government.

Ambassador William Reinhardt questioned whether the State Department should yet get involved directly. He feared that such action might appear to Mattei as an "attempt to bludgeon him." But Reinhardt shared the view that "the availability of alternative sources of low-priced crude" (from Esso and others that might follow) could bring the necessary leverage to quench Mattei's thirst for Soviet oil.[9] The Americans, as they had done more generally for all the European allies in the early 1950s, were to compensate the Italians for the costs of forgoing trade with the Soviet Union. It was hoped that divergent economic interests thus could be made to converge.

In the immediate term the Stott–Mattei negotiations produced no further movement toward an Italian boycott. There was some speculation that at the time of his death in a plane crash on October 28, 1962, Mattei was reconsidering the costs and benefits of his adversarial relationship with the majors. The actual change in policy came under Mattei's successor, Marcello Boldrini. Boldrini had been his vice-president and pledged fealty to the fallen hero's policies. But as a seventy-five-year-old statistics professor with no independent political base, he hardly commanded the power or stature of a condottiere. Moreover, changing economic factors were compelling a reassessment of Italian oil policy and of ENI's corporate strategy.

By late 1962 ENI was in severe financial straits. The overwhelming size of its assets, some questionable accounting methods, and the profitability of its natural gas operations hid the fact that its oil operations were suffering huge losses. The Gela, Po Valley, and offshore oil explorations had cost huge sums of capital yet had returned little black gold. Other than the Egyptian joint venture, all of Mattei's international crude operations had proven costly rather than profit-

[8]Cable, Rusk to Reinhardt, April 20, 1962, in NSF, Countries: Italy, Box 120, Kennedy Presidential Library.
[9]Cable, Reinhardt to Rusk, April 25, 1962, in ibid.

able. As a result, ENI's debt-servicing requirements almost equaled its total available capital. With domestic capital markets crowded by the Fanfani government's high-priority social and economic development projects, ENI could acquire needed capital only by selling off assets or attracting foreign investors. Within six weeks of Mattei's death the new vice-president of ENI, Eugenio Cefis, was in New York courting American investors.

The financial-commercial squeeze on ENI resulted also from its massive investment strategy of 1957–62. In 1962 ENI's domestic crude requirements were 6.5 million tons, of which Soviet oil and its own production could meet close to 75 percent. But with two refineries coming on line in 1963 in Italy and numerous others in ENI's international operations, by 1964 ENI would require 17 million tons of crude oil annually. To meet these requirements, ENI would have to increase its Soviet imports and its own production almost 300 percent in two years. It was not certain that the Soviets could fulfill such a requirement even if American pressures against such a deal could be resisted. In early 1963 there were reports of the first cancellation of a Soviet oil shipment to Italy due to Soviet production shortfalls and of the first increase in Soviet oil prices since 1958.[10]

Under these economic conditions, the majors began to look more and more like attractive business partners. Only they could meet Italy's rapidly increasing crude requirements. Thus within a month of Mattei's death ENI dropped two lawsuits against SONJ. The rapprochement was consummated by a contract announced on March 22, 1963, under which ENI would import 12 million tons of crude from SONJ over four years.[11] This amount came to 25 percent of ENI's estimated needs. The terms of trade were discounted by as much as 25 percent off posted prices. And in the Soviet style, SONJ accepted some barter payment in the form of drilling equipment made by an ENI subsidiary and tankers built in government-owned shipyards.

A second important contract was signed between Shell and Montecatini, Italy's second largest private enterprise. Montecatini was especially hard hit by the recession that began in 1963 and faced a severe shortage of capital. Shell agreed to put up $150 million to finance a joint petrochemical company. Then in February 1964 Gulf and ENI announced a contract even larger than the one between ENI

[10]The best English-language source on this period is the *Christian Science Monitor*. See reports in the following editions: December 18, 1962, p. 10; April 2, 1963, p. 14; April 27, 1963, p. 11.
[11]*New York Times*, March 23, 1963, p. 1; *Christian Science Monitor*, April 2, 1963, p. 14.

and SONJ. Gulf agreed to provide ENI with 17.5 million tons of crude over five years. The price of $1.05 a barrel was lower than even the Soviet oil price. The Gulf deal had an added value because 5 million tons of oil would go from Gulf's Ragusa fields in Sicily directly to ENI's nearby Gela petrochemical and refinery complex.[12]

When the ENI–SONJ deal was publicly announced, a State Department spokesman was willing only to "note with satisfaction" that Italy was "turning to Free World sources." But in a telegram dated March 20, two days before the public announcement, Under Secretary of State George Ball informed Ambassador Reinhardt that SONJ Vice-President Stott had kept him abreast of the negotiations and had informed him of the deal. "This is understood," Ball noted, "to have pre-empted the purchase by ENI of comparable amounts of Soviet crude."[13]

ENI spokesmen claimed publicly that no "political interpretation should be made of what is a commercial agreement."[14] It was hard to avoid such an interpretation, however, given the manner in which the agreement came about and the decline in oil imports from the Soviet Union that ensued (see Table 4.1). The 8.9 percent increase in 1963 was the lowest rate of growth since 1957. In 1964 and 1965 the import volume fell in absolute terms. And in relative terms, by 1965 the Soviet share of the Italian oil market had shrunk from its peak of 22 percent in 1962 to 10 percent.

At this much lower level of trade there was little threat that Soviet political influence would flow along with Soviet oil. A 10 percent market share just wasn't enough of a flow to crack the dikes of containment. The instrument that had enabled the United States to achieve this important objective had been the leverage that came with its compensatory economic resources. Italy could reduce its imports of Soviet oil virtually cost-free because of the substitute supply made available in assured quantities and at below market prices by American corporations. SONJ and others were willing to make the concessionary offers that they did because it was in their own economic interests to do so. These economic interests almost perfectly complemented the Kennedy administration's political interests to be served by stanching the flow of Soviet oil into Italy. Accordingly, not only did American politics exert no domestic contraints on American eco-

---

[12]*Christian Science Monitor*, November 25, 1963, p. 14; December 21, 1963, p. 10; February 17, 1964, p. 7; February 26, 1964, p. 7.

[13]*New York Times*, March 23, 1963, pp. 1–2; April 28, 1963, sec. III, pp. 1, 5.

[14]Ibid., April 27, 1963, p. 33; Dow Votaw, *The Six-Legged Dog* (Berkeley: University of California Press, 1964).

Table 4.1. Volume and growth rate of Italian imports of Soviet oil, 1957–1965

Year	Volume (thousands of metric tons)	Growth rate (percent)
1957	502.3	—
1958	1,082.0	115.4%
1959	3,035.9	180.6
1960	4,702.5	54.9
1961	6,165.8	31.1
1962	7,076.7	14.8
1963	7,712.6	8.9
1964	7,695.0	−0.2
1965	7,345.4	−4.5

SOURCE: Derived from Robert E. Ebel, *Communist Trade in Oil* (New York: Praeger, 1970), pp. 386–426.

nomic coercive power, but it was the public–private domestic partnership that made it possible to reduce the multilateral constraints.

THE POLITICAL SOURCES OF AMERICAN LEVERAGE OVER WEST GERMANY

In June 1962, when NATO passed a resolution imposing a partial boycott on oil, the United States also had tried to get agreement on an embargo of wide-diameter pipe. However, it achieved only an agreement to study the issue further and an advisory recommendation that in the interim, member nations "exercise, to the extent possible, restraint on export of those goods to the Soviet bloc."[15]

The October 5 West German–Soviet contracts for an additional 162,000 tons of pipe demonstrated that this advisory embargo clause was not very binding. To the contrary, these new West German contracts, if honored, would almost put the Soviets over the top on their wide-diameter pipe requirements. American intelligence estimates were that the Soviets were short as little as 200,000 tons of wide-diameter pipe.[16] The new West German contracts, if fulfilled, would

[15]Telegram, Finletter to Rusk, December 18, 1962, in NSF, Box 223, File: NATO Pipe Embargo, Kennedy Presidential Library.

[16]Estimates were that 600 miles of pipeline remained to be laid, requiring a total of 730,000 metric tons of 40-inch pipe. Existing Soviet inventories consisted of 125,000 tons. New factories were expected to come on line with a production capacity of as much as 275,000 tons in 1963. Another 130,000 tons were to be imported from Rumania. See State Department memoranda, "Large Diameter Pipe Shipments to the USSR," March 21, 1963, and "Western Efforts to Prevent Large Diameter Linepipe Exports to the Soviet Bloc" (RES-13), April 3, 1963, in NSF, Box 223, File: NATO Pipe Embargo, Kennedy Presidential Library.

account for most of this needed volume. Japanese manufacturers reportedly were coming close to signing contracts for another 43,500 tons.[17] Sweden also was interested in new contracts, and there were intimations that Britain also might be becoming interested.

Up to this point the one country that the United States had been able to leverage into at least a partial pipe embargo had been Italy. The lever was the extraterritorial application of American laws. Both of the Italian pipe manufacturing firms had imported production equipment and technology from the U.S. Steel Corporation. In approving U.S. Steel's export license, the Commerce Department had required a clause in the contract restricting the sale of any wide-diameter pipe produced with this technology to "friendly countries." In October 1961 the Kennedy administration invoked this licensing restriction against Italy.[18] For a year this issue remained as unsettled as the oil import issue (and not unrelated to it, as one of the pipe producers, Nuovo Pignone, was a subsidiary of Mattei's ENI). Finally, in early November 1962 American leverage began to register on the pipe embargo issue as well. Italy agreed to reduce deliveries of pipe from the 100,000 tons contracted for to 40,000. It also agreed to support in NATO the next American effort to pass a stronger embargo resolution. In return the United States agreed to drop its extraterritorial claims over the exports already made.[19]

Further NATO action came in a secret session on November 21, 1962, when it was resolved that "member countries, on their own responsibility, should, to the extent possible: (1) Stop deliveries of large diameter pipe (over 19″) to the Soviet bloc under *existing* contracts; (2) Prevent new contracts for such deliveries." The "stop" and "prevent" commands still were preceded by the loophole-making qualifiers "on their own responsibility" and "to the extent possible." Nevertheless, the November resolution was a significant step beyond the June pledge to study the issue. Moreover, among those voting for the embargo resolution was West Germany. There were no votes against, only an insistence by the British that their approval be qualified—the explanation and implications of which we will come back to.

The real test for West German policy came when Chancellor Adenauer's government next had to take the necessary regulatory actions

[17]Telegram, State Department to American Embassy, Japan, December 14, 1962, in ibid.

[18]Commerce Department, *58th Quarterly Report under the Export Control Act,* p. 26.

[19]Memorandum, "Western Efforts to Prevent Pipe Exports," pp. 3, 15–16, Kennedy Presidential Library.

to impose these controls agreed to secretly and in a multilateral forum on West German exporters. When on December 19 the firms holding the new 162,000-ton contracts applied for the necessary licenses, normally a perfunctory process, they were shocked to be informed by Minister of Economics Ludwig Erhard that for reasons of national security, the licenses would not be granted.[20] The issue was not settled there, though, because the same law that gave the executive the authority to deny licenses also gave the Bundestag veto power. The legislature had three months in which to act. Only a majority vote of the members present was required to override the executive decision, so long as there was a quorum.

The provision for Bundestag review was the opening for opponents of the embargo. The Social Democrats (SPD) opposed it both because of its negative impact on employment and as an overt case of American infringement on the Federal Republic's sovereign right to determine its own foreign policy. They were joined by the Free Democrats (FDP), even though they were partners of the Christian Democrats (CDU) in the governing coalition. The FDP's opposition was based on its advocacy of bilateral German-Soviet efforts at détente separate from relations at the superpower level.

The issue was compounded by the NATO resolution's call for the renunciation of existing contracts as well as a ban on future ones. Because these contracts were signed before the NATO resolution, the Soviets and the affected German firms had grounds to invoke the sanctity of existing contracts. Such an argument was strengthened by the fact that the pig iron that was bartered as partial payment for the pipe already had been imported into Germany. Moreover, the 162,000 tons of pipe were valued at $28 million, which translated into handsome profits and thousands of jobs.

The Soviets were not at all averse to making sure that the trade consequences were widely known within West Germany. Executives of the three pipe manufacturers made a secret trip to Moscow. Collateral influence was sought through other West German exporters by what an American embassy official called the "dangling of East–West trade plums before the hungry eyes of German industrialists."[21] A shipbuilding firm in Kiel which held an important contract for fishing

[20]The best account of these events is Angela Stent, *From Embargo to Ostpolitik: The Political Economy of West German–Soviet Relations, 1955–1980* (New York: Cambridge University Press, 1981), pp. 93–126. See also Robert W. Dean, *West German Trade with the East: The Political Dimension* (New York: Praeger, 1974), pp. 134–36.
[21]Telegram, American Embassy, Bonn, to Rusk, January 9, 1963, in NSF, Box 223, File: NATO Pipe Embargo, Kennedy Presidential Library.

vessels was told that the contract was suspended pending resolution of the pipeline issue.[22]

The Soviets also appealed to German pride and nationalism. Their formal protest note claimed that "it is not pipes that matter but a major principle of relations between states." They also questioned how such an action could be reconciled "with the sovereign right and State prestige of the Federal Republic," unless it was "an openly hostile act aimed at worsening relations."[23]

The Adenauer government formally answered the Soviet protest note by reaffirming its commitment to the embargo as a policy consistent with West German interests. But when the foreign trade committee of the Bundestag voted against applying the embargo retroactively to the October 5 contract, doubt was cast on Adenauer's ability to carry out this reaffirmation of his commitment. Together the SPD and FDP commanded 257 of the 499 votes in the Bundestag, a clear majority.

Faced with certain defeat if the issue came to a vote, the CDU devised an effective if less than savory parliamentary strategy. It first managed to delay debate on the embargo long enough so that the vote could not be scheduled until the last day of the three-month review period. At that point the 242 CDU deputies walked out of the Bundestag, making it impossible for the quorum necessary for any vote to be achieved. The opposition political parties branded this move a "blow to parliamentary democracy." *The Economist* termed it "parliamentary malarky." But without a quorum, the review period expired and the embargo became the law of the land.[24]

As opponents had predicted, the economic costs of cooperating with the United States did prove to be substantial. German pipe manufacturers had increased and modernized production capacity specifically in anticipation of continued growth of the Soviet market. Mannesmann, the largest contractor, lost over $25 million. Hoesch was forced to cut its welding capacity by two-thirds, and Phoenix-Rheinrohr shut down an entire plant.[25] German exports to the Soviet Union fell by 25 percent and the bilateral balance went from surplus to deficit. Total exports to the Soviet Union would not again reach 1962 levels until 1968.

---

[22]*New York Times*, March 19, 1963, p. 15.

[23]Ibid., April 7, 1963, p. 28.

[24]Stent, *From Embargo to Ostpolitik*, pp. 104–9; Dean, *West German Trade with the East*, pp. 134–36.

[25]Memorandum, "Western Efforts to Prevent Pipe Exports," p. 13, NSF, Box 223, File: NATO Pipe Embargo, Kennedy Presidential Library.

Why, then, did the Adenauer government take and then stand by a decision that was so detrimental to German economic interests and that threatened its governing coalition? There is no evidence of explicit or implicit American economic compensation, as with Italy. Instead, American leverage over West Germany was based on more political factors relating to American prestige as the alliance leader. As Wolfram Hanrieder stresses, more than those of any other West European country, the two major political parties of West Germany continued to be defined by their positions on the issue of relations with the United States.[26] The Christian Democrats and Adenauer himself originally came to power under American sponsorship. They had stayed in power ever since in large part because of public support for close ties with the United States. The argument stated by the CDU parliamentary leader, that one could not "call on NATO for one's protection on one side and ignore its clear decision on the other," proved to be a powerful one.[27] For among the West Germany populace as well as within the Christian Democrat leadership, the United States continued to enjoy immense prestige. It is quite revealing in this regard that only three months after the Bundestag pipeline embargo debate, John F. Kennedy received overwhelmingly warm and enthusiastic receptions across the Federal Republic. The adulation with which his "Ich bin ein Berliner" speech was greeted was perhaps the most graphic demonstration possible of continued high American prestige, pipe embargo notwithstanding.

The leverage value of American prestige was reinforced by two events that formed part of the pipe embargo's context. One was the Cuban missile crisis of October 1962. While there is no documentary evidence one way or the other, it is interesting that NATO finally approved the pipe embargo resolution on November 21, within a month of the Cuban missile crisis and after having previously been willing to pass only a much less stringent resolution. In the tense atmosphere of having just been to the brink, the American case for the economic defense and deterrence values of blocking the Friendship oil pipeline was much more compelling.

In addition, as Angela Stent emphasizes, the coincidental timing of the signing of the Franco-German Treaty of Cooperation on January 22, 1963, made the pipe embargo not only a test of *Westpolitik* vis-à-vis *Ostpolitik* but also of *Atlantikpolitik* vis-à-vis Gaullism. According to

[26]Wolfram Hanrieder, *West German Foreign Policy, 1949–1963* (Stanford: Stanford University Press, 1967).
[27]*New York Times*, March 16, 1963, p. 3.

Stent, "the United States interpreted Adenauer's signing of the treaty as an anti-American act because it emphasized the desire of Germany and of France for greater independence from the United States."[28] Criticism of the Franco-German treaty in the Bundesrat reflected similar domestic concerns. For the first time in eight years Adenauer was forced to make a personal appearance in the upper chamber in order to defend his treaty. Even then, the Bundesrat attached to the resolution of endorsement an understanding that the treaty did not signify any change in Germany's U.S.-oriented foreign policy.

Thus, for Adenauer's West Germany of 1962–63, the export of wide-diameter pipe, which had begun largely as an economic issue, now had been leveraged into a foreign policy issue. The fundamental question, even for the CDU deputies from the steel region who voted the party line, was allegiance to the United States. As Foreign Minister Gerhard Schroeder put it, "My heart is completely with the iron and steel industry, with full employment and the full utilization of our capacity. . . . But I must choose here between the interests of foreign policy and the interests of our economy. Thank God in a limited sphere. So I am choosing foreign policy."[29]

BRITAIN AND THE LIMITS OF AMERICAN LEVERAGE

German collaboration made it easier for the United States to keep other potential alternative traders in line. Italy followed through on its vote in NATO and the extraterritoriality compromise by turning down a Soviet offer of a new contract for 300,000 tons. The Japanese government initially resisted somewhat, contending that since the decision had been made in NATO, of which it was not a member, it had no grounds on which to impose more stringent regulations on its exporters. Under Secretary Ball cabled to Ambassador Edwin O. Reischauer that the "Embassy may wish to suggest" that noncollaboration might reverberate negatively against other pending issues more important to Japan, such as membership in OECD. While Ball did tell Reischauer to "of course avoid any implication or threat to withdraw U.S. support," it was difficult to avoid such an implication. By early January two Soviet offers for pipe contracts had been turned down by Japanese companies.[30]

[28]Stent, *From Embargo to Ostpolitik*, p. 95.
[29]Cited in ibid., p. 107.
[30]Telegrams, Finletter to Rusk, December 7, 11, and 18, 1962; Ball to Reischauer, December 15, 1962; American Embassy, Bonn, to Secretary of State, January 6, 1963, all in NSF, Box 223, File: NATO Pipe Embargo, Kennedy Presidential Library.

The most unconditional support for the pipe embargo came from France. De Gaulle's government gave the United States a written commitment not to use the new equipment it purchased from U.S. Steel for its most modern pipeline manufacturing plant at Dunkirk for export to the Soviet Union. It also rebuffed Soviet offers to purchase wide-diameter pipe in December 1962 (right after West Germany joined the embargo) and in March 1963, when a new three-year trade agreement was signed with the Soviet Union.[31]

This was the same Charles de Gaulle who concomitantly declared his hostility toward "a huge Atlantic community dependent upon and under the direction of America."[32] Yet as we noted earlier, collaboration with the United States on the issue of East–West oil trade was consistent with France's structural economic position as an energy producer nation. Under de Gaulle French energy policy was geared to two goals. One was self-sufficiency, in the sense of reserving as much of the domestic oil market as possible for the French oil companies CFP and CFR. The other was maintaining high oil prices; while they were not in the interests of consumers, it was only through artificially high prices that the operations of CFP and CFR could be financed.[33] A pipeline bringing Russian oil closer to France was inconsistent with such economically nationalistic objectives.

The most curious policy, and the one most vexing for the Kennedy administration, was the British. Initial concern about Britain's dissent within NATO was limited. Britain had never before exported wide-diameter pipe to the Soviets. Its NATO position was seen more as a symbolic upholding of its position as principal Western supporter of the American economic coercion strategy than as an expression of substantive policy from which actions would flow. Implicit in this prognosis was the assumption that Britain's position as an oil producer second only to the United States in its foreign holdings would lead it in practice to continue to oppose the development of the Soviet oil industry. In any case, it was known that Britain had very limited

---

[31]Memorandum, "Western Efforts to Prevent Pipe Exports," pp. 10, 17, and telegram, American Ambassador to Rusk, December 28, 1962, both in ibid.; Memorandum RSB-109, "Bilateral Trading Agreements between EEC and European Communist Countries," Hughes to Rusk, December 18, 1964, Special Committee on U.S. Trade Relations with Eastern European Countries and the Soviet Union, Lyndon B. Johnson Presidential Library, accessed through *Declassified Documents Quarterly Catalog* (Washington, D.C.: Carrollton Press), microfiche.

[32]Jean-Baptiste Duroselle, "De Gaulle's Designs for Europe and the West," in *Changing East–West Relations and the Unity of the West*, ed. Arnold Wolfers (Baltimore: Johns Hopkins University Press, 1964), p. 178.

[33]M. A. Adelman, *The World Petroleum Market* (Baltimore: Johns Hopkins University Press, 1972), p. 238.

capacity to produce wide-diameter pipe. The only known producer was the South Durham Steel and Iron Company, and its annual capacity was estimated at only 100,000 tons. South Durham also had a reputation for not being price-competitive and for inferior product quality.

Contrary to such predictions, Britain intensified rather than abated its opposition to the embargo policy. On January 8, 1963, German Foreign Minister Schroeder met with Lord Privy Seal Edward Heath to request British compliance with a policy for which the German government already had paid a dear political price. Schroeder reminded Heath of German support for British membership in the EEC, pointing out that cooperation "might improve Britain's image as a 'good European.'" Heath, however, was not forthcoming.[34]

In February the British took additional steps toward becoming an alternative pipe supplier. South Durham Steel accepted a pilot contract from the Soviets for 300 tons while negotiations continued over a larger contract. Soviet negotiators spoke of orders for $70 million of British ships, steel, and pipe. Such offers were particularly enticing because both the steel and shipbuilding sectors were in deep trouble, operating at less than 75 percent of capacity. The Macmillan government was interested enough in these prospective exports to consider even waiving the long-standing restrictions on imports of Soviet oil.

David Bruce, American ambassador to London, advised Secretary of State Rusk to "lay off for awhile."[35] He proposed to work quietly and gradually through established diplomatic channels. But his counsel was rejected because of the concern that Germany's compliance would soon evaporate in the face of British defection.[36] At this point the issue was bucked up to the White House level. McGeorge Bundy commissioned Christian Herter, already familiar to the British as a former secretary of state and the current trade negotiator, to go to London. President Kennedy wrote a personal letter of appeal to Prime Minister Macmillan on February 21. These diplomatic efforts also proved ineffective. Ambassador Bruce cabled that the British position on this issue "flows from Macmillan himself and has his full support."[37]

---

[34]Telegram, American Embassy, Bonn (Dowling), to Rusk, January 30, 1963, in NSF, Box 223, File: NATO Pipe Embargo, Kennedy Presidential Library.

[35]Telegram, Bruce to Rusk, January 29, 1963, in ibid.

[36]"Any attempt by a NATO or other free world country to fill the gap in Soviet orders left by the Germans would not only cause the agreement to collapse but would also have adverse political effects in the Federal Republic in view of the extraordinary efforts made by the Federal government" (memorandum, "Western Efforts to Prevent Pipe Exports," p. 13, in ibid.).

[37]Telegram, Bruce to Rusk, March 25, 1963, in ibid.

The next American strategem was to resort to economic compensation. John McCloy was the administration's emissary to the oil companies. Despite concern over price and quality, the oil companies agreed to buy 10,000 tons of 20-inch pipe and unspecified amounts of steel plate from South Durham Steel. This proposal was presented by Under Secretary of State George Ball to British Ambassador David Ormsby-Gore. It also was transmitted to Ambassador Bruce in London, who passed it on to Heath and to Frederick Erroll, president of the Board of Trade.[38]

South Durham Steel rejected the American compensatory scheme as insufficient; an order of 50,000 tons was more what they had in mind. That far the oil companies were not willing to go. At this point Ambassador Finletter floated the idea that maybe the stick of the multinationals' purchasing power should be tried and South Durham bids be ruled out for the pipelines being planned in Britain. The German ambassador again appealed to Heath at a meeting that Ambassador Bruce described as "cool if not unpleasant."[39] Foreign Minister Schroeder put British defection on the agenda of the North Atlantic Council meeting in Ottawa in the late spring.

Britain seemingly was resolute in its policy. In May a twenty-two-member trade mission made a ten-day trip to the Soviet Union. The mission head forecast that trade "should be doubled or even more than doubled." When the pipe issue was brought up at the June COCOM meeting, Britain again vetoed an embargo. By this time the United States had pretty much given up hope of changing the British position. Rusk told Bruce to encourage the British to keep their statements "bland and brief without emphasizing divisive aspects among NATO countries."[40]

Ironically, in the end the British never actually sold the Soviets any wide-diameter pipe. The South Durham deal got hung up on disagreements over price and the Soviets' concern for the quality of the pipe. But the fact that in the end no pipe was sold was secondary to the political damage done within the Western alliance (words often being more politically potent than deeds) by the anti-embargo position taken by Britain. Resentment was particularly strong in West Germany. When Britain publicly repudiated the NATO embargo resolution only days after the Bundestag had upheld West German col-

[38]Telegram, Ball to Bruce, March 19, 1963; memorandum by Rusk, March 23, 1963, Telegram, Bruce to Rusk, March 25, 1963, all in ibid.
[39]Telegrams, Finletter to Rusk, April 29, 1963, and Bruce to Rusk, May 17, 1963, both in ibid.
[40]Telegram, Rusk to Bruce, May 17, 1963, in ibid.

laboration, the newspaper *Bild Zeitung* expressed national sentiment with the headline "Outrageous!" The article went on to draw the lesson that if this was what happened when the Federal Republic sacrificed its own national interests, "then we, too, one day will put our interests before those of the Community."[41]

Why, then, did American leverage fail with British policy whereas it had succeeded with Italian and West German policy? One reason was that British economic problems were such that the compensation offered was insufficient to offset the perceived costs of trade controls. I say "perceived costs" because while on paper strict comparisons can be established between the costs of trade forgone and the benefits offered, these calculations are less important than how the relative balance is perceived. In Britain in 1963 these perceptions were colored by an unemployment rate that had increased 80 percent in the past year; by a $2.1 billion trade deficit, the highest in the industrial world; and by a currency that was on the verge of devaluation. In originally opposing the embargo the British delegate to COCOM had cited the "current special difficulties" in the British economy.[42] A riot of unemployed workers in front of Big Ben on the day that George Ball was meeting with Prime Minister Macmillan dramatized the problem. As the *New York Times* stated in its report of the incident and the failure of the Ball negotiations, Britain had a tremendous "need for all the business she can get these days."[43] After the defeat of Britain's bid for membership in the EEC, this feeling was reflected in the musing of Board of Trade President Erroll that as a trade partner the Soviet Union could be "no worse . . . than our closest friends."[44]

The second set of reasons involved the tarnished state of American prestige in British eyes. In contrast to the still healthy state of American–West German relations, Britain and the United States recently had been engaged in a number of conflicts and controversies. There was the Skybolt affair, in which both national pride and Prime Minister Macmillan's political standing suffered serious wounds.[45] The norms of the special relationship had been violated; whether because of Washington's bureaucratic politics or because of the junior partner mentality, the damaging effect on bilateral relations was the same.

---

[41]Quoted in *Economist*, March 10, 1963, p. 1212.

[42]Telegram, American Embassy, Paris, to State Department, June 20, 1963, in NSF, Box 223, File: NATO Pipe Embargo, Kennedy Presidential Library.

[43]*New York Times*, April 1, 1963, p. 60.

[44]Quoted in Michael P. Gehlen, "The Politics of Soviet Foreign Trade," *Western Political Quarterly* 18 (March 1965): 110.

[45]For an account of the Skybolt affair, see Richard Neustadt, *Alliance Politics* (New York: Columbia University Press, 1970).

There also was the inability of the United States to help Britain become a member of the Common Market. The United States may have won the Cuban missile crisis, but it clearly lost against de Gaulle on this issue. Thus Macmillan's predisposition to rebuff the United States on foreign policy contrasted markedly with Adenauer's perceived need to embrace American policy.

SUMMARY: MIXED LESSONS

The lessons of the 1962–63 oil trade sanctions case (and its subcases) were therefore decidedly mixed. On the one hand, in leveraging Italy and West Germany the United States did show that the resources on which it could draw to influence its allies' East–West trade policies still were formidable. With Italy American economic compensatory power countered the divergent economic interests that had led to the policy conflict. With West Germany it was the leverage value of American political prestige that overrode the economic interests at stake.

Once American leverage had transformed multilateral constraints into multilateral collaboration, the United States scored some success in achieving its immediate objectives of containment and economic defense. By luring Italy away from increasing its imports of Soviet oil, the United States averted the prospect that Soviet political influence would flow along with Soviet oil. Because this was a major concern of the Kennedy administration, in the overall context of East–West competition the import boycott component of the oil trade sanctions deserved to be considered a significant success.

On the pipe embargo side the United States also enjoyed some success in regard to the economic defense objective of disrupting construction of the Friendship oil pipeline. The State Department estimated that the embargo denied the Soviets 278,400 tons of pipe.[46] Some substitute pipe came from Sweden, which in keeping with its official policy of neutrality refused to collaborate with the NATO resolution; but the Swedes supplied only 61,000 tons.[47] And despite the

[46]Memorandum, "Large Diameter Pipe Shipments," p. 3, NSF, Box 223, File: NATO Pipe Embargo, Kennedy Presidential Library.

[47]The American ambassador is said to have met with representatives of the Swedish Foreign Office and "demanded that Sweden should immediately cooperate. According to well-informed sources, this demand was so bluntly stated that the Ambassador was, in a diplomatic manner, shown out of the Foreign Office" (Gunnar Adler-Karlsson, *Western Economic Warfare, 1947–1967* [Stockholm: Almquist & Wiksell, 1968], pp. 131–32).

Soviets' boasts of moving toward their own production capacity, the two new pipe mills that they brought on line in early 1963 were reported to be "experiencing difficulty both in volume and in quality of production."[48] Thus, while the FOP eventually was completed, the NATO pipe embargo did manage to delay it beyond the immediate period of tensions (Berlin, Cuba) in which the Kennedy administration was most concerned about the completed pipeline's military significance.

Some success was also achieved in terms of the more ongoing economic warfare objective of limiting the growth of the Soviet oil industry. A CIA report two years later found that pipe shortages still persisted and were principally responsible for the fact that the whole national oil pipeline system was operating at only 53 percent of planned carrying capacity.[49] As late as February 1966 an editorial in *Pravda* singled out for criticism the persisting shortages of wide-diameter pipe.[50] In addition, continued sanctions in related sectors of the Soviet oil industry were exacerbating problems there. Soviet refineries were inferior to their Western and especially American counterparts, lacking the technology necessary for secondary distillation (the process for producing the highest octane fuels and petrochemicals). Soviet drilling technology was not adequate for the deeper penetrations required as declining productivity of the wells in the Ural and Volga regions forced a shift to the vast but more recalcitrant reserves of the Central Asian and western Siberian regions of the USSR. A 1965 CIA analysis found that at depths of 15,000 feet Soviet drill pipe tended to crack under the extreme pressure and that manufacture of the diamond drill bits needed to pierce the rock cover of much of Siberia was only 10 percent of the demand forecast by Gosplan, the Soviet state planning agency. On the basis of this and other evidence, the CIA concluded that "without exception there is no single major item of oilfield equipment which is available to the Soviet bloc industry in sufficient quantity and quality."[51]

---

[48]Memorandum, "Large Diameter Pipe Shipments," p. 1, NSF, Box 223, File: NATO Pipe Embargo, Kennedy Presidential Library.

[49]Directorate of Intelligence, Office of Research and Reports, "Petroleum in the Soviet Bloc: Problems and Prospects," CIA/RR ER64-63, December 1964, Special Committee on U.S.–Soviet Trade Relations, Johnson Library, via *Declassified Documents Catalog*.

[50]Stent, *From Embargo to Ostpolitik*, p. 274, n. 89. George Ball later recounted that Soviet Ambassador Anatoly Dobrynin boasted that the American sanctions had an infant-industry-like stimulative effect on the Soviets' capacity to produce wide-diameter pipe. As the statistics cited here show, however, Dobrynin's boast was no more than that.

[51]Central Intelligence Agency, Office of Research and Reports, "Petroleum Equip-

As in the 1950s, however, the impact of economic sanctions on the Soviet economy was not nearly so disruptive as the United States had anticipated, or at least hoped. The Soviets' annual oil production growth rate did fall in the second half of the 1960s from 12.8 to 8.9 percent, but even this latter rate amounted to significant progress. Moreover, the rapid increase in natural gas production (11 percent annual growth, and an increase in the natural gas share of total national energy output from 15.5 percent in 1965 to 19.1 percent in 1970) further strengthened the Soviet domestic energy position.[52] Once again, in effect, the Soviet Union was demonstrating the extent to which the vastness of its resources endowed it with the capacity to soften the economic impact of sanctions. Thus, even when the United States was able to minimize the multilateral constraints, its coercive power to disrupt the Soviet economy extensively was still checked by the unilateral constraint of Soviet capacity to draw on its own resources.

The fourth objective of the oil trade sanctions had been to reinforce the overall Western deterrence posture. The United States had sought to achieve this objective both through the signal that Western collective action would send and by capitalizing on the oil trade issue to reassert more generally its dominance over Western policy in regard to Eastern trade. But the controversy fanned by Britain's defection from the pipe embargo blurred the forcefulness of the intended signal. Even more important, it soon became evident that the leverage that was exerted proved to be more of a last hurrah than a lasting precedent. The first sign of this came the following year, when, over the Johnson administration's opposition, the Europeans began to extend long-term credits to the Soviet Union.[53] Greased by this financing, Western European exports to the Soviet Union more than doubled between 1963 and 1968. New large-scale joint ventures such as the $1.5 billion Fiat-Togliatti auto plant were undertaken. And, as Chapter 5 will show, by the late 1960s Western European–Soviet energy trade was beginning to grow rapidly again.

Compounding the long-term problem for the United States was Congress's rebuff of initiatives taken by Presidents Kennedy and

---

ment Technology in the USSR and Eastern Europe," March 24, 1965, p. 3, via *Declassified Documents Catalog.*

[52]J. Richard Lee, "The Soviet Petroleum Industry: Promises and Problems," in U.S. Congress, Joint Economic Committee, *Soviet Economic Prospects for the Seventies,* Joint Committee Print, 93d Cong., 1st sess., 1973, p. 284.

[53]Jules Davids, *The United States in World Affairs, 1964,* Council on Foreign Relations Series (New York: Harper & Row, 1965), p. 91.

Johnson to liberalize American–Soviet trade. The short-term successes of the oil trade sanctions notwithstanding, the Kennedy administration had begun a comprehensive policy review as early as May 1963. The result of this review (which was led by Harriman, Ball, Under Secretary of Commerce Franklin D. Roosevelt, Jr., and Walt Rostow, director of the State Department's Policy Planning Council) was a 107-page report titled "U.S. Policy on Trade with the European Soviet Bloc."[54]

This report (hereafter referred to as the Rostow report, for its principal author) built the case for trade liberalization on three principal arguments. First, while economic impact could still be shown in specific instances, as in the pipeline embargo, the more general economic warfare rationale now was called "absurd." "Quite clearly, an almost total lack of American products since 1948 has not caused the Soviet economy to 'grind to a halt' or even to slow down; nor has it in any other discernible way brought the day of final reckoning closer for the ruling regime." The Rostow report argued that "even under conditions of a maximum interdiction of East–West trade, the USSR would have the capability (a) to maintain and probably to improve in its own favor the present balance of world power, (b) to preserve its internal social and political order, and (c) to continue relatively rapid economic growth."[55]

The report acknowledged that sanctions achieved some success as an "important symbol of our Cold War resolve and purpose" and as expressing "our moral disapproval of the USSR." It also acknowledged, however, that while in this light sanctions were cast as an American reaction to Soviet provocations, the Soviets perceived them as an American provocation. "No Soviet leader, in either private or public discussions of problems related to an improvement of international relations, has failed to point to 'U.S. discriminatory practices' as proof of U.S. hostility and as a bellwether of U.S. unwillingness to seek a 'genuine relaxation of tensions.'"[56] Whether the Soviet view was justified or not, the point was that if the United States was interested in improving relations, it had to take this view into account.

Moreover, such an improvement in relations was deemed now possible, desirable, and at least in part dependent on liberalized trade relations. After the two countries had been to the brink over the missiles in Cuba, the hot line had been established, both symbol and

---

[54]State Department, Policy Planning Council, "U.S. Policy on Trade with the European Soviet Bloc" (draft report), July 8, 1963, in NSF, Subjects: Trade, East–West, Box 310, Kennedy Presidential Library.
[55]Ibid., pp. 34, 3.
[56]Ibid., pp. 4, 35.

substance of a mutual commitment to crisis management. The test ban treaty was nearing completion. President Kennedy had made his historic "make the world safe for diversity" speech at American University. Other overtures had been made by both sides and initiatives taken. In this situation of "cold war movement," Rostow wrote,

> all of the peculiar values that attach to the control policy, except insofar as it affects items of direct strategic importance, fall away. At the same time, the control policy would be particularly useful, *and almost uniquely so,* as a means of furthering the movement process . . . controls would be *an enticing inducement for the USSR.* In them the US has one of the few commodities which it can afford to give up that the USSR would be interested in buying.[57]

Direct linkages of trade benefits to any specific political quid pro quo still would not work, offensive as they would be to Soviet sensitivity to being coerced. But "if during the course of a 'general negotiation' the U.S. indicated that it was prepared to change its basic approach to trade with the USSR in the interests of a settlement of outstanding issues, the USSR would be more forthcoming in contributing from its side items of value in the negotiating package."[58]

Moreover, given the progress that already had been made, progress that was greater than at any time since the anti-Hitler alliance, there was the danger that a lack of forward movement would mean backward regression. So whatever doubts remained about whether the inducements of trade actually would bring political influence, there was the danger that "unless the U.S. should be willing to give up controls, the movement process would necessarily be of short duration. The Soviet leaders have made clear they equate 'peaceful relations' with 'trade relations'; they would insist on consideration of controls in any serious negotiations; and they would consider U.S. attitudes on this issue as a decisive test of U.S. intentions."[59] Even when propagandistic motivations and Khrushchev's characteristic volatility are taken into account, Soviet protest ensuing from the pipe embargo were quite strong.[60] Such reactions could not help pulling in the

---

[57]Ibid., p. 6 (emphasis added).
[58]Ibid., p. 40.
[59]Ibid., p. 6.
[60]A classic Khrushchev reaction was a speech he made in the midst of the pipeline controversy: "Of course, anything one pleases can be regarded as strategic material, even a button, because it can be sewn onto a soldier's pants. A soldier will not wear pants without buttons, since otherwise he would have to hold them up with his hands. And then what can he do with his weapon? If one reasons thus, then buttons also are a particularly strategic material. But if buttons really had such great importance and we

direction opposite from arms control, crisis management agreements, and conciliatory speeches.

The Rostow report's third point against the strict sanctions strategy concerned the intra-alliance tensions that the oil embargo-boycott made so evident. The "combination of circumstances" that had endowed the United States with "leverage to influence their [the allies'] policies . . . are now drastically changed and *our leverage in this field greatly diminished.*" The Europeans remained willing to collaborate with controls on exports with direct military applications. But "except under a crisis situation . . . or perhaps under the greatest of pressure in specific cases [e.g., wide diameter pipe] they will not join with us in any common endeavor to curtail trade with the Bloc for political or economic warfare reasons." It would be more politic to concentrate controls where there was little dispute over basic strategy and "employ the capital previously expended to hold the trade line on more constructive undertakings."[61] Thus, whatever limited and short-term successes had been registered, there was a sense that over the longer term the costs of exerting leverage might be even greater. The United States had held the line on the oil pipe embargo but not without exacerbating the already raw nerves of its allies.

The policy shift envisioned in the Rostow report, however, encountered domestic opposition. When a few months later President Kennedy tried to take a first step by authorizing the sale of $250 million in grain to the Soviet Union, one of his congressional liaison aides reported back that "the full range of strident anticommunism was let loose in the oratory on this point. The implicit charge is that condoning the sale amounts to being soft on communism just when we should show our mettle."[62] Interestingly, it was none other than Richard Nixon who attacked the Kennedy grain sale as "the major foreign policy mistake of this administration—even more serious than fouling up the Bay of Pigs." Nixon went on: "what we're doing is subsidizing Khrushchev at a time when he is in deep economic trouble. . . . It pulls his economy out of a very great hole and allows him to divert the Russian economy into space and other military activities

could find no substitute for them, then I am sure that our soldiers would even learn to keep their pants up with their teeth, so that their hands would be free to hold weapons" (cited in Stent, *From Embargo to Ostpolitik,* p. 93).

[61]State Department, Policy Planning Council, "U.S. Policy on Trade with the Soviet Bloc," p. 12, NSF, Subjects: Trade East-West, Box 310, Kennedy Presidential Library (emphasis added).

[62]Memorandum, Fred Dutton to McGeorge Bundy and Lawrence O'Brien, "Congressional Consultations on Possible Wheat Sale," September 30, 1963, p. 2, in NSF, Box 314, Kennedy Presidential Library.

that he otherwise would have to keep in agriculture." Nor, even more interestingly, were those economic interest groups that stood to benefit the most necessarily supportive. Ten Republican members of the House Agriculture Committee, claiming to speak for their farm belt constituents, stated that "we oppose this action because we believe the vast majority of American farmers, like the vast majority of all Americans, are unwilling to sell out a high moral principle, even for solid gold."[63] The sale itself could not be blocked because it fell within existing presidential discretion.[64] But Congress could and did pass legislation making such deals more difficult to negotiate in the future.[65]

Two years later President Lyndon Johnson tried to go even further in the direction of liberalization with his East–West Trade Relations Act of 1966.[66] Once again the opposition was formidable. Representative Wilbur Mills refused to schedule hearings on the bill in his Ways and Means Committee (where all legislation that in any respect involves tariffs must originate). "I want to make my position clear," Mills said. "I am not for it."[67] Gerald R. Ford, House Republican leader, and Everett Dirksen, Senate Republican leader, opposed any trade liberalization unless "the Communists stopped aggression in South Vietnam and elsewhere." George Meany, president of the AFL-CIO, denounced businessmen interested in the Soviet market for their "greed for profit." And the front lines were manned by such

[63]Congressional Quarterly, *1963 Almanac*, p. 328.

[64]The Latta amendment to the Agricultural Act of 1961 had declared it to be the policy of Congress that the United States should "in no manner either subsidize the export [of], sell or make available any subsidized agricultural commodity" to communist countries. But an opinion written by Attorney General Robert F. Kennedy interpreted the Latta amendment as a nonbinding policy declaration, to be considered but not necessarily conformed to. A similar interpretation was made of the Johnson Act of 1934, which prohibited loans by private persons or business entities to any foreign government in default on debts to the U.S. government. The financing of President Kennedy's wheat deal was on normal commercial credit terms, which according to Attorney General Kennedy did not constitute a loan and therefore was not subject to the Johnson Act's restrictions.

[65]Key was the provision pushed by the AFL-CIO and International Longshoremen's Association requiring 50% of the grain to be carried in American ships. This provision raised the price to the Soviets rather substantially, especially since other Western grain exporters did not impose such restrictions. Commerce Secretary Hodges recalled thinking at the time, "I would not blame the Russians if they never bought a single bushel of wheat from the United States again" (Oral History interview, p. 100, Kennedy Presidential Library). And in fact they did not, at least for the next seven years.

[66]Johnson based this legislation on the report of a blue-ribbon commission he had appointed. See "Report to the President of the Special Committee on U.S. Trade Relations with East European Countries and the Soviet Union," in *Department of State Bulletin* 54 (May 30, 1966).

[67]Congressional Quarterly, *1965 Almanac*, p. 503.

groups as the Young Americans for Freedom, who organized protests and boycotts against traders with the enemy.[68]

Johnson coined the term "building bridges" as the political rationale for trade liberalization. In part this strategy actually was old-fashioned rollback through different means, in that it targeted those Eastern European countries that seemed most restive in an effort to encourage greater independence in foreign policy. It also built on Rostow's arguments (and presaged the Nixon-Kissinger strategy) for trying to induce the Soviet Union to, as Johnson put it, "shift from the narrow concept of coexistence to the broader vision of peaceful engagement."[69]

But it was extremely difficult for an administration that simultaneously was evoking the anticommunist ethic and invoking the national security imperative as the bases for committing huge sums of money and huge numbers of troops to fight a war in the jungles of Asia also to make the case for peaceful engagement with the Soviet Union. "Do we want to help the Soviet Union," as one congressman asked rhetorically when he introduced additional legislation to close existing loopholes allowing the president to extend some Export-Import Bank credits to the Russians, "while it is the principal supplier of war material to North Vietnam? The administration's trading with the enemy policy shows more concern with cash than with American lives being lost in Vietnam."[70]

Thus the ideological bias against "trading with the enemy" still was widely held and deeply felt. To go back to Alexander George's definition of normative legitimacy, trade liberalization initiatives were not "consistent with fundamental national values and contribut[ing] to their enhancement";[71] they violated the fundamental national ethic of anticommunism and did nothing to enhance national security. The Vietnam War only exacerbated both sentiments.

While there was more support in the American business community for East–West trade than in the past, it was not the kind of intensive

[68]Congressional Quarterly, *1966 Almanac*, pp. 439–40, and Marshall I. Goldman, *Détente and Dollars* (New York: Basic Books, 1975), pp. 64–65.

[69]See Johnson's 1966 State of the Union address and his October 7, 1966, speech to the National Conference of Editorial Writers, in *Public Papers of the Presidents: Lyndon B. Johnson* (Washington, D.C.: Government Printing Office, 1967), 1: 3–13 and 2: 1125–30.

[70]*Congressional Record,* 90th Cong., 2d sess., vol. 114, pt. 2, February 6, 1968, p. 2303.

[71]Alexander L. George, "Domestic Constraints on Regime Change in U.S. Foreign Policy: The Need for Policy Legitimacy," in *Change in the International System*, ed. Ole R. Holsti, Randolph M. Siverson, and A. L. George (Boulder, Colo.: Westview Press, 1980), p. 235.

support that sparked assertive lobbying efforts. Several key trade associations had gone so far as to testify in support of trade liberalization at hearings held by the Senate Foreign Relations Committee.[72] But as a survey conducted by Marshall Goldman and Alice Conner revealed, doubts about the commercial risks still were widespread in the business community. Legal issues concerning contracts still were unsettled, marketing was difficult, and other barriers made doing business with the Soviet bloc seem excessively problematic. And American firms still were tremendously concerned, as one marketing executive put it, about "the reactions of our stockholders and customers."[73]

Any shift in American policy thus was being constrained by the lack of a strong supportive domestic political coalition. The same factors that for so long had kept domestic constraints on economic coercion to a minimum now were imposing severe constraints on initiatives toward a shift to an economic inducement strategy. The paradoxical and problematic result, as the 1960s drew to a close, was that the multilateral Western alliance constraints on a coercive strategy were increasing but the American domestic constraints on an inducement strategy were not decreasing.

[72]Pro-trade testimony came from the U.S. Chamber of Commerce, the Committee for Economic Development, the National Foreign Trade Council, the Bankers Association for Foreign Trade, and the Machinery and Allied Products Institute. See U.S. Congress, Senate Foreign Relations Committee, *East–West Trade: Hearings*, 88th and 89th Congs., 1964–65.

[73]Marshall I. Goldman and Alice Conner, "Businessmen Appraise East–West Trade," *Harvard Business Review*, January–February 1966, p. 6.

CHAPTER FIVE

Energy Trade and Détente in the 1970s

THE FATE OF THE NIXON-KISSINGER ECONOMIC INDUCEMENT STRATEGY

It was ironic that it was Richard Nixon, whose political career had been so closely identified with the Cold War, who became the moving force behind the shift in American policy from economic coercion to economic inducement. On closer analysis, though, it also makes sense. For as John Lewis Gaddis has stressed, détente broke with past policy more by its means than by its ends.[1] The principal ends still were containment of Soviet influence and deterrence of nuclear war. The difference was that now, instead of pursuing these objectives strictly through Cold War confrontational policies, the Nixon administration also was attempting to condition Soviet behavior through a combination of negotiated arms control agreements, annual summitry, great power triangular diplomacy, and economic incentives. All of these initiatives were considered necessary to create an optimal mix of deterrents against aggression and inducements for cooperation. Trade was particularly important in this last regard because, as the administration explained in an August 1972 policy statement,

> our purpose is to build in both countries a vested economic interest in the maintenance of a harmonious and enduring relationship. A nation's security is affected not only by its adversary's military capabilities but by

[1]John Lewis Gaddis, *Strategies of Containment* (New York: Oxford University Press, 1982), pp. 274–344.

132

the price which attends the use of those capabilities. If we can create a situation in which the use of military force would jeopardize a mutually profitable relationship, I think it can be argued that security will have been enhanced.[2]

In addition to this long-term vision of what came to be dubbed "the structure of peace," trade also was seen as having more direct, immediate, and instrumental value as a bargaining tool. Henry Kissinger recounts in his memoirs how the administration opposed congressional moves in 1969 to liberalize the Export Control Act unilaterally and without any connection, or "linkage," to superpower politics. It was not that Kissinger wanted the linkage to be explicit; as we shall see, when the issue was the emigration of Soviet Jews, the administration proved far more willing than Congress to keep the quid pro quo implicit. But if the Kremlin wanted access to the economic benefits of trade with the United States, it first "would have to show restraint on its international conduct and arrange for progress on key foreign policy issues." Economic concessions would be offered only "after the Soviet Union cooperated with us in the political field."[3]

In their official pronouncements Soviet leaders repeatedly and staunchly opposed any linkages of trade to politics.[4] But on some key issues they proved more accepting in private of these linked terms of trade.[5] In the negotiations leading to SALT I, for example, there is some evidence that pledges by the Nixon administration to liberalize

[2]Peter G. Peterson, *U.S.–Soviet Commercial Relations in a New Era* (Washington, D.C.: Government Printing Office, 1972), pp. 3–4. As Henry Kissinger characterizes Peterson as someone who performed "with ability and finesse," one of the few personal compliments to be found in the thousands of pages of his memoirs, and as he also states that Peterson "subjected all such economic decisions to our foreign policy strategy," it is safe to conclude that this report represented official doctrine (*White House Years* [Boston: Little, Brown, 1979], p. 840).

[3]Kissinger, *White House Years*, p. 155. In 1969 Congress did pass the Export Administration Act, over administration objections. The change of name from Export Control Act was indicative of the new, more liberal approach embodied in the legislation. But the extent of decontrol achieved was much less than its sponsors, Senators Edmund Muskie and Walter Mondale, had sought when they introduced their original bill, the Export Expansion and Regulation Act. As Kissinger notes, while the new law "declared it U.S. policy to favor expansion of peaceful trade with the Soviet Union and Eastern Europe . . . much of its implementation was left to presidential discretion" (ibid.).

[4]Adam B. Ulam, *Dangerous Relations: The Soviet Union in World Politics, 1970–1982* (New York: Oxford University Press, 1983), p. 59; Franklyn D. Holzman and Robert Legvold, "The Economics and Politics of East-West Relations," *International Organization* 29 (Winter 1975): 295–96.

[5]For further development of the arguments that follow and the supporting evidence, see my "Political Basis for Trade in U.S.–Soviet Relations," *Millennium: Journal of International Studies* 15 (Spring 1986): 27–47.

existing controls on exports of both grain and industrial machinery led the Soviets in May 1971 to abandon their insistence that an ABM treaty precede any agreement to limit offensive strategic missiles.[6] A few months later, when the longshoremen and maritime unions refused to load grain destined for the Soviet Union, Seymour Hersh quotes Charles Colson as saying he received a call directly from the president telling him to work on the unions because "SALT depends on it." And through another White House aide Hersh attributes to Soviet Ambassador Anatoly Dobrynin the threat that "there would be no SALT agreement unless the grain deal was worked out."[7]

Trade inducements also appear to have contributed to progress made before and at the May 1972 summit on another top American priority, the Vietnam War. When Nixon went ahead with bombing and mining operations against North Vietnam on the eve of the summit, Kissinger and other foreign policy experts were convinced that as in the 1960 U-2 incident, the Soviets would cancel the summit, citing American aggression as the reason. That they did not, like the failure of the proverbial dog to bark, said a great deal. The American journalist Stanley Karnow tells of being tapped by a Soviet embassy official to deliver the message to Washington that "we've done a lot for those Vietnamese, but we're not going to let them spoil our relations with the United States."[8] In Marshall Goldman's interpretation, "in the Soviet scheme of things, the toleration of the escalation of U.S. violence in Vietnam was an unfortunate part of the price the Soviet Union was prepared to pay to obtain the American imports it needed."[9] Adam Ulam concurs on this point, pointing out that by May 1972 the Soviets already were aware of the severity of their harvest failure and therefore had American grain very much on their

---

[6]Seymour M. Hersh, *The Price of Power: Kissinger in the Nixon White House* (New York: Summit Books, 1983), pp. 334–49. While Kissinger does not mention the executive order of June 10, 1971, liberalizing grain exports, he does acknowledge decontrolling the gear-cutting machinery ordered by the Soviets for their $1 billion Kama River truck foundry, then under construction (*White House Years*, p. 840).

[7]Hersh, *Price of Power*, p. 347.

[8]Stanley Karnow, *Vietnam: A History* (New York: Viking Press, 1983), p. 646. The *Wall Street Journal* also reported (October 30, 1972, p. 12) that Soviet Trade Minister Patolichev was at the home of Commerce Secretary Peter Peterson when Nixon's speech announcing the mining and bombing operations was broadcast on television. "After hearing Mr. Nixon's tough words, he [Patolichev] turned to his host [Peterson] and said, 'Well, let's get back to business.' And a couple of days later he posed happily with the President, a clear signal to Hanoi that Moscow put its own interests first."

[9]Marshall I. Goldman, "Interaction of Politics and Trade: Soviet–Western Interaction," in U.S. Congress, Joint Economic Committee, *Soviet Economy in the 1980s: Problems and Prospects,* Joint Committee Print, 97th Cong., 2d sess. 1982, pt. 1, p. 121.

minds when they agreed to go ahead with the summit.[10] And while from the American perspective much would go wrong later, Nixon was sufficiently pleased to join with Brezhnev in a joint communiqué at the June 1973 summit in which "the two sides expressed their deep satisfaction" with the Paris Peace Treaty.[11]

This is not to say that economic inducements were the only reason for Soviet interest in détente with the United States. The Soviet Union was not about to be the glaring exception to Morgenthauian principles. Clearly its own strategic and political objectives also were being served. But the economic motivation clearly was an important one. The 24th Party Congress (1971) and Ninth Five-Year Plan (1971–75) marked the institutionalization of trade with the West in Soviet policy and planning. No longer were Soviet leaders content to rely exclusively on the economic strategy of regional integration and semi-autarky embodied in the Council for Mutual Economic Assistance (CMEA). Nor was there any more blustering about economically burying the West. Instead, such officials as Minister of Foreign Trade Nikolai Patolichev sounded more like David Ricardo than like Karl Marx in stressing that trade with the West allows the Soviet Union "to make fuller and more rational use of its own resources and possibilities, and at the same time to acquire, by way of commercial exchange, goods of other countries that are not produced in our country or whose production would cost more than it does to import them."[12]

This view, while not unanimously held in the Kremlin, did have the critical support of Premier Alexei Kosygin and especially of General Secretary Leonid Brezhnev, whose internal power then was on the rise. "We have entered a stage of economic development," Brezhnev declared in 1970, "that no longer allows us to work in the old way but calls for new methods and new solutions."[13] The Liberman reforms of 1965, a major effort by Kosygin and Brezhnev to solve internal economic problems, had proven both economically ineffective and

[10]Ulam, *Dangerous Relations*, p. 90.
[11]Raymond L. Garthoff, *Détente and Confrontation: American–Soviet Relations from Nixon to Reagan* (Washington, D.C.: Brookings Institution, 1985), p. 332.
[12]Cited in Herbert S. Levine, "Soviet Economic Development, Technological Transfer, and Foreign Policy," in *The Domestic Context of Soviet Foreign Policy*, ed. Seweryn Bialer (Boulder, Colo.: Westview Press, 1981), p. 190.
[13]Cited in M. Elizabeth Denton, "Soviet Perceptions of Economic Prospects," in Joint Economic Committee, *Soviet Economy in the 1980s*, p. 32. Raymond Garthoff cites a speech on West German television in 1973 in which Brezhnev explicitly repudiated autarky and stated that Soviet economic policy "proceeds from the premise" of growing economic relations with the West (*Détente and Confrontation*, p. 88).

politically risky. In comparison with stirring up the party and ministerial bureaucracies, any dangers associated with increased trade with the West seemed quite manageable.

While much of the industrial machinery and equipment in which the Soviets were interested was available from Western Europe, in two respects the United States was positioned to be the crucial trade partner. First, as we have already noted, the disastrous 1971–72 grain harvests left the Soviets in need of huge volumes of grain.[14] This was a need that only the American farm belt could satisfy. Second, and even more relevant to our particular concerns, was American energy technology. In some product areas, as the CIA noted, Western European and Japanese industry were "approaching the U.S. level of technology" (e.g., wide-diameter pipe, where they already were "abreast").[15] But for the most part American producers still held a significant technological lead in equipment and technology for oil and gas exploration (e.g., computerized seismic surveying equipment), production (e.g., deep well and rock drilling), processing (e.g., oil refineries, gas desulfurization), and transmission (e.g., turbine-powered compressor stations for natural gas pipelines).

With the Soviets' increasing need to turn to their rich but difficult-to-tap reserves in western Siberia, American export strengths matched Soviet import priorities. As Table 5.1 shows, the Ninth Five-Year Plan called for increases in western Siberian oil production from the existing level of 31 million metric tons to 125 million metric tons by 1975. This increase in volume translated into an increase from 8.9 to 25.2 percent of total national production. Or, from another angle, the annual increase of 94 million tons in western Siberian production equaled 63.9 percent of the total national total annual increase. The planned increase in gas production fitted the same pattern: from 9 billion cubic meters (bcm) to 44 bcm, 4.5 to 13.7 percent of total national output, and 28.7 percent of the total annual increment. These figures are on a smaller scale than those for oil, but as we shall see, they increase rather dramatically beginning in the second half of the 1970s.

[14]On the political economy of the American–Soviet grain trade, see Robert L. Paarlberg, *Food Trade and Foreign Policy: India, the Soviet Union, and the United States* (Ithaca: Cornell University Press, 1985); I. M. Destler, *Making Foreign Economic Policy* (Washington, D.C.: Brookings Institution, 1980); and Dan Morgan, *Merchants of Grain* (New York: Viking Press, 1979).

[15]Central Intelligence Agency, Directorate of Intelligence, Office of Economic Research, "Potential for Soviet Trade with the United States in Industrial Raw Materials," Intelligence Report ER IR 71-27, December 1971, p. 12, accessed through *Declassified Documents Quarterly Catalog* (Washington, D.C.: Carrollton Press), microfiche.

Table 5.1. Western Siberian oil and natural gas production, 1970, and Ninth Five-Year Plan targets, 1975

	1970		1975 plan	
	Volume	Percent of Soviet production	Volume	Percent of Soviet production
Oil	31 mmt[a]	8.9%	125 mmt[a]	25.2%
Gas	9 bcm[b]	4.5	44 bcm[b]	13.7

[a]Millions of metric tons.
[b]Billions of cubic meters.
SOURCE: J. Richard Lee, "The Soviet Petroleum Industry: Promise and Problems," in U.S. Congress, Joint Economic Committee, *Soviet Economic Prospects for the Seventies,* Joint Committee Print, 93d Cong., 1st sess., 1973, pp. 283–90.

The Nixon administration was well aware of the Soviet energy situation. The confidential December 1971 CIA report cited above also stated that "the USSR urgently needs modern petroleum facilities and has shown a strong interest in U.S. equipment and technology, generally the most advanced in the West." The report noted that at the Dartmouth Conference held in Kiev the previous July, Premier Kosygin repeatedly had stressed the potential for developing American–Soviet trade in the energy sector. Soviet officials also had put out feelers during Commerce Secretary Maurice Stans's trip to Moscow in November. The estimates being bandied about reportedly were $500 million in initial exports related to oil and up to $500 million annually for at least the following few years, and $1 billion in projects related to natural gas.[16] There also had been some preliminary discussion of a joint project for the development of Siberian natural gas reserves, the construction of processing facilities for liquefied natural gas (LNG), and the shipment by 1980 of as much as 2 billion cubic feet (bcf) of LNG per day back to the United States.

It is interesting to note, especially in light of later events, that in assessing these prospects for American–Soviet energy trade and cooperative ventures, the CIA and the Nixon administration in general dismissed the notion that American security interests might be threatened. In another confidential report written in February 1972, the CIA advised that the Soviet Union was "as reliable a source of supply as almost any foreign country." The Soviets "had a good record of honoring contractual obligations." They "have a stable government." And their "desire to realize . . . earnings of hard currency" over the

[16]Ibid., pp. 2, 8.

long term would be "the best guarantee that the Soviet Union would [continue to] be a reliable supplier." Therefore, far from representing risks to American security and other foreign policy interests, such ongoing commercial relations as the LNG joint project "would give both countries a vested interest in continued cooperation."[17]

The United States was seen as deriving substantial economic benefits from such trade. In 1970 American domestic oil production had begun to decline. With energy consumption rates still rising and other domestic sources (coal, nuclear, Alaskan natural gas) encountering their own sets of problems, dependence on foreign sources of supply would continue to increase. Given the international supply and marketing control still exercised by the major American oil corporations, the United States was not about to lose altogether its position as an energy-producing nation. But more than at any time in the past, it was beginning to think like an energy-consuming nation. This process would be accelerated rather markedly by the October 1973 OPEC oil shock. But even before the OPEC shock it was coming through in the assessments of the potential economic benefits to be gained from Soviet energy sources. The CIA's February 1972 report also concluded that Soviet LNG had the advantage of "affording some slight diversification of supply."[18] And *U.S.–Soviet Commercial Relations in a New Era*, an administration document released in July 1972, emphasized the economic gains that could be expected to accrue to the United States from the Soviet energy trade:

> The United States, which historically has spent its energy and material resources like a drunken sailor, can now feel the hole in the bottom of its pocket. With the tremendous increases that are projected in our energy requirements by the end of this century, it may be very much in our interest to explore seriously the possibility of gaining access to, and in fact to aid in the development of energy fields as rich as those possessed by the Soviet Union.[19]

The Soviets' behavior (as distinguished from their rhetoric) during the 1973 OPEC embargo reinforced this thinking. Quietly but no less significantly, they broke the embargo by providing the United States and the Netherlands with some alternative supplies of oil. In 1972 the United States imported only $7.5 million worth of Soviet oil. This

---

[17]Central Intelligence Agency, Directorate of Intelligence, Office of Economic Research, "Soviet Liquefied Natural Gas for the United States?" Intelligence Memorandum ER IM 72-21, February 1972, pp. 15, 3, via *Declassified Documents Catalog*.

[18]Ibid., p. 16.

[19]Peterson, *U.S.–Soviet Commercial Relations*, p. 14.

figure increased to $76.2 million in 1973 and $37.3 million in the first two months of 1974 (an annual rate of $200 million).[20]

In effect, then, American-Soviet energy trade was seen as an integral part of the overall inducement strategy because it offered great economic value to the Soviet Union while posing no threat to American security *and* promising benefits to the American economy. Consequently, with the sole exception of grain exports, energy equipment exports and technology transfers grew faster than any other sector of American–Soviet trade. Table 5.2 lists some of the major contracts for energy equipment exports signed in the first eighteen months after Nixon and Brezhnev declared at the May 1972 summit that "the U.S.A. and U.S.S.R. regard commercial and economic ties as an important and necessary element in the strengthening of their bilateral relations and thus will actively promote such ties."[21] Table 5.3 shows the major technical and economic cooperation agreements in the energy sector signed during this period. But it was the proposed North Star and Yakutsk LNG cooperative ventures that really were indicative of the extremely high expectations of both governments in regard to energy relations.

The details of these two projects are sketched in Table 5.4. They were to be by far the most ambitious undertakings in the history of American–Soviet commercial relations.[22] The North Star project in-

Table 5.2. Value of major contracts for exports of U.S. energy equipment to the USSR, 1972–73, by firm (millions of dollars)

Firm	Exports	Value
General Electric	Gas turbine compressors	$250
Caterpillar Tractor	Pipelayers	40
Dresser Industries	Gas turbine compressors	27.5
International Harvester	Gas turbine compressors	26
TRW	Submersible pumps	20
Borg-Warner	Submersible pumps	6

SOURCES: Marshall I. Goldman, *Détente and Dollars* (New York: Basic Books, 1975), pp. 292–97; Christopher E. Stowell, *Oil and Gas Development in the U.S.S.R.* (Tulsa: Petroleum Publishing Co., 1974), Appendix IV.

[20]Arthur Jay Klinghoffer, *The Soviet Union and International Oil Politics* (New York: Columbia University Press, 1977), p. 175.

[21]*Department of State Bulletin* 66 (June 26, 1972): 898–99.

[22]The best source of information on these projects is the hearings held in 1974 as part of Senator Frank Church's more general investigation of the relationship between the activities of American multinational corporations and American foreign policy. See U.S. Congress, Senate, Committee on Foreign Relations, Subcommittee on Multina-

Table 5.3. Major technical and economic cooperation agreements between U.S. firms and the USSR, 1972–73

Firm	Services to be supplied
Occidental Petroleum	Oil and gas exploration technology, in return for Soviet raw materials
Dresser Industries	Increase in well-logging efficiency for offshore and Arctic oil operations; manufacture of gas turbine compressors
General Electric	Joint development of electric power generating technology
Brown & Root	Managerial methods and organization for engineering and construction of gas pipeline projects
Bechtel	Managerial methods and organization for engineering and construction of gas pipeline projects
Armco	Manufacture of oil field equipment
General Dynamics	Construction of ships for the transport of liquefied natural gas
Cooper Industries	Production and transmission of natural gas

SOURCES: Marshall I. Goldman, *Détente and Dollars* (New York: Basic Books, 1975), pp. 292–97; Christopher E. Stowell, *Oil and Gas Development in the U.S.S.R.* (Tulsa: Petroleum Publishing Co., 1974), Appendix IV.

volved development of the Urengoi natural gas reserves in western Siberia by the American consortium of Tenneco, Texas Transmission, and Brown & Root. At the time Urengoi was the largest natural gas deposit in the world, by itself equal to 80 percent of total American natural gas reserves. The American companies were to build a 1,600-mile pipeline to an LNG plant in the city of Murmansk, on the Barents Sea. From this port a fleet of twenty LNG tankers would load 2.1 bcf per day for twenty-five years beginning in 1980 for shipment to the east coast of the United States. This minimum guarantee of gas, a volume calculated to be sufficient to satisfy 10 percent of projected levels of natural gas consumption from Maine to Kentucky, would be partial payment for the LNG plant and pipeline.

A second consortium composed of Occidental Petroleum, the El Paso Gas Company, the Bechtel Corporation, and several Japanese firms drew up plans with the Soviet government to develop the Yakutsk gas reserves of eastern Siberia. This project involved a 2,400-mile pipeline to the Soviet Pacific port of Nakhodka, where an LNG plant would be constructed. The gas would be shipped from there to Japan and the west coast of the United States. Here again payment would be partially in the form of future gas deliveries, estimated at 1

tional Corporations, *Multinational Corporations and U.S. Foreign Policy: Hearings,* 93d Cong. 2d sess., 1974, pt. 10.

Table 5.4. Details of North Star and Yakutsk natural gas projects, as proposed in 1973–74

	North Star	Yakutsk
U.S. companies involved	Tenneco, Texas Eastern Transmission Co., Brown & Root	El Paso Natural Gas, Occidental Petroleum, Bechtel[a]
Volume and destination	2.1 bcf[b] per day to U.S. east coast for 25 years,[c] beginning 1980	1 bcf[b] per day to U.S. west coast, 1 bcf[b] per day to Japan for minimum of 25 years, beginning 1982
Location	Urengoi gas fields, western Siberia	Yakutsk area, eastern Siberia
Projected U.S. exports (millions of dollars)	$3,700	$962[d]
Financing (millions of dollars)		
U.S. Export-Import Bank:		
direct loans	$1,000	$433
loan guarantee	1,000	433
Soviet down payment, private unguaranteed loans	1,700	96
Japanese financing	—	962
All financing	$3,700	$1,924
Other U.S. production generated: LNG[e] ships and port facilities (millions of dollars)	$2,600	$1,350

[a]In collaboration with a Japanese consortium.
[b]Billions of cubic feet.
[c]Equivalent to 10% of the area's projected gas requirements in 1980.
[d]An additional $962 million in exports projected for Japan.
[e]Liquefied natural gas.
SOURCES: U.S. Congress, Senate, Committee on Foreign Relations, Subcommittee on Multinational Corporations, *Multinational Corporations and U.S. Foreign Policy: Hearings*, 93d Cong., 2d sess., 1974, pt. 10, pp. 5–7, 66–71, 77–78, 86–90; Christopher E. Stowell, *Oil and Gas Development in the U.S.S.R.* (Tulsa: Petroleum Publishing Co., 1974), Appendix IV.

bcf per day for twenty-five years to the United States and the same volume to Japan, beginning in 1982.

At their June 1973 summit Nixon and Brezhnev issued a joint communiqué generally favoring "further and more permanent economic cooperation" and singling out "the delivery of Siberian natural gas to the United States" as one of the specific projects to be pushed. The communiqué continued: "The President indicated that the United States encourages American firms to work out concrete proposals on these projects and will give serious and sympathetic consideration to proposals that are in the interests of both sides."[23] The two governments also signed initial protocols in support of the projects at this time.

The signing of intergovernmental protocols, however, was not sufficient to get these projects off the ground. A key remaining obstacle involved intragovernmental relations—specifically, the domestic constraints of opposition within the U.S. Congress. For these projects to be at all commercially feasible, Export-Import Bank financing of the exports and most-favored-nation (MFN) tariff treatment for the Soviet gas were necessary. Both had been promised the Soviets by President Nixon. The bilateral trade treaty signed October 18, 1972, included a pledge to grant MFN status. An executive order issued the same day had opened the way for initial Eximbank financing. Ultimately, though, neither commercial concession could be granted without congressional approval.

The MFN issue got caught up in the controversy over Soviet Jews' freedom to emigrate. The Nixon administration's preferred position was reflected in Kissinger's private remark during the Moscow summit: "How would it be," he asked rhetorically, "if Brezhnev comes to the United States with a petition about the Negroes in Mississippi?"[24] In later public statements he took a less strident but no less firm position against the linkage of trade and Jewish emigration. He urged a Senate committee to understand that "the domestic practices of the Soviet Union are not necessarily related to détente which we primarily relate to foreign policy." Such a position was not "moral callousness" but rather a recognition of the "limits on our ability to produce internal change in foreign countries."[25]

Leading the other side was Senator Henry Jackson (D-Wash.). Jackson was a long-time hawk, an outspoken critic of all aspects of détente, who, among other things, had been searching for a legislative vehicle to block the new economic relationship. He first raised the issue of old World War II lend-lease debts, only to have the Russians consent to a compromise agreement. Soon thereafter, in fact just eight days before President Nixon signed the original bilateral trade treaty in October 1972, he introduced his first bill linking MFN to Jewish emigration.

[23]Ibid., p. 109.

[24]William Safire, *Before the Fall* (New York: Doubleday, 1975), p. 451.

[25]Testimony before U.S. Congress, Senate, Committee on Finance, *Hearing on the Emigration Amendment to the Trade Reform Act of 1974*, 93d Cong., 2d sess., 1974, p. 72; and testimony before Senate Committee on Foreign Relations, September 19, 1974, included in Henry A. Kissinger, *American Foreign Policy*, 3d ed. (New York: Norton, 1977), p. 145.

Jackson also had 1976 presidential politics on his mind. The political beauty of the Jewish emigration issue was that it appealed to antidétente conservatives and at the same time evoked the traditional Wilsonian values of liberals and served the interests of the Jewish constituency (a key source of Democratic campaign contributions). Thus, with Congressman Charles Vanik (D-Ohio) as the House cosponsor, Jackson's amendment rapidly gathered supporters on Capitol Hill.[26]

The Soviets' reactions were exemplified by President Nikolai Podgorny's response: "Questions of sovereignty and of our internal affairs," he said, "have never been and will never be a matter for political bargaining."[27] As on SALT and Vietnam, however, their actions somewhat belied their words. For at the same time that they stepped up their antilinkage rhetoric, the number of exit visas issued increased from 13,020 in 1971 to 31,681 in 1972 and almost 35,000 in 1973.[28] The 60,000 quota insisted on by Senator Jackson was not reached; the very idea of a quota decreed by the United States was patently unacceptable, irrespective of the number attached to it. But President Gerald Ford recounts that Dobrynin privately gave him an oral guarantee of 55,000.[29]

Once again, then, it appeared that the Soviets wanted the quo of American trade badly enough to bargain with political quids that, while less than the original asking price, were substantially more than any previous Soviet government had been willing to pay. Yet, as became all too clear as the issue played itself out, there were definite limits to how far economic incentives would push the Brezhnev leadership. In 1972–73 increases in Jewish emigration were intended to send a signal to the American Congress that tying MFN to Jewish emigration was unnecessary, that the Soviets already were cooperating. When the Congress went ahead anyway—the House passed the Jackson-Vanik amendment in December 1973 and there was little doubt that Senate passage would follow—it no longer was possible for the Soviets to give ground and hide the fact. The choice was narrowed to overt compliance or blatant noncompliance. The Soviets chose the

[26]The definitive account of the Jackson-Vanik amendment is Paula Stern, *Water's Edge: Domestic Politics and the Making of American Foreign Policy* (Westport, Conn.: Greenwood Press, 1979). For a different perspective see Henry A. Kissinger, *Years of Upheaval* (Boston: Little, Brown, 1982), pp. 985–98. See also Dan Caldwell, "The Jackson-Vanik Amendment," in *Congress, the Presidency, and American Foreign Policy*, ed. John Spanier and Joseph Nogee (New York: Pergamon Press, 1981), pp. 1–21.

[27]Cited in Garthoff, *Détente and Confrontation*, p. 466.

[28]Robert O. Freedman, ed., *Soviet Jewry in the Decisive Decade* (Durham, N.C.: Duke University Press, 1984), Annex 1.

[29]Gerald R. Ford, *A Time to Heal: The Autobiography of Gerald Ford* (New York: Harper & Row, 1979), pp. 138–39.

latter. During 1974, as a very different signal to an American Congress on the verge of going too far, the Soviets slashed the number of exit visas issued to a level (20,628) 41 percent lower than that of 1973. When the Senate gave Jackson-Vanik final passage, rather than accept the new conditionality, the Soviets renounced the 1972 bilateral trade treaty. There was to be no MFN status for LNG or any other Soviet export to the United States. And Jewish emigration fell to 13,221 in 1975.

Thus one of the lessons of Jackson-Vanik was that when trade is used as a bargaining instrument, *tactics matter*. It showed that there is a point of diminishing returns beyond which pressure becomes counterproductive even if the reward for cooperation is a valued one. The Soviets did prove susceptible to instrumental influence on the Jewish emigration issue, but only up to a point. When American tactics became too overt and "loud," they became self-defeating. Nor are such parameters of pressure peculiar to the Soviet Union. Numerous studies of economic coercion involving other nations have shown that the more overt the tactics, the less likely their success in bringing a coercer state political influence over its target state.[30]

A second lesson was that the ideology that shaped American–Soviet relations had become ambiguous. On the one hand, the Cold War ideology finally had been weakened sufficiently to make it possible to begin liberalizing trade with the Soviet Union. Part of the reason for this change was that the early successes of détente seemed to show that it was possible to reach some accords and accommodation with the Soviet Union. In this context the old national security imperative became less encompassing as an approach to superpower relations and therefore less prohibitive of superpower trade relations. Moreover, the symbolism of it all, from the cordial toasts at the summits to the Apollo-Soyuz mission to such scenes as Leonid Brezhnev embracing the American television cowboy Chuck Connors, contributed to the intangible but no less significant process of weakening the old anticommunist ethic. This softening of the image of the Soviet threat interacted somewhat synergistically with the more general discrediting of the old Cold War ideology as a consequence of the Vietnam War. Vietnam cracked the old consensus both at the leadership level

---

[30]See Johan Galtung, "On the Effects of International Economic Sanctions, with Examples from the Case of Rhodesia," *World Politics* 19 (April 1967): 378–416; Richard Stuart Olson, "Economic Coercion in World Politics: With a Focus on North–South Relations," *World Politics* 31 (July 1979): 471–94; and Jerrold D. Green, "Strategies for Evading Economic Sanctions," in *Dilemmas of Economic Coercion: Sanctions in World Politics*, ed. Miroslav Nincic and Peter Wallensteen (New York: Praeger, 1983), pp. 61–85.

and among the general public.[31] As a result, the legitimacy of Cold War foreign policy, once so compelling, was being called into question more strongly than at any time since the hopes of One World had been so quickly dashed at the end of World War II.

Thus there now was at least room for debate over whether or not to trade with the Soviet Union. Détente policies in general and economic inducement in particular could get more of a hearing and attract more support than in the past. This response stopped well short, however, of a new détente-based consensus. Even those who no longer accepted the old Cold War ideology were not necessarily prepared to embrace détente as Nixon and Kissinger preached it. They took exception to its realpolitik thrust as ignoring human rights and other related normative concerns—such as the emigration of Soviet Jews. Their views ran to post–Cold War liberal internationalism and semi-isolationism, both of which rejected the old Cold War conservative internationalism but neither of which was disposed to provide unconstrained support to the Nixon-Kissinger strategy.[32]

Then, of course, there were the persisting Cold War internationalists, the opponents of détente who believed ever more fervently that, as Henry Jackson put it in a television interview, "the Cold War is still on."[33] Nor, as Jackson himself exemplified, were the ranks of those opposed to détente confined to the Republican right. These traditional conservatives were joined by the "neoconservatives," traditional Democrats who, like Jackson, separated themselves from the ascendant post–Cold War internationalist wing of their party. Among other things, these neoconservatives organized the Committee on the Present Danger, which became a particularly influential mechanism for opposing détente in virtually all its aspects.[34]

[31]Ole R. Holsti and James N. Rosenau, *American Leadership in World Affairs: Vietnam and the Breakdown of Consensus* (Boston: Allen & Unwin, 1984); John A. Rielly, ed., *American Public Opinion and Foreign Policy, 1975* (Chicago: Chicago Council on Foreign Relations, 1975); Michael Mandelbaum and William Schneider, "The New Internationalisms: Public Opinion and American Foreign Policy," in *Eagle Entangled: U.S. Foreign Policy in a Complex World,* ed. Kenneth A. Oye, Donald Rothchild, and Robert J. Lieber (New York: Longman, 1979), pp. 34–88; Rielly, *American Public Opinion, 1975;* and Robert W. Tucker, William Watts, and Lloyd A. Free, *The United States in the World: New Directions for the Post-Vietnam Era?* (Washington, D.C.: Potomac Associates, 1976).

[32]Holsti and Rosenau, *American Leadership in World Affairs,* use the terms "post–Cold War internationalism," "Cold War internationalism," and "semi-isolationism." Mandelbaum and Schneider, "New Internationalisms," use the terms "liberal internationalism," "conservative internationalism," and "neo-isolationism." While the definitions vary, for the most part the terms are interchangeable.

[33]Stern, *Water's Edge,* p. 21.

[34]Charles Tryoler II, *Alerting America: The Papers of the Committee on the Present Danger* (New York: Pergamon-Brassey, 1984); Norman Podhoretz, *The Present Danger* (New York: Simon & Schuster, 1980).

Still, the Cold War ideology had been weakened enough for American exports to the Soviet Union to exceed $2 billion in the less than two years between the first Nixon–Brezhnev summit and the passage of Jackson-Vanik. This figure represented over 70 percent more than had been exported in the previous twenty-five years combined. But political factions that could agree on little else in American foreign policy, and that had very different reasons for doing so, could and did agree to link American–Soviet trade to Soviet Jewish emigration. The Nixon-Kissinger economic inducement strategy thus became constrained by its own lack of a strong basis of ideological support amidst fundamentally competing visions of American-Soviet relations.

In addition to this ideological ambiguity revealed by the politics of Jackson-Vanik, there was the similarly constraining economic ambivalence evident in the alignment of economic interest groups on both sides of the Eximbank credits issue. Under Chairman William Casey (who would become director of the CIA in the Reagan administration) the Eximbank already had granted the Soviets $476 million in loans and loan guarantees. But congressional action was needed to increase Eximbank lending authority. This was especially important for the North Star and Yakutsk natural gas ventures. Both consortiums were wary of making heavy investments without some government participation. The North Star consortium wanted $1 billion in direct credits and $1 billion in guarantees. The Yakutsk consortium already had applied for $49.5 million in credits and $49.5 million in guarantees; if initial explorations proved that the project was commercially feasible, an additional $1 billion in Eximbank commitments was to be requested.[35]

The support for this and other energy projects coming from major American energy multinationals was in striking contrast to the role of Exxon/SONJ et al. in the 1962–63 oil sanctions case. A decade earlier any oil trade with the Soviet Union had been opposed because the Soviets were considered competitors for world markets. Now, with OPEC having permanently and unfavorably altered investment terms in the Middle East and with the omnipresent threat of political instability in the region, the Soviets appeared as an attractive partner for trade and joint ventures. Exxon, Gulf, Atlantic Richfield, Occidental, and Union Oil of California all were charter members of the U.S.–USSR Trade and Economic Council. As Table 5.2 indicates, a number of oil companies signed technical cooperation agreements

---

[35]Senate Foreign Relations Committee, *Multinational Corporations and American Foreign Policy*, pt. 10, pp. 43–48, 77.

with the Soviets. Others, including Exxon, were engaged in discussions concerning joint offshore oil explorations.

Two other groups of energy companies were even more enthusiastic about the Soviets as commercial partners. The Soviets had the potential to be the source of the vastly increased volumes of natural gas needed by such distributors as El Paso, Texas Eastern, and Tenneco to meet their rising domestic demand. A Tenneco executive testified at congressional hearings that unless new gas supplies were found within five years, existing contracts could no longer be fulfilled. And with the risks inherent in turning to such OPEC countries as Algeria also for gas, the Soviet Union was put forward as a partner whose reserves were vast enough to meet American consumption needs and whose gas would diversify the American import portfolio so as to enhance energy security.[36]

The other set of companies pushing the energy trade were such energy equipment manufacturers as General Electric (compressor stations and turbines for natural gas pipelines), Dresser Industries (compressors and diamond rock drill bits needed for the difficult Siberian terrain), and Caterpillar Tractor Company (pipelayers and other pipeline construction equipment). In the first full year of liberalized trade, energy equipment exports to the Soviet Union had soared from $10.6 million to $90.7 million. The North Star and Yakutsk projects were seen as having enormous potential for even more rapid export growth. Moreover, with exploration and production slowing within the United States, export sales were becoming an increasingly prominent item on the balance sheet.

Aligned on the other side of the issue was a coalition of groups and legislators who viewed the Soviet energy trade as threatening to their economic interests. One key coalition member was labor. While concerned enough about unemployment to push the protectionist Burke-Hartke Foreign Trade and Investment Act, the AFL-CIO had not bought the economic rationale for trading with the Russians. George Meany still lambasted détente as a "one-way street," and another labor leader lashed out at "businessmen and bankers, whose salaries are well over $100,000 per year, [who] flock to Moscow as if they were penurious Polish peasants beseeching the Czar for economic favors."[37] The fledgling consumer movement also had come to oppose East–West trade, in large part because of the inflationary conse-

[36]Testimony of Jack Ray of Tenneco in ibid., pp. 3–61.

[37]Meany is quoted in Morgan, *Merchants of Grain*, p. 258; Frank Barnett is quoted in Alan Wolfe and Jerry Sanders, "Resurgent Cold War Ideology: The Case of the Committee on the Present Danger," in *Capitalism and the State in U.S.–Latin American Relations*, ed. Richard R. Fagen (Stanford: Stanford University Press, 1979), p. 51.

quences of the "great grain robbery" of 1971. Though the grain deal had been heralded as offering benefits for the economy in general as well as for grain traders, the actual result was that the Soviet purchases left the American consumer with short supplies and higher prices. Consumers also were understandably offended that the Russians could get 6 percent interest from the Eximbank while their banks charged 12 percent for a car loan.

It was largely in response to these interests that liberal Senate Democrats took the lead in restricting Eximbank lending to the Soviet Union. Senator Adlai Stevenson III (D-Ill.) was the principal sponsor of an amendment to the new Eximbank authorization bill which limited total new Eximbank credits to $300 million. Additional credits now would require prior congressional approval. The Stevenson amendment also gave Congress veto authority over any single credit greater than $50 million.[38] Of even greater significance to the North Star and Yakutsk projects were two additional amendments sponsored by Senator Frank Church (D-Idaho). One imposed a $40 million subceiling on credits related to energy research and exploration; the other put an outright ban on any lending related to the production, processing, or distribution of energy.

Here again the broad context must be kept in view if the American domestic politics of the Soviet energy trade issue is to be understood. In the summer of 1974, when the credit requests of North Star and Yakutsk brought the issue to a head, Senator Church was chairing extensive investigative hearings on alleged wrongdoings by American multinationals. These investigations uncovered a great deal of evidence of undue influence over American foreign policy and a pattern of economic behavior that appeared to show that the public economic weal was not always served very well by the multinationals' pursuit of their private, particularistic interests. This deep suspicion of corporate motives and of the veracity of the benefits they forecast for the North Star and Yakutsk projects came through Church's questioning of witnesses during six days of hearings devoted exclusively to this issue.[39]

Church (and other liberals) also viewed the issue from the perspective of the lesson taught by the 1973 OPEC crisis, that dependence on any foreign source for energy supplies was dangerous. He contended

---

[38]Stern, *Water's Edge*, pp. 117–18, and Stanley J. Marcuss, "New Light on the Export-Import Bank," in *U.S. Financing of East–West Trade*, ed. Paul J. Marer (Bloomington: Indiana University Press, 1974).

[39]Senate Foreign Relations Committee, *Multinational Corporations and Americans Foreign Policy*, pt. 10, passim.

that the United States should be dedicating the limited supply of energy equipment that its industry was capable of producing to increased domestic exploration and production. "If we are serious about wanting to decrease American dependence on foreign energy supplies," he told his Senate colleagues, "it is folly to subsidize Soviet purchases of the very equipment we need to do it."[40] In addition, he argued, the long-term, set-price contracts for liquefied natural gas imported from the North Star and Yakutsk projects would lock American consumers in at prices that would be artificially high once the markets had adjusted to the 1973 shock and prices had fallen.

Without MFN and credits, the North Star and Yakutsk projects languished. Supporters in the consortiums still pushed them, but to no avail.[41] By 1980, though, the North Star project had reemerged in somewhat altered form. It then became known as the Yamal natural gas pipeline and involved a Western European–Soviet cooperative venture. But we are getting ahead of the story.

CARTER'S ECONOMIC DIPLOMACY VARIANT

The Democrats' critique of Kissingerian economic inducement became the basis for the shift to an *economic diplomacy* strategy in the new administration of President Jimmy Carter. If something less than a reversion to Cold War economic warfare, as embodied in Presidential Directive (PD) 18, signed by Carter in August 1977, economic diplomacy was something more than economic inducement.

According to its principal author, ranking NSC official Samuel Huntington, the economic diplomacy strategy had three essential elements.[42] First was the expansion of the political agenda of issues linked to trade to include both human rights in the Soviet Union and Soviet intervention in the Third World. Carter had made human rights a central theme of his presidential campaign, and in his first major foreign policy address as president he had promised a new foreign policy "rooted in our moral values" and attuned to "the new

---

[40]*Congressional Record*, vol. 120, pt. 17, 93d Cong., 2d sess., July 2, 1974, p. 24842.

[41]Wilton E. Scott and Jack H. Ray, "The Role of Natural Gas in East–West Trade Relations," in *Common Sense in U.S.–Soviet Trade*, ed. Willard C. Mathias (Washington, D.C.: American Committee on East-West Accord, 1979), pp. 47–53.

[42]Samuel P. Huntington, "Trade, Technology, and Leverage: Economic Diplomacy," *Foreign Policy* 32 (Fall 1978); 63–80. For an exceptional analysis of Huntington's strategy and his efforts to implement it see Jim Hoagland's article "A Carefully Primed Soviet Bear Trap," *Washington Post*, August 20, 1978, pp. A1, A14.

global questions of justice, equity and human rights."[43] While such politico-spiritual concerns were among the president's priorities, the "crescent of crisis" pattern of Soviet intervention through military aid and advisers was on the minds of Huntington and his boss, Zbigniew Brzezinski, assistant to the president for national security affairs.

The economic diplomacy strategy also departed from economic inducement in making the linkages between trade and political quid pro quo firmer and more explicit. The previous administration's so-called web of interdependence was criticized as too loose and full of holes, amounting in Huntington's view to little more than a laissez-faire approach that had allowed "economic détente and military adventurism" to go hand in hand.[44] While the carrot was not to be totally discarded, it needed to be offered more discriminately. Concomitantly, the stick of sanctions, while not to be wielded indiscriminately, nevertheless had to be unsheathed.

Another important difference was that as far as Brzezinski and Huntington were concerned, if the Soviets proved unwilling to comply with their political conditions and if the trade failed to materalize, that was not too bad an outcome either. Even before the first set of specifically politically linked sanctions were promulgated in July 1978, the Carter administration had reversed the pattern of continuous growth in nonagricultural exports to the Soviet Union. Grain exports were considered strategically harmless and, as Gerald Ford had learned and Jimmy Carter soon would learn, grain embargoes could be politically harmful.[45] But nonagricultural exports, and in particular capital goods exports and technology transfers, were seen as more potentially dangerous to the basic capabilities-limiting economic defense objective. Thus total nonagricultural exports dropped 28 percent in 1977, from $819 million to $586 million, and another 4

[43]Commencement address, University of Notre Dame, May 22, 1977, in *Public Papers of the Presidents: Jimmy Carter, 1977*, 1: 954–62.

[44]Huntington, "Economic Diplomacy," p. 69. Brzezinski never had been an East-West trade enthusiast. See, for example, his testimony during Senator Church's hearings, Senate Foreign Relations Committee, *Multinational Corporations and American Foreign Policy*, pt. 10, pp. 165–88.

[45]In the summer and fall of 1974 two major grain sales to the Soviet Union were suspended by the Ford administration and new regulations written requiring prior federal government approval of large sales (more than 50,000 tons in a day or 100,000 in a week). These regulations were not motivated by foreign policy but rather represented an effort to avoid another "great grain robbery" and its inflationary effects on the American economy; see Morgan, *Merchants of Grain*, pp. 14, 266, and Richard Gilmore, *A Poor Harvest: The Clash of Policies and Interests in the Grain Trade* (New York: Longman, 1982), p. 99. The sales eventually were allowed to go through, but even these temporary embargoes were not forgotten by American farmers when they went to the polls in November 1976.

percent in 1978, to $562 million. The decline in exports of industrial machinery and transportation equipment was even steeper: 38 and 25 percent, respectively. Exports of oil and gas equipment also declined from $108 million in 1976 to $79 million in 1978—$12 million less than the figure that in 1973 had been taken as a harbinger of far more lucrative things to come.[46]

Huntington and Brzezinski did agree with their predecessors that the formulation and implementation of East–West trade policy should be centralized in the White House. They may have agreed with the substance of the Jackson-Vanik and Church-Stevenson amendments, constraining a policy they considered ill advised, but they did not agree with the form. These amendments needed to be repealed, they argued, so that the president and not the Congress would have the discretion to determine when and under what conditions MFN and credits carrots were to be offered.

Nor did they want their own State, Commerce, or Defense Department to be closely involved. Secretary of State Cyrus Vance and the numerous post–Cold War liberal internationalist middle-level appointees at State were considered endemically soft on this and other issues—perhaps cognizant of principles but not so realistic about power as Brzezinski professed himself to be.[47] Commerce was dismissed as the prisoner of its business constituency, and, as one NSC official put it, Defense often behaved as if it had been "infiltrated by Commercies."[48] Only the NSC, according to such reasoning, could responsibly fulfill the realpolitik responsibilities as the fulcrum point for an economic diplomacy strategy.

For a number of reasons energy trade became the first test case of this new strategy. In a highly publicized study released in April 1977, the CIA had predicted the imminent decline of the Soviet oil industry.[49] The Soviets' inefficient production techniques in use at existing wells were finally taking their toll, while the geological and climatic barriers of western Siberia were keeping new oil production below Plan targets. Total production would soon peak and begin to decline until by 1985 the USSR would be a net importer of oil. While other

[46]Jack Brougher (Department of Commerce), "1979–1982: The United States Uses Trade to Penalize Soviet Aggression and Seeks to Reorder Western Policy," in U.S. Congress, Joint Economic Committee, *Soviet Economy in the 1980s: Problems and Prospects*, Committee Print, 97th Cong., 2d sess., December 1982, pt. 2, pp. 421, 445.

[47]The allusion is to the title chosen by Brzezinski for his memoirs, *Power and Principle* (New York: Farrar, Straus & Giroux, 1983).

[48]Personal interview, July 1980.

[49]Central Intelligence Agency, "Prospects for Soviet Oil Production," ER 77-10270, April 1976.

analysts faulted the CIA for overestimating the potential problem, few offered a very rosy picture of the future of the Soviet oil industry.[50]

There was general agreement that whether or not the Soviets could import Western equipment and technology would be a critical factor. The administration calculated that Western equipment and technology accounted for 10 to 15 percent of total Soviet oil production as well as unspecified gains in natural gas production and in overall exploratory, refining, and transmission (e.g., pipeline) capacity.[51] Marshall Goldman, among others, agreed that "if they can obtain the foreign technology, the Soviets should be able to avail themselves of some significant output gains."[52] When in the first quarter of 1978 Soviet orders for American oil and gas equipment exceeded the total for any previous single year, administration officials were even more convinced that here lay a significant vulnerability.[53]

U.S.–Soviet political tensions again broke into conflict in July 1978 over a series of incidents, including the arrests of F. Jay Crawford, an American businessman, on black-marketeering charges and of Soviet dissident leaders Aleksandr Ginzburg and Anatoly Shcharansky on charges of crimes against the state. Consistent with PD 18, President Carter tightened export controls in an attempt to compel a change in Soviet behavior. Of particular note was the new requirement that all equipment and technology exports for energy exploration and production be subjected to executive branch review, followed by a freeze on Dresser Industries' application for an export license for a $144 million sale, including the technology and equipment for a "turnkey" rock drill bit factory.[54]

The embargo decision split the Carter inner circle. Brzezinski, De-

---

[50]See, for example, Marshall I. Goldman, *The Enigma of Soviet Petroleum: Half-Full or Half-Empty?* (London: George Allen & Unwin, 1980); David Wilson, *Soviet Oil and Gas to 1990* (London: Economist Intelligence Unit, 1980); Leslie Dienes and Theodore Shabad, *The Soviet Energy System: Resource Use and Policies* (New York: Wiley, 1979); and U.S. Congress, Senate, Select Committee on Intelligence, *The Soviet Oil Situation: An Evaluation of CIA Analyses of Soviet Oil Production*, Staff Report, 95th Cong., 2d sess., 1978. To elaborate on its methodology and reasoning and to tone down its predictions somewhat, the CIA issued "Prospects for Soviet Oil Production: A Supplemental Analysis" (ER 77-10425) in July 1977.

[51]Huntington, "Economic Diplomacy," pp. 69, 72.

[52]Goldman, *Enigma of Soviet Petroleum*, p. 136.

[53]Huntington, "Economic Diplomacy," p. 70.

[54]Since the early 1970s there had been no licensing requirements for energy industry exports. A "turnkey" factory is a facility completely equipped at the time of its transfer, including technical data concerning training and operation—all that is necessary to operate it is to turn the key. The rock drill bit turnkey factory was especially important for Soviet plans to increase Siberian oil production.

fense Secretary Harold Brown, and Energy Secretary James Schlesinger all supported it, for reasons that had even more to do with the instrumental objectives of economic defense and politico-strategic deterrence than with the fate of Anatoly Shcharansky. So did political adviser Jody Powell and image manager Gerald Rafshoon, who "told the President in no uncertain terms that his domestic credibility would suffer greatly unless he was seen as taking a firm position."[55] Commerce Secretary Juanita Kreps was quoted as having "grave reservations."[56] Secretary of State Cyrus Vance also was opposed. According to Brzezinski,

> the president turned all of a sudden to Cy and said that he doesn't want new trade initiatives started by Treasury, Commerce or State, with the effect of going around his recent decision. . . . He doesn't want Marshall Shulman, Juanita Kreps, or others indicating to the Soviets in some fashion that this was just a little slap on the wrist. We want the Soviets to take this seriously, that we can do this to them, that it was meant to hurt. He was quite sharp, and I could tell that Cy was rather surprised. . . . Later that day he sent me a memo back with my comments on Blumenthal's objections, writing in the margin, "Tell Mike to support my policies."[57]

Given this reported dressing down and the corresponding political alignments, the unanswered question is why in early September Jimmy Carter announced that the Dresser sale in its entirety would in fact be licensed. No official explanation was given, even though the split between the Vance and Brzezinski factions had been reported widely by the press. Carter totally passes over the issue in his memoirs, and Brzezinski conveniently skips over the decision to license Dresser and moves on to the Afghanistan embargo, erroneously giving the impression that his recommendation held sway from the outset.[58]

It quickly became apparent, though, that the Dresser decision, rather than being an isolated case, marked another major shift in policy. The validated licensing requirement for all oil and gas exploration and production equipment and technology was kept on the books, but as a matter of policy it had little impact between September 1978 and January 1980. In the two months following the Dresser

---

[55]Brzezinski, *Power and Principle*, pp. 322–23.
[56]*Washington Post*, July 19, 1978, p. A1.
[57]Brzezinski, *Power and Principle*, p. 322.
[58]Nor did interviews conducted with a number of key actors turn up anything definitive, or even a strong hypothesis.

decision, all thirty license applications received were approved. At the December meeting in Moscow of the Joint U.S.–USSR Commercial Commission, Secretary of Commerce Kreps announced the approval of the twenty-two license applications then pending. Treasury Secretary Blumenthal assured those assembled of expeditious action on future license applications. He also stated that it was "the overall policy of the President to share technology and equipment with other countries to develop energy resources around the world."[59]

The message, in essence, was that the validated licensing regulation was not to be mistaken for an obstacle to energy trade. No formal new policy announcement ever was made. But between August 1978 and March 1979, 113 applications were made for the export of energy equipment and technology worth $368 million. Not a single application was denied.[60] Nor were any applications denied during the remaining months of 1979.[61] As a result, after two consecutive years of decline, exports of oil and gas equipment more than doubled in 1979. There even was speculation that the North Star project might be resurrected.

Why such a major change of policy? The proximate cause was an upturn in U.S.–Soviet relations, manifested initially by a swap of Dresser for Crawford. The Soviets suddenly moved up Crawford's trial date to September 5 and sent word through diplomatic channels that Crawford would be convicted but then allowed to return to the United States. On September 6 Carter announced his decision to permit the Dresser sale. On September 8 Crawford was on a plane headed for the United States.

It also is possible that some linkage to SALT II was extracted from the process, for after more than a year of no progress, a meeting with

[59]Herbert E. Meyer, "Helping the Soviet Union to Avoid an Energy Crisis," *Fortune*, January 29, 1979, p. 90. On this point Brzezinski's account also is misleading. He claims that a liberalization initiative by Vance, Blumenthal, and Kreps on November 18 came "completely out of the blue" and was rejected by the president on his recommendation. He cites a November 28 directive sent to the secretaries that they could promise "expeditious license review" and "a generally favorable attitude towards U.S.–Soviet trade" but could make no binding commitments or promises indicating revocation of existing controls. The secretaries' statements in Moscow may have conformed with the letter of this directive, but their actions hardly were limited by its spirit. See Brzezinski, *Power and Principle*, pp. 324–25.

[60]Testimony of Secretary of Commerce Juanita Kreps, U.S. Congress, Senate, Committee on Banking, Housing, and Urban Affairs, *U.S. Export Control Policy and Extension of the Export Administration Act: Hearings*, 96th Cong., 1st sess., March 1979, pt. 1, p. 66.

[61]Jack Brougher, "1979–82: The United States Uses Trade to Penalize Soviet Aggression," in U.S. Congress, Joint Economic Committee, *Soviet Economy in the 1980s: Problems and Prospects*, Joint Committee Print, 97th Cong., 2d sess., December 1982, pt. 2, p. 448.

Soviet Foreign Minister Andrei Gromyko in late September made even Brzezinski think that "the end was in sight."[62] In ensuing meetings the human rights issue was not totally resolved but the Soviets did agree to allow some dissidents, including Aleksandr Ginzburg (but not Shcharansky), to emigrate. The cycle of détente culminated in the Carter–Brezhnev summit of June 1979, at which SALT II was signed, objectives for SALT III were discussed, and a sense of positive momentum in the overall relationship was generated. In a pattern similar to that of 1972–73 (Huntington's condemnation of the Nixon-Kissinger approach as laissez-faire notwithstanding), total exports to the Soviet Union in 1979 reached $3.6 billion, a 60 percent increase over 1978. In the third and fourth quarters—the six months after the Vienna summit—exports were being shipped at the equivalent of an annual rate of $4.3 billion. Carter even had begun testing the waters for an effort to repeal or modify the Jackson-Vanik and Church-Stevenson amendments.[63]

A second reason for the change of policy, and one especially relevant to energy trade, had less to do with Soviet behavior than with the international economic context. In January 1979 the shah of Iran was forced into exile and the revolution of the Ayatollah Khomeini began. The Ayatollah was neither willing nor able to maintain oil production, and by the summer of 1979 the world was rocked by an oil crisis far more severe than even the 1973 embargo. In the months that followed, a political uprising in Saudi Arabia, war between Iran and Iraq, and the inability to resolve the Palestinian issue provided ample reason to believe that the political future of the world's principal oil-producing region would be even less stable than its already chaotic present.

In this context an economic-based but nevertheless strategic argument was beginning to develop for helping the Soviet Union avoid the production decline predicted by the CIA. Whatever else it was, it was a non-OPEC supplier. The reequilibration of world markets and the avoidance of another crisis required new energy supplies from as many non-OPEC sources as possible. As Assistant Secretary of Energy Duane Sewell told a congressional committee, "from an energy perspective, U.S. exports of energy-related equipment and technology can play a major role in increasing worldwide supplies of energy and

---

[62]Brzezinski, *Power and Principle*, p. 327.

[63]Question-and-answer session with the National Governors Association, February 27, 1979, and press conference, April 30, 1979, in *Public Papers of the Presidents: Jimmy Carter, 1979*, pp. 358–59, 749. Huntington himself by this time had returned to Harvard.

improving the efficiency of energy use. Promoting the transfer of useful and constructive energy technologies is an essential element in the administration's internal energy policy." Another Energy Department official told the same committee that while other aspects of U.S.–Soviet relations necessarily would have to be considered, the two superpowers shared a "common interest" in increasing world energy supplies. In contrast to those who saw a decline in Soviet energy production as an opportunity to roll back communism in Eastern Europe, he argued that "it would be in the U.S. interest to have Soviet exports of oil [continue] for Eastern Europe, because it reduces their demand on the overall world supply."[64] Further, any help that would enable the Soviet bear to satisfy his energy appetite within his own borders would serve to dissipate possible incentives for intervention in the Middle East–Persian Gulf region.

A third reason for the policy shift, and another way in which economic interests came into play, related to the growing export consciousness in the United States. Economists both within government and in academia increasingly were pointing to the widening trade deficit as a central cause of America's economic problems. The $42.3 billion trade deficit of 1978 forced the Carter administration to devalue the dollar, with negative consequences both for international confidence in American leadership (political as well as financial) and for domestic inflation. Unemployment, the budget deficit, and tax increases also were traced at least in part back to the trade deficit. To resolve these problems, on September 26, 1978, President Carter proposed a set of initiatives for a national export policy. "It is important for this Nation's economic vitality," the president declared, "that both the private sector and the Federal Government place a higher priority on exports."[65] Included in this export promotion package were two directives with particular relevance to East–West trade: foreign availability was to be given greater emphasis as a reason for decontrol, and the equivalent of an economic impact statement was to be considered before export controls were invoked for foreign policy purposes.

When the Export Administration Act came up for renewal in 1979, the administration worked with the key subcommittee chairmen, Congressman Jonathan Bingham (D.-N.Y.) and Senator Adlai Stevenson (D.-Ill.), to defeat more restrictive bills introduced by conservatives, such as the Technology Transfer Ban Act of 1979, and to

---

[64]Senate Banking Committee, *U.S. Export Control Policy*, pp. 84, 110.
[65]U.S. Congress, House, *Export Administration Act of 1979*, Conference Report no. 96–482 (to accompany S. 737), 96th Cong., 1st sess., 1979, pp. 1–2.

liberalize the existing legislation.[66] The Export Administration Act of 1979, passed by Congress and signed by the president, reads as much like a bill intended to promote American exports as one intended to impose controls. Six of the nine declarations in the preamble were statements about the importance of exports to the American economy, including the following:

> The restriction of exports from the United States can have serious adverse effects on the balance of payments and on domestic employment. . . .
> Uncertainty of export control can curtail the efforts of American business to the detriment of the overall attempt to improve the trade balance of the United States. . . .
> It is the policy of the United States that export trade by United States citizens be given a high priority.[67]

Senator Stevenson, who five years earlier had been a prime mover of legislation restricting trade with the Soviet Union, had changed his position as a function of both his general commitment to export promotion and his disillusionment with unilateral American controls. As he stated on the Senate floor,

> Despite the growing trade deficit, new export controls have been adopted with insufficient consideration of their cost and effect. The United States is in danger of acquiring a reputation as an unreliable supplier, a reputation it can ill-afford in an increasingly competitive world. . . . Other nations see clearly the increased production and jobs exports yield. We too frequently succumb instead to seductive notions of "leverage" or theological calls to purification through self-denial. . . . Ill-conceived refusals to export deprive the United States of influence as well as sales.[68]

Commerce Secretary Juanita Kreps took this argument even further, making the case that a healthy domestic economy was a necessary condition for national security—and one that no longer could be presumed.

> Our physical security and foreign policy interests are, of course, paramount. But economic performance and political and military power are

---

[66]See Jonathan Bingham and Victor C. Johnson, "A Rational Approach to Export Controls," *Foreign Affairs* 57 (Spring 1979): 894–920.

[67]Conference Report, *Export Administration Act of 1979*, pp. 1–2.

[68]*Congressional Record*, 96th Cong., 1st sess., March 22, 1979, p. 53184.

ultimately inseparable. In today's world, our economic vitality is increasingly dependent on our ability to export. Today's environment requires that we take more seriously than ever before the erosion in our power and influence that can come from a failure to meet the export challenge.[69]

Administration and congressional supporters also stressed the extent of foreign availability of comparable equipment and technology, even in a sector traditionally as American-dominated as energy. When NL Industries of Texas lost a $226 million contract for gas lift equipment to the French company Technip because of licensing delays, this point was driven home. William Verity, chairman of Armco Inc., presented a congressional committee with extensive documentation of foreign availability in most energy industry product lines. Verity accompanied these data with estimates of the effects on the balance of payments, employment, and capital formation of major projects for which American companies were in the running.[70] The message was that the United States stood to be a double loser—sanctions would not bring political influence because of the availability of alternative trade partners, and business would be lost.

But when the Soviets invaded Afghanistan in late December 1979, all such calculations changed. The economic value of export promotion had not gone away. In fact, a record trade deficit, staggering double-digit inflation, and unemployment drastic enough to turn blue-collar voters a year later to a presidential candidate who supported right-to-work laws showed that the American economy needed all the business it could get. Nor had energy market considerations changed. The gasoline lines were gone but memories of them were all too vivid. But no nation "committed to world peace and stability," President Carter told the nation, "can continue to do business as usual with the Soviet Union."[71] Accordingly, renewed trade sanctions were prominent among the retaliatory steps proposed by the president.[72] Grain exports were reduced from the 25 million

[69]Senate Banking Committee, *U.S. Export Control Policy*, p. 37.
[70]For example, Verity estimated the economic consequences of NL Industries' lost contract at $15 million in capital formation, $225 million in the balance of payments, and 10,000 jobs. See U.S. Congress, Senate, Committee on Banking, Housing, and Urban Affairs, *Use of Export Controls and Export Credits for Foreign Policy Purposes: Hearings*, 95th Cong., 2d sess., 1978, pp. 62–136.
[71]*Public Papers of the Presidents: Jimmy Carter, 1980*, 1:23.
[72]Other measures included draft registration, withdrawal of SALT II from the Senate, the recall of the American ambassador to Moscow, a military and economic aid package for Pakistan, and higher priority for development of the Rapid Deployment Force.

metric tons on order to the 8 million tons guaranteed by the Long-Term Supply Agreement signed back in 1975. All existing licenses for high-technology exports, including Dresser Industries' license to export rock drill bits, were suspended. All future applications to export technology were to be subjected to a presumption of denial, with some of the strictest standards applied to oil and gas, unless there was overwhelming evidence of foreign availability.

The immediate objective of these sanctions was to compel the Soviets to get out of Afghanistan; but they also were intended to demonstrate American will and resolve in the hope of deterring the Soviets from taking similar actions elsewhere. Before the year was out, however, as the high economic costs and low political returns of the Afghanistan sanctions became apparent, Jimmy Carter would be assailed as an incompetent rather than a courageous leader. On both sides of the congressional aisle, critics lined up against this latest in a string of Carter foreign policy failures. Business groups came out of their temporary closet to call into question these as well as all export controls that imposed economic costs on an already beleaguered American economy. And in the American heartland, farmers vented their anger by voting in overwhelming numbers for the Republican presidential candidate, Ronald Reagan. While some economists later would argue that the net costs imposed even on farmers were minimal, that clearly was not the perception that prevailed on the first Tuesday after the first Monday in November 1980.

THE POLITICAL ECONOMY OF EURO-SOVIET DÉTENTE AND ENERGY TRADE

In contrast to the on-again–off-again pattern in American policy—decried by private citizen George Shultz in 1979 as "light switch diplomacy"[73]—Western European–Soviet trade relations increased steadily during the 1970s. As Table 5.5 shows, American exports fluctuated often, severely, and principally for political reasons—up 120 percent in 1973 (détente at its zenith), down 43 percent in 1974 (Jewish emigration), up 185 percent in 1975 (Vladivostok accord and Ford-Brezhnev summit), down 31 percent in 1977 (breakdown of SALT negotiations and tensions over human rights), up 57 percent in 1979 (Salt II signed, Carter–Brezhnev summit held), down 59 percent in 1980 (Soviet invasion of Afghanistan). In contrast, Western

[73]*Business Week,* May 28, 1979, pp. 24–26.

Table 5.5. Value of exports to the Soviet Union from the United States and four European COCOM countries, 1971–1980 (millions of dollars)

Year	United States	West Germany	France	Italy	United Kingdom
1971	$ 161	$ 460	$ 256	$ 295	$ 206
1972	542	712	340	269	216
1973	1,194	1,183	574	351	230
1974	650	1,856	656	618	257
1975	1,850	2,824	1,147	1,020	459
1976	2,350	2,686	1,118	981	431
1977	1,600	2,789	1,496	1,128	606
1978	2,300	3,140	1,455	1,133	811
1979	3,604	3,619	2,007	1,220	891
1980	1,664	4,811	2,712	1,271	1,162

SOURCE: United Nations, Statistical Office, *Yearbooks of International Trade: 1974, 1977, 1981* (Geneva, 1975, 1978, 1983).

European exports declined rarely (once for West Germany and the United Kingdom, twice for France, and three times for Italy), minimally (the greatest drop was Italy's 8.8 percent in 1972), and principally for commercial reasons (massive grain imports in 1976, necessitated by the Soviets' disastrous harvest, left them little hard currency for importing industrial equipment from Western Europe).

This is not to say that the Europeans did not have a political agenda. In fact, one of the key differences between the growth of Euro-Soviet trade in the 1970s and the 1960s was that now foreign policy considerations also were a motivating factor. This was especially true for West German Chancellor Willy Brandt's *Ostpolitik.* Throughout the Adenauer–Christian Democrat era, foreign policy had been based on the belief that progress on those issues of special importance to West Germany ("the German question" of national reunification or at least normalized relations) could best be achieved through a united Western front behind the American diplomatic lead. The essence of *Ostpolitik,* however, was that such progress now required West Germany to take its own initiatives to improve its bilateral relations with the Soviet Union.[74] As he had no weapons systems to trade off,

[74]This policy was not to be equated with neutrality or a drift out of NATO. But as Brandt expressed the sentiment in his memoirs, a certain national pride came with reaching this stage in national political rehabilitation: "An essential ingredient of our *Ostpolitik* was that we applied ourselves to our own affairs in a new and more positive manner instead of relying solely on others to speak for us. This meant that, while remaining in touch with our allies and retaining their confidence, we became the advocate of our own interests vis-à-vis the governments of Eastern Europe" (Willy Brandt, *People and Politics: The Years 1960–1975* [Boston: Little, Brown, 1976], p. 168).

Brandt was even more inclined than Nixon and Kissinger to rely on trade as a possible inducement for détente. And while in some respects Brandt overestimated the potential for political influence through trade, the Soviets' interest in West German trade did prove to be an important factor in their final agreement to the Renunciation of Force and Four Powers treaties in 1970.[75]

Nor were the Germans alone in pursuing the political benefits of a bilateral détente. In France de Gaulle's successors, while less flamboyant on the world stage, continued the traditions of French foreign policy independence from the United States and of competition with West Germany for the role of preeminent European international actor.[76] In late 1971 Brezhnev used the occasion of the signing of a new ten-year trade agreement to proclaim a "special relationship" between the Soviet Union and France.[77] In Italy, especially after the revelations of American covert attempts to influence Italian elections, the political survival of the Christian Democrats required some distancing from the United States. And in Britain, both Labour and Conservative governments continued to hope to offset with independent initiatives the junior-partner status implicit in the "special relationship" with the United States.

When in the late 1970s American policy began moving further and further away from détente, the Europeans were reluctant to go along. They did concur that the NATO military deterrent had to be strengthened. Accordingly, they agreed in 1978 to 3 percent annual real growth in defense spending and in 1979 to the dual-track policy of arms-control negotiations and the deployment on European soil of a new generation of intermediate-range nuclear weapons. Following the Soviet invasion of Afghanistan, the allies also participated in a series of flag-showing NATO military maneuvers. West German Chancellor Helmut Schmidt weathered domestic criticism and authorized German participation in NATO naval maneuvers in the North Atlantic and Indian oceans. British Prime Minister Margaret Thatcher agreed to a joint Anglo-American squadron as part of the Rapid Deployment Force. And in France, Socialist François Mitterrand

[75]Angela E. Stent, *From Embargo to Ostpolitik: The Political Economy of West German–Soviet Relations, 1955–1980* (New York: Cambridge University Press, 1980), pp. 179–86, and Robert W. Dean, *West German Trade with the East: The Political Dimension* (New York: Praeger, 1974), pp. 219–22.

[76]A. M. De Porte, *Europe between the Superpowers: The Enduring Balance* (New Haven: Yale University Press, 1979), and Edward A. Kolodziej, *French International Policy under de Gaulle and Pompidou* (Ithaca: Cornell University Press, 1974).

[77]Department of State, Weekly Summary, "Union of Soviet Socialist Republics/France," July 21, 1972, p. 422B, via *Declassified Documents Catalog*.

made a tough anti-Soviet posture a central element in his successful presidential campaign.[78]

But further than that the Europeans were unwilling to go. For they did not share the American conclusion that détente was some sort of hoodwinking of the West by the Soviets. Détente was in need of some toughening and buttressing, perhaps, but was not so tattered as to be written off as a failure. While the political benefits were less than had been hoped, they nevertheless had been direct and tangible. Moreover, the Europeans were committed to preserving détente for the same reason that they agreed to an increase in defense spending and to the deployment of intermediate-range nuclear weapons. Détente was an alternative to a military conflict that, if fought, would more than likely have the European continent as its epicenter.

The Europeans also contended that it was precisely when tensions were high that they needed to maintain trade in order to manage and contain the crisis. Consequently, they did not heed Jimmy Carter's urgings to embargo trade with the Soviet Union following the invasion of Afghanistan. While American exports fell 54 percent in 1980, French exports increased 35 percent, West German 32 percent, British 30 percent, and Italian 4 percent (Table 5.5). Both French President Giscard d'Estaing and West German Chancellor Schmidt met with Brezhnev in 1980 and signed new trade agreements. Even the pledge not to undermine the American sanctions directly by picking up the business forgone did not hold up. The West German firm Klockner-Werke snapped up the contract for a $311 million aluminum plant in Siberia for which Alcoa had been in line. The French firm Creusot Loire took over a $350 million contract for construction of a steel mill that Armco had been forced to give up by the Carter sanctions.[79] European farmers saw their grain exports to the Soviet Union jump from 220 million tons in 1979 to 820 million in 1980.[80]

---

[78]Frans R. Bax, "Energy Security in the 1980s: The Response of U.S. Allies," *Energy and National Security: Proceedings of a Special Conference,* ed. Donald J. Goldstein (Washington, D.C.: National Defense University Press, 1981), pp. 38–39.

[79]*New York Times,* September 18, 1980, p. D5, and November 15, 1980, p. 1. The issue struck an especially sensitive nerve because Creusot Loire was controlled by a holding company of which a leading stockholder was Mme Valéry Giscard d'Estaing. The Carter administration retaliated by banning the import into the United States of many of Creusot Loire's products.

[80]*Economist,* February 27, 1982, p. 50. Before August 1980 Canada had cooperated with the grain embargo by not picking up any of the contracts forfeited by American companies. But when evidence was discovered that American companies were flooding the Canadian market with their embargoed grain, Canada protested and terminated its tacit cooperation. By the year's end Canadian grain sales to the Soviet Union had increased 250% over 1979.

And in June 1980—in fact, only a few weeks after the Western summit in Venice—Chancellor Schmidt went to Moscow and signed an initial agreement concerning construction of what would prove to be an even greater point of conflict within the Western alliance: the western Siberian natural gas pipeline.

Had the Europeans shared Jimmy Carter's perception of the Afghanistan invasion as the greatest threat to peace in the postwar era, their responses surely would have been quite different. A fundamental dispute over foreign policy strategy had opened up—one that, as Chapters 6 and 7 will show, grew more serious over time.

The second factor motivating European policy in the 1970s was the increased economic importance that trade with the Soviet Union came to have. Once again the economic value was especially pronounced in the energy sector. This time, though, it was less in the oil trade than in the newly developing natural gas trade. As Table 5.6 shows, Western European imports of Soviet oil did not follow a consistent pattern in the 1970s. Italy actually was importing less Soviet oil in 1980 than 1973. West Germany experienced a modest increase. French imports increased the most, but even these amounted to only an 8.4 percent market share by 1980. This limited growth pattern could be linked in part to the leveling off of Soviet oil production. It was not a decline of the crisis proportions predicted by the CIA, but production growth rates did slow from the 1970–75 average annual rate of 7.7 percent to 5.2 percent in 1976–78 and 2.6 percent in 1979–80. This meant that after Soviet domestic and Eastern European consumption requirements were met, less surplus was available for export to Western Europe. Thus, after four years of steady growth from 386 million barrels per day (mbd) in 1974 to 921 mbd in

Table 5.6. Volume of Soviet oil imported by three European COCOM countries and percentage of total oil consumed, 1973, 1975, and 1980 (millions of barrels per day)

	West Germany		Italy		France	
Year	Volume	Percent	Volume	Percent	Volume	Percent
1973	116	4.2%	163	9.0%	95	4.1%
1975	148	6.2	123	6.0	57	3.0
1980	138	5.8	138	7.7	168	8.4

SOURCES: Volumes from Central Intelligence Agency, Directorate of Intelligence, *International Energy Statistical Review,* March 26, 1985, p. 24; percentages from data provided by Jochen Bethkenhagen, German Institute for Economic Research, West Berlin.

1978, Soviet oil exports to Western Europe fell to 865 mbd in 1979. By 1981 they had fallen to 845 mbd.[81]

A second reason for the limited growth in East–West oil trade was Western Europe's increased emphasis on conversion from oil to natural gas. This planned switch had already begun before the 1975 OPEC oil crisis. Natural gas as a percentage of total primary energy consumed had increased from 2 percent in 1950 to 10 percent in 1973.[82] Understandably, following the 1973 oil crisis there was interest in speeding up the rate of conversion to gas. Much of the gas then still was expected to come from European sources. The Dutch Groningen reserves, discovered in 1959, were the principal source. Their production already had increased from 1.7 billion cubic meters (bcm) in 1965 to 31.4 bcm in 1970. Exports to fellow EEC members had followed a similar path, from 0.13 bcm in 1966 to 11.3 bcm in 1970.[83] In addition, Norwegian gas from the newly discovered North Sea fields was expected to come on line by 1976–77. Britain also had its North Sea gas fields. And West Germany, France, and Italy all had some small gas production of their own.

Nevertheless, there was an economic logic in the turn to the Soviet Union as an additional gas supplier. Between 1960 and 1970 its gas production had increased from 45 bcm to 198 bcm annually. Its gas reserves were enormous: the newly discovered Urengoi field in western Siberia was 50 percent larger than the Dutch Groningen field.[84] At first the pattern of European–Soviet gas trade mirrored the initial development of European–Soviet oil trade in the late 1950s. In December 1969 Italy became the first NATO-COCOM member to sign a gas import contract. The gas was to be shipped through a pipeline to be built with Italian wide-diameter pipe (now measured at 60 inches).[85] Two months later the Brandt government signed a comparable con-

---

[81]As the CIA had forecast, the cause of the slowdown was falling production in the older producing regions. Urals-Volga production peaked at 4.52 mbd in 1975 and by 1980 had fallen to 3.82 mbd. Other non-Siberian production (Central Asia, Azerbaijan SSR, North Caucasus, other) declined from 2.4 mbd in 1973 to 2.34 mbd in 1975 to 1.96 mbd in 1980. However, the CIA underestimated the size of the increase in western Siberian oil production: 1.75 mbd in 1973 to 2.96 mbd in 1975 to 6.25 mbd in 1980. These data are from the CIA's *International Energy Statistical Review*, March 26, 1985, pp. 24–25.

[82]George W. Hoffman, *The European Energy Challenge: East and West* (Durham, N.C.: Duke University Press, 1985), Appendix A, pp. 157, 159.

[83]*Petroleum Press Service*, September 1971, p. 324. See also Malcolm Peebles, *Evolution of the Gas Industry* (London: Macmillan, 1980), pp. 122–25.

[84]*Petroleum Press Service*, May 1968, p. 167.

[85]Jeremy L. Russell, *Energy as a Factor in Soviet Foreign Policy* (Lexington, Mass.: Heath, 1976), pp. 183–84.

Table 5.7. Volume of Soviet natural gas imported by four European COCOM countries and percentage of total natural gas consumed, 1973, 1975, and 1980 (billions of cubic meters)

Year	West Germany		Italy		France		Great Britain	
	Volume	Percent	Volume	Percent	Volume	Percent	Volume	Percent
1973	0.4	1.2%	—	—	—	—	—	—
1975	3.1	7.5	2.3	10.3%	—	—	—	—
1980	10.7	18.2	7.0	24.8	4.0	13.9%	—	—

SOURCE: Jonathan Stern, *Soviet Natural Gas Development to 1990* (Lexington, Mass.: Heath, 1980), p. 59 for 1973 and 1975 volumes; 1980 volume from International Energy Agency, *World Energy Outlook* (Paris: OECD, 1982), p. 192; market share percentages from data provided by Jochen Bethkenhagen, German Institute for Economic Research, West Berlin.

tract.[86] Because West Germany was closer to the Siberian gas fields from which the exports would flow, it could begin to receive gas even sooner than Italy. The target date, ironically, was October 1973.

France also was a gas-consuming country, but in the early 1970s Algeria was meeting most of its import needs. Imports from Algeria had begun in 1965 at the rate of 0.5 bcm a year. In 1970 a new fifteen-year agreement was signed guaranteeing an increase to 3.5 bcm by 1972.[87] The price was favorable, the supply seemed secure, and the increased volume would satisfy much of France's total import requirements. Soviet gas was less price-competitive for France than for West Germany or Italy because France would be the last stop on a very long pipeline. Any arrangements also would require the cooperation of the governments of the countries that such a pipeline would traverse. Consequently, when the Franco-Soviet Economic Cooperation Agreement was signed in 1971, energy was given only passing mention.

Two conclusions can be drawn from the gas import figures in Table 5.7. First, like the oil trade a decade earlier, European–Soviet gas trade in the early 1970s developed selectively. As consumer countries, West German and Italy had a much greater economic interest in Soviet gas than did European producer countries. Second, it was only after the 1973 OPEC crisis that the European–Soviet gas trade began

[86]Stent, *From Embargo to Ostpolitik*, pp. 163–69. In a forerunner to this trade agreement, West Germany produced wide-diameter pipe as a subcontractor in the 1968 Austrian–Soviet natural gas trade agreement. For details see *Petroleum Press Service*, October 1967, p. 387, and July 1968, pp. 247–48, and Robert E. Ebel, *Communist Trade in Oil and Gas* (New York: Praeger, 1970), pp. 135–37.

[87]*Petroleum Press Service*, January 1970, p. 8.

to grow rapidly. This is evident in the increases in West German and Italian imports and especially in the post-1973 shift in French policy. France, which depended on OPEC oil for 67 percent of its total energy requirements, was perhaps most shaken by the 1973 OPEC crisis and its aftermath. During the supply cutbacks occasioned by the embargo the French government had pressured the major French oil companies, CFP and ELF-Erap, to cut deliveries to other destinations and sustain France's supply at normal levels. But even the French *dirigiste* state could not ensure its oil supply in such a severe crisis.[88] Thus in December 1974 President Valéry Giscard d'Estaing signed France's first major natural gas trade agreement with the Soviet Union. The gas actually was part of a four-way swap in which France bought Dutch gas on Italy's account and Italy bought additional gas from the Soviet Union on France's account. The lack of efficient pipeline distribution still was an obstacle to more direct trade, but of greater significance was the fact that the terms of this agreement went well beyond any past trade in oil or natural gas between France and the Soviet Union.

In late 1975 France and West Germany (and Austria as well) took this relationship a step further by signing a triangular gas trade agreement with the Soviet Union and Iran. The original terms had Western European equipment being sold to Iran, Iranian gas to the Soviet Union, and Soviet gas to Western Europe. In 1977 the agreement was expanded to include construction of a 1,440-kilometer pipeline known as IGAT II, linking the Kangan gas fields of southern Iran to the Soviet border at Astara.[89] About 35 percent of the gas transported (annual capacity was to be 25 bcm by 1983) was to be retained by Iran for domestic consumption. Another 25 percent was to be consumed by the Soviet Union and Czechoslovakia. The remaining 10.9 bcm per year was to go to Western Europe via the Soviet Union: 5.5 bcm to West Germany, 3.6 bcm to France, and 1.8 bcm to Austria.[90]

IGAT II, however, was killed by the Iranian revolution of 1978–79. The Western Europeans, who already had exported much of the

[88]Robert J. Lieber, "Energy Policies of the Fifth Republic: Autonomy versus Constraint," in *The Fifth Republic at Twenty*, ed. William G. Andrews and Stanley Hoffmann (Albany: State University of New York Press, 1981), pp. 316–17.

[89]IGAT I, built between 1966 and 1970 by the Soviet Union and Iran, became the major natural gas supply line for Azerbaijan, Georgia, and Armenia. The gas was payment for a steel mill built by the Soviets at Isfahan as well as for the pipeline. See Goldman, *Enigma of Soviet Petroleum*, pp. 81–82.

[90]U.S. Congress, Office of Technology Assessment, *Technology and Soviet Energy Availability* (Washington, D.C.: Government Printing Office, 1981), p. 358.

Table 5.8. Percentage of energy consumed and imported by four European COCOM countries represented by OPEC oil, 1978

Country	Oil as percent of total energy consumed	Percent of oil imported	OPEC oil as percent of total imports	OPEC oil as percent of total energy consumed
West Germany	54%	95%	58%	29.8%
France	63	99	84	52.4
Italy	68	99	80	53.8
United Kingdom	45	55	67	16.6

SOURCE: David A. Deese and Linda B. Miller, "Western Europe," in *Energy and Security,* ed. David A. Deese and Joseph S. Nye (Cambridge, Mass.: Ballinger, 1981), p. 187.

equipment and technology, were left with unpaid bills for their exports and worthless paper pledges for natural gas imports.[91] Worse were the ravaging effects of the 1979 oil crisis, which also was a consequence of the Iranian revolution. The energy supply shortages were more extensive and the price hikes more astronomical than those of 1973. That this time it was internal revolution rather than external war that precipitated the oil crisis served only to make affected nations feel even less secure about being dependent on OPEC. And as Table 5.8 shows, levels of dependency on OPEC were dangerously high. With the exception of the United Kingdom, oil still was the principal energy source for European economies, virtually all of it imported, and most of the imported oil came from OPEC. OPEC oil accounted for over 50 percent of total energy consumption in France and Italy and almost 30 percent in West Germany.

Europe's need to restructure its pattern of energy trade was no longer just a matter of economic interest but a fundamental issue of economic security. It had to shift away both from oil and from OPEC. One option, in theory at least the most attractive, was to turn increasingly to European producers of natural gas. This step would enable the Western Europeans to turn away from oil and to deal with suppliers who were far more politically reliable than OPEC. The problem, though, was that anticipated demand far exceeded planned supply. Fearing that the Groningen reserves might be depleted by the year 2000, the Dutch government had begun to cut sales to other European countries. From a peak of 53.4 bcm in 1976, exports to the

[91]Jonathan P. Stern, *Soviet Natural Gas Development to 1990* (Lexington, Mass.: Heath, 1980), pp. 79–80, and Goldman, *Enigma of Soviet Petroleum,* pp. 157–58.

Table 5.9. Percentage of natural gas requirements of three European COCOM countries supplied by European and other sources, 1980 and 1990 (projected)

Country and source	1980	1990
West Germany		
Domestic production	30.1%	22.3%
Netherlands	36.6	15.7
Norway	15.7	22.3
All European sources	82.4%	60.3%
Other	17.6	39.7
All sources	100.0%	100.0%
France		
Domestic production	27.5%	8.0%
Netherlands	37.6	8.0
Norway	9.1	13.0
West Germany	4.0	—
All European sources	78.2%	29.0%
Other	21.8	71.0
All sources	100.0%	100.0%
Italy		
Domestic production	46.8%	17.0%
Netherlands	24.3	13.6
All European sources	71.1%	30.6%
Other	28.9	69.4
All sources	100.0%	100.0%

SOURCE: Adapted from *Financial Times*, February 1, 1982, p. 2.

rest of Europe were expected to shrink to 13 bcm by 1995 and to zero by the end of the century.[92] At the same time French, German, and Italian domestic production also would be declining. Expected increases in British and Norwegian North Sea gas were not even enough to counteract these declines in production, let alone to fuel the anticipated 11 percent annual increase in demand for gas.[93] The effect, as Table 5.9 indicates, was that European gas consumer nations were going to have to look increasingly outside of Europe for their gas. It was estimated that European sources could supply only about 30 percent of the gas required by France and Italy by 1990. While West Germany's aggregate dependence on non-European imports would be lower, the disproportionate regional dependence of

[92]"North Sea Gas: Alternative to the Soviet Deal?" *Dun's Business Month,* November 1982, pp. 69–73. See also "Western Europe Facing Shortfall in Gas Supply," *Oil and Gas Journal,* July 14, 1980, pp. 39–43. Groningen production had peaked in 1977 and declined thereafter. See Central Intelligence Agency, Directorate of Intelligence, *International Energy Statistics Review,* February 22, 1982, p. 21.

[93]Estimates from International Energy Agency, *World Energy Outlook: 1982* (Paris), p. 380, 391.

Bavaria (for which northern European gas sources were un-economical) would make that nation's problem no less severe.

In terms of volume, these figures amounted to increases in consumption from 25 bcm to 45 bcm for Italy, from less than 20 bcm to 45–50 bcm for France, and from 60 bcm to 80 bcm for West Germany.[94] Where would all this gas come from? Algeria? Turning to a country that had participated in two embargoes and boosted its prices skyward would hardly serve to enhance energy security. Moreover, in the wake of the 1979 oil crisis Algeria demanded that its gas be given f.o.b. parity with high-grade crude oil, the equivalent of up to a 100 percent increase in existing gas prices. When its demands were not met, it reneged on its contracts with Italy and cut its exports to France by over 50 percent.[95] Iran and its ayatollah? "No one can tell me," one West German official cogently remarked, "that the Straits of Hormuz is a safer energy channel than a gas pipeline from Russia."[96]

Then there was the Soviet Union with its 27 bcm of natural gas reserves (fully a third of the world total), with a projected increase in gas production from 435 bcm in 1980 to 600–640 bcm by 1985, with promises of orders for billions of dollars' worth of exports and with the prospect of energy trade strengthening détente at a time when it was on the verge of collapsing.

It was in this context that negotiations began on the Siberian natural gas pipeline.

SUMMARY: CONSTRAINTS ON ECONOMIC INDUCEMENT

By the end of the 1970s there could be little doubt that the American experiment with an economic inducement strategy had collapsed. Explaining why, however, was a complex matter. As with the coercive sanctions strategy, part of the difficulty of pursuing political influence through trade promotion stemmed from the Soviets' reluctance to accept the principle of linkage—in effect, the unilateral constraint of Soviet behavior. There was a multilateral constraint as well: Western

---

[94]Miriam Karr and Roger W. Robinson, Jr., "Soviet Gas: Risk or Reward?" *Washington Quarterly*, Autumn 1981, p. 7. See also *Oil and Gas Journal*, July 14, 1980, pp. 39–43.
[95]*Financial Times*, September 28, 1982, p. 38; *Journal of Commerce*, January 25, 1982, p. 5A; Ghislaine Cestre, "Algeria's Unhappy Gamble: The Crude Oil/Natural Gas Pricing Link," *Geopolitics of Energy*, January 1984, p. 5; and Jonathan P. Stern, *International Gas Trade in Europe* (London: Heinemann, 1984), pp. 74, 88, 97. Apparently the Dutch also had tried similar tactics in the past; see *Dun's Business Month*, November 1982, p. 73.
[96]*New York Times*, August 6, 1981.

European governments were pursuing their own détente and economic relationships with the Soviet Union. As their economic interests in importing Soviet natural gas increased and the diffusion of energy technologies made them more capable of supplying the equipment needed by the Soviet energy sector, the allies' relevance as alternative trade partners also increased. While Euro-Soviet energy trade was not totally delinked from Euro-Soviet political issues, the allies' agenda was not always the same as the American one.

But the most significant constraint came from American domestic policies. The combination of the additional political demands imposed by Jackson-Vanik and the reduced economic benefits left by the Eximbank restrictions undermined the original Nixon-Kissinger strategy. In John Gaddis' terms, "it overloaded the 'linkage' mechanism."[97] Previously, on such issues as SALT I, Vietnam, and even Jewish emigration, trade inducements had enhanced American bargaining influence. It is interesting to note that some authors who otherwise disagree on the causes of the general failure of détente concur on the severe damage done by Jackson-Vanik and the Eximbank restrictions. Harry Gelman cites these factors as "the central cause" of Soviet disillusionment with détente, a "watershed" in the deterioration of Soviet–American relations. Alexander George singles them out as "a major blow to the further development of détente." Raymond Garthoff stresses the particular embarrassment they caused Brezhnev, who "personally accepted and pushed more vigorously than any other top leader the policy of maximizing East–West trade." And Adam Ulam remarks that even "if the Kremlin had been ready to swallow its injured national pride" after Jackson-Vanik, "it certainly would not do so for a paltry" few million dollars.[98]

The impact of domestic constraints on the economic inducements the United States could offer the Soviet Union therefore is not to be underestimated. They were not the only constraints. Nor is there any guarantee that the structure of peace would not have collapsed under the weight of the other tensions and conflicts that still marked American-Soviet relations. But one also must be wary of arguments that point to the 1970s experience as a refutation of the economic induce-

[97]Gaddis, *Strategies of Containment*, p. 315.

[98]Harry Gelman, *The Brezhnev Politburo and the Decline of Détente* (Ithaca: Cornell University Press, 1984), pp. 122–23, 148–51; Alexander L. George, "Détente: The Search for a 'Constructive Relationship,'" in his *Managing U.S.–Soviet Rivalry: Problems of Crisis Prevention* (Boulder, Colo.: Westview Press, 1983), p. 22; Garthoff, *Détente and Confrontation*, p. 88; Ulam, *Dangerous Relations*, p. 123.

ment strategy. For as Gaddis points out, the domestic constraints "made it impossible to test" the validity of the inducement strategy.[99]

This, however, was not the way Ronald Reagan and his administration saw the lessons of the 1970s. They saw the failure of détente as proof positive that no inducements could succeed with the Soviet adversary. Continued trade between the United States—or, for that matter, its allies—and the Soviet Union would only fulfill Lenin's prophecy that the capitalist nations would be so blindly greedy as to sell the communists the rope to hang them with.[100]

---

[99]Gaddis, *Strategies of Containment*, p. 315.

[100] Carl Gershman, "Selling Them the Rope: Business and the Soviets," *Commentary* 67 (April 1979): 35–45.

CHAPTER SIX

The Reagan Administration's Sanctions against the Siberian Natural Gas Pipeline, 1981–1984

THE OVERALL REAGAN COERCIVE STRATEGY: ENERGY, HIGH TECHNOLOGY, AND CREDITS

It was touted as "the deal of the century." A 5,000-kilometer pipeline with an annual carrying capacity of 40 bcm, bringing natural gas from the supergiant reserves of the Yamal Peninsula in western Siberia across vast permafrost terrain, over the Ural Mountains, through dense forest, bridging some seven hundred river crossings, and finally to homes, factories, and utilities throughout Western Europe.[1] The Carter administration had taken a position of "muted skepticism."[2] It warned the Europeans against the dangers of dependence on the Soviet Union for energy but stopped short of actively and overtly pressuring them not to go ahead with the Siberian natural gas pipeline (SNGP). The Reagan administration's position was both more skeptical and less muted. "It is simply no longer convincing," Assistant Secretary of Defense Richard N. Perle argued as a general point, "to suggest that trade will moderate Soviet behavior or deflect it from its buildup of military power." Quite to the contrary, there

---

[1]High costs and engineering difficulties led to a change of plans so that the already tapped Urengoi reserves, 150 miles to the south and only slightly less extensive, became the source of gas for this project. See *Petroleum Economist*, January 1982, p. 13, and U.S. Congress, Office of Technology Assessment (OTA), *Technology and Soviet Energy Availability* (Washington, D.C.: Government Printing Office, 1981), pp. 19–76, and 370–82.

[2]Jonathan Stern, "U.S. Controls and the Soviet Pipeline," *Washington Quarterly* 5 (Autumn 1982): 53.

were several reasons why he deemed the SNGP in particular a serious threat to Western security:

> First, it will generate substantial hard currency earnings for the Soviet Union that will finance a number of Soviet developments inimical to our interests. With the pipeline in full operation, several billion dollars annually will flow into the Soviet treasury. . . .
>
> Second, the revenues available to the Soviets will help to forge an economic link with Europe that will inevitably increase Moscow's influence among our allies. And where jobs and profits emanate from Moscow, it would be naive to believe that politics will stay far behind. . . .
>
> Third, we believe that Europe will incur a dangerous vulnerability to the interruption of supplies of natural gas from the Soviet Union. . . . Even in the absence of a crisis severe enough to lead to a Soviet cutoff, there is the day-to-day influence that must flow, like the gas itself, through a pipeline to which there will be no practicable alternative. . . .
>
> Is there any doubt that our allies listen more carefully to kings and rulers who supply them with energy than to those who do not?[3]

It was not until after the imposition of martial law in Poland on December 13, 1981, that the Reagan administration actually imposed sanctions against the Siberian gas pipeline. The president's pronouncements stressed two objectives, the symbolic one of "speaking for those who have been silenced" and the instrumental one of "helping those who have been rendered helpless" by compelling the Soviets and their Polish quislings to end the repression.[4] Both the timing and the content of Perle's statement, however, indicate that American coercive objectives ran much deeper than the symbolic and compellence objectives associated with the issue of martial law in Poland. Perle made his remarks during testimony at a congressional hearing on November 12, 1981—one month and one day *before* martial law

---

[3]Congressional testimony of November 12, 1981, reprinted in *Defense '82* (February 1982), pp. 15–19.

[4]The preexisting (from the Carter administration) licensing requirement for oil and gas exploration and production equipment was extended to cover refining and transmission equipment (e.g., pipelayers, pipeline compressor stations); all existing licenses for all high-technology exports including oil and gas equipment were suspended, and no new licenses were to be issued; the offices of the Soviet Purchasing Commission were closed; Aeroflot flights were suspended; exchange agreements on energy and science and technology would not be renewed; negotiations for a new maritime agreement were suspended; and negotiations for a new long-term grain agreement were postponed. All of the conditions announced for a lifting of the sanctions were related to the situation in Poland: an end to martial law, the freeing of labor leader Lech Walesa and other political prisoners, and the Polish government's initiation of a dialogue with the Catholic church and Solidarity, the union headed by Walesa.

was declared in Poland. Moreover, Perle was quite explicit about the ways in which the Siberian pipeline threatened the objectives of containment, deterrence, and economic defense. It was "naive," he argued, to think that Soviet political influence would not flow along with Soviet gas, thus bringing the Soviets closer to their long-held goal of breaking through the dike of containment and splitting Western Europe from the United States. Too, a move that subjected Europe to a "dangerous vulnerability" to a threatened or actual cutoff of gas in a time of crisis would weaken the overall Western deterrence posture. And on a more continuing basis, the $5 to $10 billion in hard currency that the Soviets would earn from the pipeline would finance the acquisition of Western technology with possible military applications, free up internal resources to be reallocated to the military buildup, and otherwise contribute to "developments inimical to our interests."

The Soviets seemed to have become uniquely vulnerable to energy trade sanctions. Their earnings from oil and gas exports had increased from $444 million and 18.3 percent of total hard-currency earnings in 1970 to $14.7 billion and 62.3 percent in 1980. Now, however, the Soviets were being squeezed by plummeting world oil prices and their own stagnant production. In 1981 oil revenues increased by only $292 million, or 2.4 percent; demand for hard-currency imports was increasing much more rapidly—grain imports alone cost almost $2 billion more in 1981 than in 1980, and other agricultural products an additional $700 million. As a partial offset, imports of machinery and equipment were slashed from $6 billion to $4.5 billion.[5] But such cuts in imports of Western industrial technology only added to problems of declining productivity.[6]

Thus the Reagan administration saw energy trade as something of a linchpin in the entire Soviet economic relationship with the West.

---

[5]Joan Parpart Zoeter, "U.S.S.R.: Hard Currency Trade and Payments," in U.S. Congress, Joint Economic Committee, *Soviet Economy in the 1980s: Problems and Prospects*, Joint Committee Print, 97th Cong., 2d sess., 1982, pt. 2, pp. 501–2.

[6]Herbert S. Levine generalizes a 3:1 productivity ratio in favor of imported machinery; see his "Soviet Economic Development, Technology Transfer, and Foreign Policy," in *The Domestic Context of Soviet Foreign Policy*, ed. Seweryn Bialer (Boulder, Colo.: Westview Press, 1981), pp. 187–88. Microeconomic studies of the Soviet chemical industry attribute disproportionate shares of fertilizer, plastic, and textile production to imported plants. Similar findings have been made in regard to machine tools, computers, and automobiles, as well as oil and natural gas. See OTA, *Technology and East–West Trade* (Washington, D.C.: Government Printing Office, 1979), pp. 228–42; George D. Holliday, "Western Technology Transfer to the Soviet Union: Problems of Assimilation and Impact on Soviet Imports," in Joint Economic Committee, *Soviet Economy in the 1980s*, pt. 1, pp. 521–24. See also Organization for Economic Cooperation and Development, *East–West Technology Transfer* (Paris, 1984).

Steady increases in the hard-currency earnings of oil and gas were essential to fund the imports of both grain and industrial technology on which the Soviet economy relied. But increases in oil and gas production in turn required Western equipment and technology. As a study by the Office of Technology Assessment (OTA) documented, the Soviets continued to rely on Western equipment and technology for key functions at virtually every stage of the energy production process: computers for exploration, deep well and diamond rock drill bits, turnkey refineries, submersible pumps and wide-diameter pipe and turbine-powered compressor stations for natural gas pipelines. The OTA study went on to point out that "with few exceptions, adequate quantities of the energy equipment sought by the USSR are produced and available outside the United States, and the quality of these foreign goods is generally comparable to that of their U.S. counterparts."[7] But while for the OTA and others this availability was a reason not to attempt an embargo, for the Reagan administration it was a reason only to increase pressure on the Western Europeans to collaborate with expanded controls on the export of energy equipment and technology.

Events in Poland therefore were more precipitating than causal. In fact, the objectives to be served by blocking the Siberian pipeline not only were more complex than a mere response to the Polish situation, but in a more fundamental way were part and parcel of an overarching strategy to purge from American policy all remnants of economic inducement and revert to Cold War–style economic coercion.

There were early hints to this effect in the very appointment of Perle and of Lawrence Brady to the key middle-level positions in the export control bureaucracy. As Henry Jackson's chief staff aide in the 1970s, Perle had earned a reputation as the man who "did as much as any other American to doom détente during the 1970s." Among other things, he had helped draft and engineer passage of the Jackson-Vanik amendment. Brady had garnered his anti-Soviet trade credentials during the Carter administration. Then a lower-level Commerce Department official, he had gone to Congress (specifically, to testify before a Senate subcommittee chaired by Henry Jackson and staffed by Richard Perle) with accusations that his superiors were not strictly enforcing safeguards against Soviet diversion of industrial technology exports to military purposes. After one such accusation in January 1980 regarding the use of trucks made at the Kama River

[7]OTA, *Technology and Soviet Energy Availability,* pp. 35–37, 46–48, 53–55, 62–64, 67–70, 392.

truck foundry (a multibillion-dollar project built in part with American technology) to transport soldiers and supplies during the invasion of Afghanistan, Brady was fired for insubordination. Brady's appointment at a higher level (as assistant secretary of commerce for export administration) made a statement from the start about where the new administration was headed.[8]

Other administration officials shared this basic disposition. Ronald Reagan himself long had been a critic of the economic inducement strategy. "Why shouldn't the Western world quarantine the Soviet Union," one of his 1980 campaign stump speeches went, "until they decide to behave like a civilized nation?" During the campaign and then once in office Reagan modified his tough talk on economic sanctions by making an exception for grain exports. Various rationales were developed as justification. The Carter grain embargo was said to have unfairly imposed more than a fair share of the burdens of American foreign policy on American farmers. There even were some rather counterintuitive calculations purporting to show that grain exports actually had a strategic value because they absorbed Soviet hard currency, which otherwise could be spent on more militarily relevant industrial equipment and technology.

In reality, though, the grain exception was a graphic demonstration of domestic constraints. Much had changed since 1963, when farm belt congressmen condemned the Kennedy grain sale as selling out patriotism for a profit. Then the ideological prohibition against trade was strong while the economic interests at stake were weak. Farm income then was increasing at a rate of 11.8 percent. And at only 21 percent of total grain output, exports in general were of marginal importance. By 1980–81, however, farm income was mired in the worst decline since the dust bowl days of the Great Depression. And not only had total exports increased to 40 percent of total grain output, but exports to the Soviet Union amounted to 15.6 percent of total exports, or about 6.2 percent of total grain production.

Though much of this loss was made up by increased exports to other world customers and through various emergency subsidies extended by the Carter administration,[9] the grain embargo set off a

[8]The characterization of Perle is from Fred Hiatt, "Richard Perle's War against Arms Control," *Washington Post*, national weekly ed., January 21, 1985, p. 6. On Brady see Christopher Madison, "Sweet Revenge," *National Journal*, May 9, 1981, p. 822.

[9]Robert L. Paarlberg, "Lessons of the Grain Embargo," *Foreign Affairs* 59 (Fall 1980): 144–62; H. Stephen Gardner, "Assessing the Cost to the U.S. Economy of Trade Sanctions against the U.S.S.R.," in *The Politics of East–West Trade*, ed. Gordon B. Smith (Boulder, Colo.: Westview Press, 1984), pp. 175–97.

wave of prairie fever that was among the key factors in Jimmy Carter's overwhelming defeat in the 1980 presidential election. Appropriately chastened by the political lessons, Ronald Reagan promptly
delivered on his campaign promise and lifted the grain embargo. By
August 1983 his administration had gone as far as to sign a new grain
agreement with the Soviets which included the firm and explicit
pledge never to embargo grain again. It is hard to imagine more
impressive evidence of the potency of domestic constraints than an
American president, especially one who only months earlier had condemned the Soviet Union as an "evil empire" and who on all other
fronts was vigorously prosecuting the Cold War, pledging not to impose sanctions under any conditions on the one American export on
which the Soviets relied heavily.[10]

Grain, however, remained the exception and not the rule. The
strategy of simultaneously pushing hard for sanctions on most industrial equipment and technology while exempting grain would cause
major problems both within the Western alliance and in domestic
politics. But to the Reagan administration (with some exceptions, notably Secretary of State Alexander Haig) the objectives to be served by
nonagricultural sanctions seemed compelling.[11] The Soviet economy
appeared to be suffering through its most serious crisis since the end
of World War II. Growth rates were at an all-time low. Efforts to
reverse the decline in productivity were making little progress. Think
what could happen if the Soviets now were denied the benefits of
trade with the West and thus forced to suffer the stagnation that is the
ultimate consequence of the inefficiencies of their economic system.
Secretary of Defense Caspar Weinberger outlined the possibilities. At
minimum such economic burdens would make it much more difficult
for them to sustain high military spending: "Without constant infusion of advanced technology from the West, the Soviet industrial base
would experience a cumulative obsolescence, which would eventually

[10]Article II of the new Long-Term Agreement on Grain Supplies reads: "During the
term of this Agreement, except as otherwise agreed by the Parties, the Government of
the USA shall not exercise any discretionary authority available to it under U.S. law to
control exports of commodities purchased for supply to the USSR in accordance with
Article I." When Secretary of Agriculture John Block, upon signing the agreement,
condemned the 1980 embargo as a "distasteful chapter" in American–Soviet relations,
Zbigniew Brzezinski, national security adviser in the Carter administration, retorted,
"What is truly distasteful is Secretary Block crawling on his knees to Moscow" (*New York
Times*, August 26, 1983, pp. 1, 28).

[11]Haig opposed the lifting of the grain sanctions as a unilateral concession that could
have been an effective bargaining chip. For his account of the decision to lift the grain
embargo, see Alexander M. Haig, *Caveat: Realism, Reagan, and Foreign Policy* (New
York: Macmillan, 1984), pp. 110–16.

also constrain the military industries. . . . By allowing access to a wide range of advanced technologies, we enable the Soviet leadership to evade this dilemma." It might even become possible, finally, for the sanctions strategy to be effective as economic warfare and undermine the very stability of the Soviet political system. Secretary Weinberger again:

> The Soviet leaders know full well by now that their central planning system is fatally flawed. But their system cannot be reformed without liberalizing Soviet society as a whole. Hence without access to advanced technology from the West, the Soviet leadership would be forced to choose between its military-industrial priorities and the preservation of a tightly controlled political system. . . . Thus, the West helps preserve the Soviet Union as a totalitarian dictatorship.

Finally, against those who built their case for economic inducement on the contention that we must seek to influence Soviet intentions rather than just limit their capabilities, Weinberger outlined the alternative path to intentions *through* capabilities: "If the Soviet Union were less totalitarian, it would also be less of a military threat, since a less controlled and more liberalized regime could not possibly allocate so much of the nation's resources to military expenditures."[12]

In addition to blocking the Soviet pipeline, the key measures in implementing this ambitious economic coercive strategy were tightening controls on high technology and on export credits. The Soviets, Assistant Secretary Perle warned, had been conducting "a raid on our technology . . . both through legal and illegal channels."[13] Loose CO-COM restrictions allowed them to acquire through perfectly legal means sophisticated equipment and technology that was applied commercially in the West but could be and was diverted to military applications in Soviet hands. In addition, the laxity of Western enforcement mechanisms allowed Soviet agents to smuggle on a massive scale. One White House official estimated that since 1976 the Soviets had acquired illegally 30,000 pieces of equipment and 400,000 technical documents of military value. Perle went even further, claiming that "virtually every new Soviet weapon system" was built at least in part with Western technology.[14]

[12]*Annual Report to the Congress of the Secretary of Defense, FY 1983* (Washington, D.C.: Government Printing Office, 1982), sec. I, pp. 22–23; sec. II, pp. 26–32.

[13]Congressional testimony of Richard Perle, reprinted in *Defense '82*, pp. 10–15. See also the report by the Central Intelligence Agency, "Soviet Acquisition of Western Technology" (declassified version), April 1982.

[14]The smuggling estimates are from *Wall Street Journal*, January 25, 1985, p. 1;

If the high-technology leakage were to be plugged, the allies were going to have to collaborate. In 1981 the United States accounted for only 3.3 percent of legal exports of Western high technology to the Soviet Union.[15] The smuggling problem required multilateral coordination to crack down on dummy corporations, reexport gambits, KGB activities, and other illegal practices. Often the Soviets operated through non-COCOM countries, such as Sweden, Switzerland, Austria, South Africa, and Hong Kong. In some cases, these non-COCOM countries could be brought into enforcement operations; Sweden, for example, played a role in intercepting the sophisticated Digital VAX 11/782 computer. The Reagan administration felt that ultimately COCOM or COCOM-style relationships would have to be devised with these and other friendly or neutral countries.[16] But most immediate was the need to tighten and enforce more effectively the existing COCOM restrictions.

In January 1982, for the first time since 1958, a high-level meeting was convened to review the COCOM embargo lists.[17] Members unanimously agreed to proceed with a review of the COCOM lists, with particular attention to high-technology items with potential military uses. The review process continued through 1983 and the first half of 1984, and an agreement was finally reached in July 1984. The results by no means were everything the Reagan administration wanted. American proposals to upgrade COCOM to formal treaty status and

Perle's statement is from his testimony before the House Armed Services Committee, cited in *Washington Post*, June 10, 1983, p. D9. See also Perle's article "The Strategic Implications of West–East Technology Transfer," in *The Conduct of East–West Relations in the 1980s—Part II*, Adelphi Paper no. 190 (London: International Institute for Strategic Studies, 1984), pp. 31–36, and the Defense Department Report "Soviet Acquisition of Militarily Significant Western Technology: An Update," September 1985.

[15]Gordon B. Smith, "The Impact of Western Technology Transfer on the Soviet Union," paper presented at Conference on Technology Transfer in the Modern World, Georgia Institute of Technology, April 26–27, 1984, p. 7.

[16]One step in this direction was the executive order issued March 23, 1984, granting the Defense Department authority over export licenses to twelve non-COCOM countries. The identity of these countries was not made public. News reports mentioned Austria, India, Sweden, Switzerland, and South Africa (*National Journal*, March 31, 1984, p. 595; *Wall Street Journal*, March 22, 1984, p. 12). There also was talk of trying to bring together Australia, New Zealand, Singapore, Hong Kong, Malaysia, South Korea, Indonesia, and the Philippines in an "Asian COCOM" (*Aviation Week and Space Technology*, August 20, 1984, p. 13).

[17]Previous list reviews had been carried out, most recently in 1974–78. But these reviews had been at the working group level of the permanent delegations to COCOM. The January 1982 meeting of subministerial-level officials was intended to demonstrate the importance and comprehensiveness of the new review process. This meeting had been agreed to at the July 1981 Ottawa summit and therefore was not strictly a response to martial law in Poland.

to create a military subcommittee in order to increase the role of defense ministers/secretaries were not adopted. Certain dual-use items that the United States wanted to add to the COCOM lists, not the least of which were oil and gas equipment and technology, were kept off.[18] Added to the COCOM lists, however, were such items as electronic-grade silicon, printed circuit boards and their technology, ceramics used in semiconductor manufacturing, large floating dry docks, technical data on superalloy production, certain robotics technologies, jet engines, inert gas, and atomizing technology. Large telecommunications switches also were added, and restrictions on them were made to apply retroactively to contracts already signed by several West German companies. And for the first time since 1976 disagreements over computer controls were bridged. The United States agreed to leave personal computers off the COCOM list in exchange for European consent to add high-speed computers, portable "ruggedized" computers (designed for harsh industrial use and thus also fit for battlefield use), and a range of software.[19]

European governments also stepped up their enforcement efforts, cracking down on suspected Soviet agents within their borders and coordinating with the United States policing operations against attempted transshipments of embargoed goods across their borders. In the first six months of 1983, sixty-five Soviet agents had been expelled from Western Europe on charges of industrial espionage.[20] All of these measures amounted to sufficient collaboration for a senior Pentagon official to comment that "we're generally pleased with it," and for a Commerce Department official to compliment the allies on their "dramatic improvement in . . . getting serious about both enforcement and licensing, and harmonizing those systems."[21]

The principal reason for this improvement in transatlantic collaboration was the shared assessment that much high-technology trade, legal and illegal, posed a serious security threat. That is to say, on this point the United States and its allies shared a guiding foreign policy strategy. Economic interests diverged somewhat, with Western Europe having a greater stake in technology exports to the Soviet Union and Eastern Europe. But as in the past (e.g., the 1954 and 1958

[18]William A. Root, "Trade Controls That Work," *Foreign Policy* 56 (Fall 1984): 67; *Wall Street Journal*, July 17, 1984, p. 35.

[19] *Aviation Week and Space Technology*, July 23, 1984, pp. 21–22; *American Metal Markets*, April 16, 1984, p. 1; *New York Times*, July 17, 1984, p. D7; *Washington Post*, July 21, 1984, pp. D1, D7; *Wall Street Journal*, July 23, 1984, p. 17.

[20]During the same period only three such agents had been expelled from the United States (*New York Times*, July 24, 1983, p. 10).

[21]*Wall Street Journal*, July 17, 1984, p. 35; *Aviation Week and Space Technology*, April 30, 1984, p. 59.

COCOM liberalizations), where technologies with the greatest military significance were concerned, economic interests were secondary to foreign policy considerations. As for the illegal flow of high tech, only the smugglers benefited economically; jobs were not created, nor was the official balance of payments improved. Thus, while European governments were still somewhat uncomfortable with the United States' broad interpretation of what constituted military significance, they had less dispute with the basic economic defense objective of limiting Soviet military capabilities, or at least not enhancing them with Western technology.

For a while it seemed that some progress also would be made on the export credits issue. Back in 1978 the OECD had tried through the twenty-two-nation Agreement on Guidelines for Officially Supported Export Credit to set minimum interest rates for all trade financing with all countries. Under this agreement (generally referred to as the Consensus), countries were categorized as rich, middle income, or poor, with corresponding minimum interest rates and maximum repayment periods. The Soviet Union originally was classified as a middle-income country, for which the minimum interest rate was 7.5 percent. This rate was increased first to 8.5 percent and then to 11.0 percent in 1980–81 as market rates went up. The key step was the agreement in May 1982 to move the Soviets into the rich category (12.5 percent minimum interest rate).[22]

For the United States the principal motivation was political. Increased interest rates would make credit more expensive and possibly also less available to the Soviets, thus adding another component to the coercive economic squeeze. For Europe, however, the principal motivation was economic. Export credits lacked the direct relevance to military capabilities which the Europeans considered necessary if trade controls were to be based on considerations of foreign policy. They originally had made export credits available to the Soviets in large amounts and often at concessionary rates for the same reasons that they extended comparable credits to other countries: to promote exports. The Soviets generally had been deemed even less of a lending risk than other countries. Now, however, this assumption was weakened by the Soviet Union's internal economic problems and especially by Poland's immense debt, for which the Soviet Union was taken to be the guarantor of last resort.[23]

---

[22]U.S. Department of State, Bureau of Public Affairs, "A Collective Approach to East–West Economic Relations," *Current Policy*, no. 495 (June 20, 1983); *Wall Street Journal*, November 2, 1982, p. 27.

[23]Richard Portes, "East Europe's Debt to the West: Interdependence Is a Two-Way Street," *Foreign Affairs* 55 (July 1977): 751–82. Debt statistics for 1982 were reported in

In addition, and somewhat ironically, the very success of the Soviets' strategy to negotiate the lowest possible interest rates to finance the equipment and technology imports for the Siberian gas pipeline was an incentive to avoid such cutthroat competition in the future. Axel Lebahn, chief negotiator for Deutsche Banke, later recounted how the Soviets "skillfully played the various countries off against each other." They would get a low bid from one country's exporters and pass it on to another country's exporters, who proceeded to lock themselves into an underbidding cycle. The same gambit was used to keep the interest rates low and the volume of credits high. Here Lebahn puts the blame squarely on the French, who offered the lowest interest rates and the most credit. He contends that West Germany had no choice but to make its terms of trade comparably attractive, with the result that the costs of building the pipeline to the Soviets were "extraordinarily low."[24] And so, consequently, were the profits for Western exporters and financiers.

As with any cartelistic agreement intended to avoid cutthroat competition, there was reason to calculate that collective rather than unilateral action was the optimal strategy for all suppliers. But collective action is optimal only if the partners stand together. It takes only one price/credit-cutting defector to undermine collective action.[25] And France remained reluctant to go along with either firm minimum interest rates or limits on total credit.[26] When at the Versailles summit President Reagan tried to move from the OECD recategorization to firmer limits on both interest rates and total credits to the Soviet Union, President Mitterrand resisted.[27] He agreed to a joint statement to the effect that "taking into account existing economic and

---

The Economist, May 22, 1982, p. 56, and *Wall Street Journal*, June 13, 1984, p. 20.

[24]Axel Lebahn, "Yamal Gas Pipeline from the USSR to Western Europe in the East–West Conflict," *Aussenpolitik* 3 (1983): 257–62, 276. The situation could be traced back to May 1980, when in an effort to boost exports the French offered the Soviets a five-year open-ended line of credit at the fixed rate of 7.8% (then the minimum interest rate). Despite the surge in world market rates, the French stood by this earlier agreement, with the government subsidizing the differential.

[25]Mancur Olson, *The Logic of Collective Action* (Cambridge: Harvard University Press, 1965); William Fellner, *Competition among the Few: Oligopoly and Similar Market Structures* (New York: Knopf, 1949).

[26]The French traditionally had used subsidized export credits as an instrument for promoting their exports to all markets. See John Zysman, "The French State in the International Economy," in *Between Power and Plenty: Foreign Economic Policies of Advanced Industrial States*, ed. Peter J. Katzenstein (Madison: University of Wisconsin Press, 1978), pp. 255–93.

[27]Mitterrand apparently wanted to link Soviet export credits also to the issue of American high interest rates and their impact on the French economy (Haig, *Caveat*, pp. 308–12).

financial considerations, we have agreed to *handle cautiously* financial relations with the U.S.S.R. and other Eastern European countries in such a way as to ensure that they are conducted on a *sound economic basis,* including also the need for *commercial prudence in limiting export credits.*"[28] But within a day of its signing (almost literally before the ink was dry), this very statement became the subject of divergent interpretations in Washington and Paris. The Reagan administration took it to be a firm commitment for a collaborative restrictive policy. The Mitterrand government claimed that it represented a pledge to consult and coordinate, but that interest rates and credit volumes remained the province of national policy.

Thus, even with economic interests somewhat convergent, collective Western controls proved difficult to sustain on the issue of export credits. The Siberian pipeline issue lacked even the degree of convergence of economic interest that the export credits issue had. And unlike the high-technology issue, which connected to shared foreign policy objectives and assessments of a mutual threat, the energy trade issue brought out fundamental differences over foreign policy strategy. Consequently, while the allies had collaborated to some extent on high-technology controls and less on export credits, they would collaborate least on energy trade controls. The multilateral constraints of allies turned alternative trade partners would be especially problematic in the Reagan administration's efforts to squeeze the Soviet economy on this front.

THE PIPELINE SPLITS THE ALLIANCE

President Reagan first raised the Siberian pipeline issue with his fellow leaders at the July 1981 Ottawa summit. West Germany, France, Italy, and Great Britain were close to concluding contract negotiations with the Soviets. The key exports involved were the 25-megawatt turbines that would power the pipeline compressor stations (three per station). Some of the European firms that were building these turbines were subsidiaries of American corporations (Dresser France), some had licensed the technology from General Electric (France's Alsthom Atlantique), and some were using parts supplied by GE (Italy's Nuovo Pignone, West Germany's AEG-Kanis, Britain's

---

[28]U.S. Department of State, Bureau of Public Affairs, "Economics and Security: The Case of East–West Relations," *Current Policy,* no. 465 (March 7, 1983), p. 2 (emphasis added).

John Brown Engineering). Because the Soviets lacked the capacity to produce such powerful pipeline compressors, the president saw an opportunity to block the pipeline or at least significantly to hamper the efficiency of its operation if the allies could be persuaded not to complete fulfillment of the export contracts. He also wanted to persuade them not to sign the gas import contracts, which in his view would strengthen the Soviets by increasing their hard-currency earnings and weaken the allies by dangerously increasing their dependence on the Soviets for such a vital commodity.

One administration official later described the president's approach at Ottawa as "consciousness raising."[29] It can be seen in part as an effort to articulate a shared foreign policy strategy, but even more clearly as an effort to bring to bear the leverage of American prestige as the alliance leader. Fresh from a stunning string of victories in domestic politics and a formidable reputation as the "Great Communicator," Ronald Reagan essentially tried to sell his fellow heads of state on his foreign policy (and on his leadership) as he had the American Congress on his economic policy. He did have some success, as when he obtained the allies' consent to hold the ministerial review of COCOM high-technology controls. But on the energy trade issue he made no progress. Instead, the commercial negotiations were pushed ahead.[30] And on September 29 the first contracts were signed. A consortium headed by Mannesmann Anlagenbau (West Germany) and Creusot-Loire (France) would deliver 22 compressor stations (each containing three 25-megawatt turbines) worth $1 billion. Mannesmann and Creusot-Loire were to be the general contractors for the whole pipeline project with AEG-Kanis (West Germany) and John Brown Engineering (Great Britain) as the subcontractors manufacturing the compressors. Two days later another contract valued at $1.1 billion was signed with Nuovo Pignone (Italy) to serve as another general contractor and also to manufacture itself the 19 additional compressor stations planned for the pipeline.

John Brown Engineering won additional Soviet orders for turbine spare parts and equipment worth approximately $60 million. The $350 million contract for computerized control equipment for the pipeline signed by the French firm Thomson-CSF was particularly controversial because of the potential military applications if the em-

[29]Personal interviews, November 7–11, 1983.
[30]The complex details of these negotiations are laid out and the Soviet negotiating strategy analyzed in Nil Ozergene, *Lessons of the Pipeline Negotiations*, ACIS Working Paper no. 40 (Los Angeles: Center for International and Strategic Affairs, UCLA, July 1983).

bodied technology were reverse-engineered. The French government considered banning the sale but despite American pressure allowed it to go through. Other pipeline-related contracts included $225 million to Creusot-Loire for nineteen refrigeration stations, $40 million to Alsthom Atlantique (France) for forty spare turbine rotor kits, $30 million to Ruston Gas Turbines (Great Britain) for forty-five gas turbine generating sets, $30 million to Plenty (Great Britain) for fuel gas conditioning facilities, $15 million to Redifusion (Great Britain) for a computer information system, and $150 million to Liebhen (West Germany) for 323 truck-mounted cranes. Contracts were also signed for huge volumes of wide-diameter pipe (now defined as 56 inches): an estimated $690 million to Mannesmann and Thyssen (West Germany) for 1.2 million tons and $230 million to Italsider (Italy) for 400,000 tons.

Negotiations on the gas import agreements also were moving ahead. In October the Italian state-owned utility SNAM (a division of ENI) signed a preliminary import agreement. In November Ruhrgas of West Germany signed a final contract. And in January 1982 Gaz de France also signed its final contract. The details of these import agreements are shown in Table 6.1. In all three cases the Siberian pipeline gas would increase the Soviet share of gas consumption quite substantially. West Germany would increase the share of its total gas supply acquired from the Soviets from 15 percent in 1980 to more than 30 percent by 1990. France's increase would go from 11.7 percent to almost 30 percent. Italy's agreement was only a preliminary one, but if consummated it would give the Soviets a 40 percent market share.

The Reagan administration's invocation of American prestige at the Ottawa summit clearly had proved ineffective as leverage. In November 1981 it resorted to another old and previously successful leverage strategy. A delegation headed by Under Secretary of State Myer Rashish went to Europe to offer an economic compensatory package intended to lead all of Western Europe away from Soviet natural gas the way Italy had been led away from Soviet oil in 1962–63. The American economic package had two key components. One was an offer of American coal as an alternative to Soviet natural gas. The other was not quite an offer, since it wasn't the United States' to give, but a suggestion of increased reliance on Norwegian gas as another substitute energy supply.

In the weaknesses of both components, as well as in the omissions from the package, we see how and why American economic leverage was so much less than it had been twenty years earlier, when Italy had

Table 6.1. Volume and percentage of natural gas imported from the Soviet Union by three European COCOM countries, 1980, and projected for import via Siberian pipeline, 1990 (billions of cubic meters)

Country	Volumes imported, 1980	Percent of total gas supply, 1980	Volume to be imported annually via Siberian pipeline	Percent of total gas supply, 1990
West Germany	9.9	15.0%	10.5	>30%
France	3.3	11.7	8.0	30
Italy	5.8	27.6	8.5[a]	40

[a]This figure, which appears in a preliminary agreement signed October 15, 1981, shrank to 4.5–6.0 bcm in the final contract, signed May 17, 1984. But it was on the preliminary figure and the corresponding projection of dependency that the Reagan administration based its policy.

SOURCES: 1980 import volumes from and percentages based on International Energy Agency, *Annual Oil and Gas Statistics, 1980/81* (Paris, 1983), pp. 482, 492; 1990 projected percentages from U.S. Congress, Office of Technology Assessment, *Technology and Soviet Energy Availability* (Washington, D.C., 1981), pp. 373–77; 1990 projected volumes from *New York Times*, November 21, 1981 (West Germany), and January 24, 1982 (France, and *Financial Times*, November 16, 1981 (Italy).

received an offer far more difficult to refuse. The problem with the coal offer was that it was speculative. This was not something the Reagan administration had in hand. It only could talk about future increases in coal production and export. And while few people underestimated the vastness of American coal reserves (30 percent of the world total), many doubted that the United States could deliver as much as it was promising. American port facilities already were pressed beyond capacity; ships already were being delayed an average of seventeen days in the major port of Hampton Roads, Virginia, creating shortage problems for foreign customers and raising their costs. The Carter administration had proposed a major program of port construction and expansion as part of its coal export policy. But as even Secretary of State Alexander Haig acknowledged, any harbor-dredging project could be subject to review by sixty-seven federal agencies and thirty-two congressional subcommittees.[31] It also was not certain that coal production could be increased as much as the administration was contemplating, given the constraints of the Surface Mining Act of 1977 and other environmental and worker safety legislation.

Coal also presented a host of problems on the consuming end. Especially as public awareness of the acid rain problem increased, resistance could be expected from European environmental groups. Equipping utilities and factories with the necessary scrubbing and other antipollution devices involved high fixed capital costs. In addition, European domestic producers and coal miners' unions, already hurt by twenty-five years of conversion from coal to gas and with much higher production costs than the United States', would not take well to another dose of competition.

The problem with the American proposal for increased reliance on Norwegian gas was that it did not have the support of the Norwegian government. Norway was hyperconscious of avoiding the dangers of social and economic disruption associated with too rapid development of its oil and gas sector. The softness of world market prices in the early 1980s only added to the incentives to keep the gas in the ground. Thus, after growing from 14.9 bcm in 1978 to 26.0 bcm in 1980, Norwegian gas production stopped growing and even fell off to 25.6 bcm in 1982. As a result, at the same time that the United States was trying to persuade the European consumer countries to turn

---

[31]The coal option is intelligently analyzed in Steven Grinspoon, "The Soviet Gas Pipeline: Boon or Boondoggle?" Cornell University paper, April 1982. Haig's comment is in *Business Week,* February 22, 1982, p. 63.

Table 6.2. Macroeconomic indicators, four European COCOM countries, 1978 and
1982

Country and year	Unemployment (percent)	Trade balance (millions of dollars)	Index of industrial production (1975 = 100)
West Germany			
1978	3.9%	$20,703	112
1982	7.7	20,534	112
France			
1978	5.2	−5,260	112
1982	9.9	−23,177	118
Italy			
1978	7.1	−398	116
1982	9.2	−13,996	125
Great Britain			
1978	5.7	−6,876	112
1982	14.0	−2,707	104

SOURCE: United Nations, *Monthly Bulletin of Statistics,* March 1983.

more to Norway, they were experiencing a 7.25 percent decline in
their imports from Norway.[32]

A further complication was that Norwegian gas was more expensive
than Soviet gas. (In 1963 the oil offered Italy by SONJ, Gulf, and
Shell undercut the Soviet price.) At one point the Reagan administration tried to persuade the Norwegian government to increase production by talking about a "security premium" added to the regular
price.[33] There was some talk of the United States' picking up the
subsidy, but even the Great Communicator could not realistically expect to get congressional support for such a scheme at a time of
unprecedented domestic budget cuts.

A further deficiency in the American economic package was its
failure to compensate for the loss of exports and their favorable effects on employment, balance of payments, and industrial production. "We would have been able to survive very comfortably without
the Soviet natural gas," a West German economics ministry official
stated. "The pipeline contract was dictated by pure misery—jobs were
the main consideration."[34] As Table 6.2 shows, economic conditions

[32]Jonathan Stern, *International Gas Trade in Europe: The Policies of Exporting and Im-
porting Countries* (London: Heinemann, 1984), pp. 4–41; David Fairlamb, "North Sea
Gas: Alternative to the Soviet Deal?" *Dun's Business Month,* November 1982, pp. 69–73;
"Perceptions of Norway," *Geopolitics of Energy* 5 (June 1983).

[33]"Perceptions of Norway," p. 2; *Washington Post,* July 24, 1982, p. A10.

[34]*Wall Street Journal,* November 2, 1982, p. 1. The same article quotes a Dutch official
as calling the Yamal pipeline "a Keynesian relic."

amounted to the worst recession in half a century; it was not a propitious time to expect European governments to bear added economic burdens. Unemployment in West Germany, only 3 percent as recently as 1978, reached a postwar peak of 7.7 percent in December 1982. British unemployment, which hit 14 percent in September 1982, already had ignited the worst urban riots that country had known in this century. The Socialist government of France had pledged to provide jobs, but upwards of 350,000 more Frenchmen were out of work in mid-1982 than at the time of Mitterrand's victory. In addition, three of the four major European countries were running trade deficits. West Germany had a trade surplus, but a smaller one (especially in real terms) than in 1978, and had just experienced in 1981 its first decline in total exports of the postwar era. Similarly, Italy, France, and Britain suffered their first years of falling exports since 1952, 1956, and 1967, respectively. In addition, overall industrial production continued to stagnate. Italy's 2 percent average annual growth since 1978 was the best achieved. Britain's production index actually had fallen.

Many of the firms whose exports were directly at stake were in even worse shape than these aggregate figures suggest. For the major exporters of wide-diameter pipe, such as Mannesmann and Italsider, the Soviet contracts were absolutely critical. The entire European steel industry was plagued by surplus capacity. This problem already was causing excruciating tensions for the European Community, as it forced production cuts averaging 15 percent to establish continent-wide quotas. Mannesmann had been forced by a lack of orders in 1981 to cut its output by 70 percent, at a loss of nearly $52 million. Italsider had lost $1.3 billion in 1981.[35] Consequently, not only did the Soviets' orders for wide-diameter pipe represent a larger absolute volume than those placed in the early 1960s; when seen in this broader context of sectoral surplus capacity and declining profits, their relative value was even greater.

Technically, at least, the contracts for wide-diameter pipe never were at issue in the American embargo. But if the turbine-powered compressors that were at issue were embargoed, the whole project could fall through. And for the engineering firms holding the turbine contracts, the economic situation was no less precarious. John Brown Engineering was located in Clydesbank, Scotland, an area with 20 percent unemployment. The Soviet pipeline contracts alone equaled

---

[35]*New York Times*, August 6, 1981, p. D15; *Economist*, May 15, 1982, p. 80; Ozergene, *Lessons of the Pipeline Negotiations*, p. 18.

the total revenues of the company's gas turbine division the previous year. Creusot-Loire only recently had turned a profit after three consecutive years of losses. Company officials estimated that as many as 50 percent of its personnel in many of its thirty factories would be kept employed by the Soviet contract for several years. AEG-Kanis was a subsidiary of AEG-Telefunken, which had not turned a profit in six years. When in the middle of the embargo controversy it became West Germany's largest corporate bankruptcy of the postwar era, it became a symbol for all of Europe.[36]

Thus, as Secretary of State Haig later would reflect in his memoirs, "in the final analysis Washington had no alternatives to offer."[37] Western Europe's economic interests in the Soviet energy trade were stronger than ever before. Yet the American compensatory offerings were weaker than ever before. This marked a profound and fundamental change in the West-West political economy of East-West trade.

As strong as these economic motivations were, it by no means should be inferred that European interest in the Siberian gas pipeline was purely economic. For the issues also involved a no less fundamental dispute between the United States and Western Europe over foreign policy strategy. It was not that the allies were turning pacifist or neutral, as top Reagan administration officials often implied. After all, at this very moment European governments were resisting intense domestic pressure and going ahead with the deployment of Pershing and cruise missiles. Rather they were dismayed by what they considered extremes and excesses in Reagan's approach. Statements emanating from Washington only exacerbated these concerns about following the American lead. In October 1981 President Reagan remarked that yes, it was possible in his estimation for nuclear weapons to be used in a tactical exchange without escalation to all-out nuclear war. Even Secretary of State Haig, who was looked to as the voice of moderation, at one point indicated that the United States was prepared to use nuclear weapons in Europe. As a "warning shot," of course—which is exactly what his statement proved to be, although to a different audience and with consequences different from those he intended.[38] There could have been no better way to build support for

---

[36]*New York Times*, August 20, 1982, p. D4, and August 27, 1982, p. D1; Ozergene, *Lessons of the Pipeline Negotiations*, p. 10.

[37]Haig, *Caveat*, p. 253.

[38]Miles Kahler, "The United States and Western Europe: The Diplomatic Consequences of Mr. Reagan," in *Eagle Defiant: United States Foreign Policy in the 1980s*, ed. Kenneth A. Oye, Robert J. Lieber, and Donald Rothchild (Boston: Little, Brown, 1983), pp. 273–309.

the peace movements in Western Europe than to continue to substantiate their arguments that the alternative to détente was a confrontation in which Europe would be the battlefield.

The Europeans also disputed the Reagan administration's analysis of the specific foreign policy consequences of the Siberian pipeline. They argued that the Americans were grossly overestimating their vulnerability to a Soviet gas embargo. A number of "safety net" measures were being developed to protect against any such eventuality. These measures included the construction of gas storage facilities as strategic reserves, requirements for interruptible contracts and dual-fired industrial burners (able to switch to oil or coal), flexible national distribution systems, and surge capacity contracts with the Dutch and Norwegians.[39] Consequently, even if they accepted the American worst case scenario of a politically motivated Soviet gas embargo during a moment of crisis or as coercive leverage in a diplomatic dispute, they felt secure in their economic ability to resist Soviet demands.

The Europeans also felt that the Americans overestimated the strategic benefits the Soviets would gain from the trade. The argument about the strategic significance of hard-currency earnings jogged memories of the admonitions of earlier American administrations that every ruble saved through the comparative advantage of trade was destined to be reallocated to the military sector.[40] As we have seen, on such issues as high-technology trade the Europeans were more accepting of the strategic arguments for controlling trade. But on energy trade they contended the same logic did not hold.

It was in this context of a major foreign policy dispute, widely divergent economic interests, and failed American attempts at leverage through the invocation of political prestige and the offering of economic compensation that the intra-alliance conflict was brought to a head by events in Poland. At an emergency meeting of NATO foreign ministers called in early January 1982, the European allies did join with the United States in a communiqué condemning the Soviets

---

[39]Stefanie Lenway and Eric Paul Thompson, "Trading with the Adversary: Managed Interdependence in East–West Energy Trade," paper presented to the Annual Conference of the American Political Science Association, Washington, D.C., August 30–September 2, 1984; Louis L. Ortmayer, "West Germany and the Soviet Gas Pipeline: Political Economy of Détente in the 1980s," paper presented to the Annual Conference of the American Political Science Association, Chicago, September 1–4; 1983; Hans W. Maull, *Natural Gas and Economic Security* (Paris: Atlantic Institute for International Affairs, 1981).

[40]On the resource-freeing rationale see Jeffrey W. Golan, "U.S. Technology Transfer to the Soviet Union and the Protection of National Security," *Law and Policy in International Business* 11 (1979): 1063–66.

for their "active support for the systematic suppression in Poland." They even imposed some selected economic sanctions against both Poland and the Soviet Union. But not against the Siberian gas pipeline. The most the Reagan administration could muster was a joint statement that "Soviet actions towards Poland make it necessary to examine the course of future economic and commercial relations. . . . The Allies will also reflect on longer-term East-West economic relations, particularly energy. . . ."[41] The "particularly energy" clause was a Pyrrhic victory for the United States; for any credibility the threats to examine and reflect may have had was diluted by statements elsewhere that the NATO resolution was nonbinding and that "each of the allies will act in accordance with its own situation and laws." In other words, communiqués might be collective but energy trade controls were going to remain unilateral.

Confirmation that this was in fact the case was not long in coming. Three days before the NATO foreign ministers' meeting, the Reagan administration denied an export license to General Electric for $175 million worth of rotors and other parts for the compressor stations for which it was a subcontractor to AEG-Kanis, Nuovo Pignone, and John Brown Engineering. Two days after the NATO meeting, West Germany's economics minister, Otto Lambsdorff, excluded from a pledge not to undermine American sanctions directly those contracts for which American firms were only subcontractors; that is, the compressor station contracts.[42] Later in January the French signed their import contracts. And in early February the French banking consortium that already had agreed to provide $850 million in low-interest credits announced that it also would finance the $140 million originally scheduled to be made as a down payment. This step put the Mitterrand government, which on arms control and other issues had taken a much harder line than its predecessors and most of its European allies, in a position of demonstrating a firmer commitment to the natural gas trade than even the West Germans. The Deutschebank consortium had rejected a similar Soviet request for 100 percent financing and was reported to be furious that the French bankers had broken a gentleman's agreement to keep the concessionary terms at least within some limits.[43]

---

[41]*New York Times,* January 12, 1982, p. A8.

[42]John Hardt and Kate Tomlinson, "Soviet Gas Pipeline: U.S. Options" (Congressional Research Service, 1982), p. 13.

[43]Ozergene, "Lessons of the Pipeline Negotiations," p. 49; Beverly Crawford and Stefanie Lenway, "Decision Modes and International Regime Change: Western Collaboration on East–West Trade and the Trans-Siberian Pipeline Dispute," *World Politics* 37 (April 1985): 375–402; and especially Lebahn, "Yamal Gas Pipeline," pp. 257–81.

Amidst such defections the Reagan administration was eager to point to Italy's decision to "pause for reflection" and not to conclude its pipeline and gas import contracts as evidence of support. But while the official position articulated by Prime Minister Giovanni Spadolini was that the pause was a reaction to events in Poland, later events and decisions demonstrated that it was more commercially than politically motivated. What Italy really was after was better terms of trade. With overall economic growth rates slowed by the recession and oil prices falling, Italy wanted to buy less gas than the volume originally projected. And with a $2 billion deficit in its bilateral trade with the Soviet Union, it wanted to pressure for increased exports. A firm contract finally was signed in May 1984, despite the fact that nothing had changed in Poland. And while the volume of gas to be imported through the Siberian pipeline was scaled down from 8.5 bcm to 4.5–6.0 bcm annually, even this reduced volume of new imports stood to bring the Soviet share of the Italian gas market to as much as 34 percent by 1990.[44] As this was a larger projected market share than France's or West Germany's, it also indicated little support for the Reagan gas dependence–containment argument. What the Italians did get from their "pause for reflection" was the Soviets' pledge of $2 billion in export contracts. The fact that the materials to be exported were destined for such major Soviet projects as a coal slurry pipeline, additional natural gas pipelines, a petroleum refining plant, and oil drilling equipment further demonstrated how little Italy shared the Reagan administration's objectives.[45]

Between January and June 1982 the United States and Western Europe continued to wrestle with the issue. When the seven heads of state arrived at the Versailles summit, it was with a common hope of settling their conflict over the Soviet pipeline. The difference, of course, was that the Reagan administration wanted it settled with collective sanctions, and the Europeans wanted an end to American pressure. Neither side got its way. The best that could be achieved was a Sunday-morning patched-together statement that the allies agreed "to pursue a prudent and diversified economic approach to the U.S.S.R. and Eastern Europe, consistent with our political and se-

[44]The press reported that Italy would purchase 4.5–5.5 bcm annually through the year 2008; see *Journal of Commerce*, May 19, 1984, p. 11A. The market share estimate is from Stern, *International Gas Trade in Europe*, p. 166.

[45]The same *Journal of Commerce* article reported that the Soviet agreement to increase purchases of Italian exports was part of the natural gas import deal. Earlier (December 16, 1983, p. 11A) the *Journal of Commerce* reported a $42 million contract for five coal-processing plants awarded by the Soviets to the state-run company Italimpank as a sweetener intended to bring Italy closer to finalizing the gas deal. The details of the export contracts are from *East European Markets*, June 11, 1984, p. 13.

curity interests." Even this agreement unraveled rather quickly. Heated transatlantic exchanges were followed by the Reagan administration's decision on June 18 to claim extraterritorial application of its export controls on a retroactive basis. This combination of extraterritoriality and retroactivity encompassed all the major contractors for the Siberian pipeline compressors. All of the companies had American connections as either subsidiaries, technology licensees, or parts users. And existing contracts were not to be exempted. Violations were to be punished by the stiffest penalties authorized by American law—ten-year prison sentences for executives of offending companies, fines of up to $100,000 for each infraction, and denial of all trading privileges with the United States.

The alleged precipitant was the disagreement with President Mitterrand over the export credits issue. And again the stated rationale involved an attempt to force the Soviets to lift martial law in Poland (i.e., the compellence objective). But once again the motives and the strategies were more complex. One Defense Department official close to Richard Perle described the central objective as moving toward a "long-term alliance strategy on East–West economic relations that has the coherence and depth of our military strategy."[46] A State Department document spoke of sending "an important message to our allies . . . about our seriousness of purpose," leaving no doubt as to where the United States stood and intended to lead.[47] More directly to the point was the calculation that a stoppage of European equipment exports could delay the whole pipeline by as much as two years.[48] Such a step could lead to a reduction in the Soviets' hard-currency earnings and an economically weaker Soviet Union (the economic warfare objective); a reduced chance of gas-induced Euroneutrality (the containment objective); and a stronger Western alliance (the deterrence objective)—all key ingredients of Reagan's overall foreign policy strategy.

The only question was whether the immediate outcry was louder in Washington or in Europe. For Secretary of State Haig it was the last straw that led to his resignation. His personal style as well as differences over other issues, notably allegations that he had given Ariel

---

[46]Donald J. Goldstein, "East–West Trade, Technology Transfer, and Western Security," in *Politics of East–West Trade,* ed. Smith, p. 164.

[47]"East–West Economic Issues: Questions and Answers," May 26, 1983, State Department Background Paper for Williamsburg Summit, sec. IV, quest. 1 (mimeo). The conservative magazine *Human Events* quoted a "high Administration source" to the effect that the real importance of the extraterritoriality decision lay in its indication that Reagan "would brave [not only] Soviet wrath but the howls of our allies and Western business interests as well" (July 3, 1982, pp. 16, 19).

[48]*Washington Post,* June 24, 1982, p. 33.

Sharon a green light for the Israeli invasion of Lebanon, already had strained Haig's relations with the president. But the extraterritorial pipeline sanctions, imposed as they were against his recommendation and at an NSC meeting held in his absence, became the issue on which he based his resignation.[49]

Western European leaders were so incensed that they displayed an uncommon unity in their responses. French Foreign Minister Claude Cheysson spoke of a "progressive divorce" because "we no longer speak the same language." West German Chancellor Schmidt angrily pledged, "The pipeline will be built." Even Conservative British Prime Minister Margaret Thatcher argued that "the question is whether one very powerful nation can prevent existing contracts from being fulfilled."[50] The European Community (EC) formally protested this "unacceptable interference" in its sovereign affairs: "Whatever the effects on the Soviet Union, the effects on European Community interests of the United States' measures, applied retroactively and without sufficient consultation, are unquestionably and seriously damaging."[51]

The European firms involved reacted with more trepidation than anger. Their position was ambivalent. They valued the export contracts with the Soviet Union, but they also were concerned about the punitive consequences of the American sanctions, and they were not sure they could fulfill their contracts without the GE rotors. Thus the Reagan administration appeared to have at least potential leverage against the companies themselves.

The problem was in making the administration's measures stick. The British, French, Italian, and West German governments challenged the legality of the American extraterritoriality claim by invoking national laws to order their companies to fulfill their contracts. The showdown began on August 26, the date on which the first compressors were to be shipped. Dresser-France had received its shipment of GE rotors before the initial sanctions, and it was the first firm to have to deal with the cross-pressures. When it went ahead with the shipment, the Reagan administration retaliated with its countersanctions. An executive order was issued prohibiting all American exports to Dresser-France and Creusot-Loire (the general contractor for the whole pipeline project).

Over the next six weeks this same shootout scenario was played out

---

[49]Haig, *Caveat*, pp. 303–16. See also Leslie Gelb's account in *New York Times*, June 22, 1982, p. 18.

[50]*Newsweek*, August 2, 1982, p. 37; *Economist*, June 26, 1982, pp. 52–53; *New York Times*, July 2, 1982, pp. A1, A4.

[51]*New York Times*, August 13, 1982, p. A21.

against Nuovo Pignone (September 4), John Brown Engineering (September 9), and AEG-Kanis (October 5) as their respective pipeline exports went on their way. At the behest of the new secretary of state, George Shultz, and Commerce Secretary Malcolm Baldridge, the countersanctions, which had originally covered all exports, were restricted to equipment, services, and technology specifically related to oil and gas. But the intensity of the dispute did not abate. The *New York Times* editorialized on September 1 against "pipeline machismo," warning that "incompetent American diplomacy has turned the disagreement into a battle over sovereignty that mocks the unity of the Atlantic alliance. The only possible beneficiary of this confrontation is the Soviet Union."[52] Matters were made worse when both sides tried to gain leverage by linking other intra-alliance disputes to the pipeline. Senator Ted Stevens, the second-ranking Republican in the Senate, introduced legislation to cut back American troops stationed in Western Europe as retaliation for noncooperation on the pipeline issue. For their part, the Europeans dragged their feet and undermined Special Trade Representative Bill Brock's efforts to put together a far-reaching agenda for the November GATT ministerial meeting.[53]

The other argument repeatedly returned to was the alleged contradiction posed by continuing American grain sales in the face of the insistence that energy trade should be halted. This long-standing dispute was exacerbated when in the middle of the pipeline imbroglio President Reagan offered the Soviets an additional 23 million metric tons of grain under promises of contract sanctity.[54] The timing of this announcement was dictated by the American electoral calendar. Things did not look good for the midterm congressional elections. All possible stops were being pulled out to limit the damage inflicted on Republican congressional candidates by association with the administration. Europe demanded to know who was taking care of whose special interest groups. To the administration response that grain sales actually weakened the Soviet Union by using up hard currency that otherwise might be spent on industrial equipment and technology, Europeans pointed to a study by Wharton Econometrics which found that grain imports actually saved the Soviets $32 billion by reducing the need for agricultural investment.[55]

By early November there could no longer be any doubt about Eu-

[52]*New York Times*, September 1, 1982, p. A22.
[53]*National Journal*, July 31, 1982, p. 1327.
[54]*Chicago Tribune*, October 16, 1982, p. 3.
[55]*Economist*, October 23, 1982, p. 25; *Washington Post*, October 10, 1982, p. C3.

rope's determination to stay its own course. President Mitterrand and Prime Minister Thatcher held a joint news conference to draw attention to an EC study refuting the American contention that the gas import contracts endangered Europe's security. They called on the Reagan administration to drop its countersanctions immediately. The following week the new West German chancellor, Christian Democrat Helmut Kohl, stressed his intention to affirm the Schmidt government's commitment to the pipeline project.[56] In Italy, 3,600 striking workers marched on the American consulate in Florence.

Finally, on November 13, the United States relented. Credit generally is given to Secretary of State Shultz for persuading the president to lift the countersanctions against European companies. The official position taken was that "substantial agreement on a plan of action" had been achieved. Therefore, the president continued, "there is no further need for these sanctions and I am lifting them today." The alleged plan of action, however, was not particularly substantial. The Europeans agreed only to hold off on *new* contracts for Soviet gas pending a study by the International Energy Agency (IEA) of the vulnerability question. They also agreed to participate in three other studies under the auspices of OECD (export credits), COCOM (high-technology controls), and NATO (overall trade). They did not agree to be bound in any way by the findings and recommendations of any of these studies. The other parts of the agreement were nothing new—to "strengthen existing controls" of militarily relevant high technology and improve "procedures for monitoring financial relations with the Soviet Union and work to harmonize our export credit policies." Nor did they have anything to do with energy trade.

Events and actions since the November 13 "compromise" have shown quite clearly that the United States did far more conceding than leveraging.[57] One indication of the extent of European non-collaboration is seen in Table 6.3 showing major energy trade contracts totaling more than $1.5 billion signed just in the ensuing five months. It was as if the floodgates had been opened. Perhaps the Soviets were rewarding the Europeans for their ulterior motives. Whatever the case, it was difficult to maintain that there was a collective Western policy in light of such a boom in exports of energy-related equipment.

---

[56]Chancellor Kohl: "One should not demand of the other what one would not like to have demanded of oneself" (*New York Times*, October 5, 1982, p. A1).

[57]The same assessment is reached in Crawford and Lenway, "Decision Modes and International Regime Change." The November 13 agreement, they write, "revealed the utter failure of the U.S. compliance strategy" (p. 397).

Table 6.3. Value of major contracts for exports of energy equipment and technology by European COCOM firms to the USSR, November 1982–March 1983 (millions of dollars)

Country and firm	Equipment	Estimated value
West Germany		
Salzgitter AG, Hoesch-Werke	Wide-diameter pipe	$240.0
Mannesmann Anlangebau	Pipe and equipment for Astrakhan gas fields	196.0
Kloeckner	Wide-diameter pipe	113.0
AEG-Kanis, MAN-GHH	Gas turbine components	96.0
France		
Technip, Creusot-Loire	Sulfur-extraction plant and gas treatment equipment for Astrakhan gas fields	662.0
Italy		
Finsider	Steel pipe tubing	200.0
All firms		$1,507.0

SOURCES: *Wall Street Journal,* December 8, 1982, p. 34; March 15, 1983, p. 3; *New York Times,* December 23, 1982, p. D3; *Oil and Gas Journal,* March 7, 1983, p. 45; *Financial Times,* December 29, 1982, p. 3; March 15, 1983, p. 6; *Journal of Commerce,* December 6, 1982, p. 5A; December 23, 1982, p. 9A.

A further manifestation was the continuing conflict within CO-COM. In February 1983, despite the seeming lessons of June–November 1982, the United States proposed that COCOM adopt about two dozen restrictions on oil and gas equipment and technology (including the turbines for gas pipeline compressor stations).[58] The Europeans, according to *The Times of London,* responded with "an unusually strong protest expressing their 'deep abiding concern' over the new American proposal."[59] Yet a month later, in a speech before the U.S.–German Industrialists' Group, Under Secretary of State Allen Wallis reiterated that "we tend to view Western sales to the Soviets of energy-related equipment—equipment for the most part they cannot produce for themselves—as seriously detrimental to Western security."[60]

The trade controls dispute spilled over into preparations for the May 1983 Williamsburg summit. Press reports before the summit and later accounts by key participants indicated that the Reagan administration's initial strategy was to press for multilateralization of all

[58]Root, "Trade Controls That Work," p. 67.
[59]*Times of London,* May 16, 1983, p. 8; see also reports in *Financial Times,* March 18, 1983, p. 3, and *New York Times,* March 7, 1984, pp. D1, D17.
[60]State Department, "Economics and Security," p. 2.

198

controls on the export of oil and gas equipment and technology and for a moratorium on future energy projects. At one point Assistant Commerce Secretary Brady went so far as to threaten that the United States would "reconsider military commitments to Western Europe" if cooperation on trade controls were not forthcoming.[61] But when stiff opposition was encountered from the allies, Brady's rather blunt and undiplomatic tactics were disavowed. Then the whole East–West trade issue was relegated to a back burner in order to project an appearance of collaboration. Yet, far from living up to the administration's goal of a strategy "that has the coherence and depth of our military strategy," the summit pronouncement that "East–West economic relations should be compatible with our security interests" was empty.[62] It could be interpreted exactly as each signee desired. It had no teeth, no specific policy content; therefore, while it projected an image of unity, it brought the allies no closer to true collaboration on trade controls.

Assessments of the gas import question are somewhat more complicated, but ultimately also corroborative. The volume of imports finally agreed to was substantially less than the amount originally talked about. Such countries as Belgium and the Netherlands, which expressed interest in Soviet gas back in 1980–81, decided against it. Italy signed on for only about 50 to 60 percent of the anticipated amount, and reportedly at a lower price. Both France and West Germany got the Soviets to agree to renegotiate at reduced levels both the volume and the price of their gas.[63] As a result, commitments for gas from the new Siberian pipeline totaled in the range of 25–30 bcm, 10–15 bcm less than the original estimates. When the reduced prices

[61]*New York Times*, May 10, 1983, p. D5. This point also was stressed in the interviews I conducted both in Washington and in Europe. Brady is quoted in *New York Times*, April 24, 1983, p. 1.

[62]State Department, "Collective Approach to East–West Economic Relations," p. 2.

[63]The actual gas prices negotiated in these deals never have been made public. What is known is that the pricing mechanism is a complex formula that includes the following factors: a minimum or "floor" price, a "basket" of reference fuels, a "take or pay" clause establishing minimum volumes, and a maximum or "ceiling" price. For further elaboration see Stern, *International Gas Trade in Europe*, pp. 151–52; Ozergene, *Lessons of the Pipeline Negotiations*, pp. 22–25; and Ed A. Hewett, *Energy, Economics, and Foreign Policy in the Soviet Union* (Washington, D.C.: Brookings Institution, 1984), p. 190. The *Wall Street Journal* (August 31, 1982, p. 29) reported the original contract prices as $4.60–4.90 per thousand cubic feet for West Germany, $4.75 for France, and $4.00 or less for Italy. The Gaz de France volume renegotiation was reported in *Journal of Commerce*, May 4, 1984, p. 11A, and *Financial Times*, May 4, 1984, p. 5. The Ruhrgas renegotiation was reported in *East European Markets*, August 20, 1984, p. 14. I also have relied on information provided by officials of Gaz de France during an interview on July 16, 1985, and on internal reports provided by Ruhrgas officials.

were taken into account as well, estimated additional Soviet hard-currency earnings dropped from $10 billion to about $5 billion per year.

The key question that needs to be answered is whether this difference between planned and actual imports of Soviet gas can be attributed to American leverage or whether it had other principal causes. As was to be expected, the Reagan administration preferred to take the credit for American leverage. Yet extensive interviews with more than seventy-five European government officials, company executives, officials of international agencies, and other researchers revealed little agreement with this interpretation outside the Reagan administration.[64] Both Ruhrgas and Gaz de France already had been ordered by their respective governments to increase strategic reserve storage capacity, negotiate assurances of surge capacity from Gasunie (Netherlands), require interruptible contracts with major industrial and utility consumers, and take other measures intended to reduce potential vulnerability. The American pressure may have reinforced the need for such measures, but it cannot take credit for initiating them. By transforming the issue into a nationalistic cause célèbre, the American pressure actually may have made it more difficult to take the vulnerability problem seriously.

The far more important influence on Western Europe's decision to scale back its imports of Soviet gas was the economic marketplace. As a blurb for a *Forbes* article said, "American diplomacy couldn't cut Russian export earnings from natural gas, but it looks like the market can."[65] One key market change was the decrease in world oil prices, which made gas relatively more expensive than original calculations had indicated. Few economists anywhere predicted that oil prices would fall from $40 a barrel in 1980 to $27 in 1983. Most predicted a slow if steady increase in oil prices. Nor did economists or government officials foresee the severity or duration of the recession of the early 1980s. But as overall national economic growth rates slowed, so did energy consumption. The net effect of both of these market changes was that between 1979 and 1982, Western European gas consumption declined 8 percent in absolute terms. Demand increased somewhat in 1983, but total gas consumption was projected to increase no more than 2 percent annually through 1987.

Table 6.4 shows that the immediate decrease in gas imports in the

[64]Interviews conducted in Washington, D.C., November 7–11, 1983, and March 5–9, 1985; and in Great Britain, West Germany, France, and Belgium, June 17–July 19, 1985.
[65]*Forbes*, April 11, 1983, p. 170.

Table 6.4. Volume of natural gas imported from all sources by three European COCOM countries, 1980 and 1982 (billions of cubic meters)

Country and year	Soviet Union	Netherlands	Norway	Algeria	Other	All sources	Soviet gas as percent of total gas imported[a]
West Germany							
1980	10.8	22.6	9.6	—	0.2	43.2	24.9%
1982	10.6	17.6	7.0	—	—	35.2	30.1
France							
1980	5.1	11.2	2.5	1.8[b]	1.3	21.9	23.3
1982	5.2	5.7	2.3	6.3[b]	0.1	19.6	26.5
Italy							
1980	8.6	8.0	—	—	2.0	18.6	46.2
1982	9.5	5.3	—	—	—	14.8	64.2

[a]These relative figures should not be confused with those in Table 6.1. Soviet gas is shown here as a percentage of total gas *imports*, there as a percentage of total gas *supply*, including domestic production.

[b]Liquefied natural gas.

SOURCES: U.S. Department of Energy, Energy Information Administration, *1981 International Energy Annual* (Washington, D.C., 1982), p. 70, and *1983 International Energy Annual* (Washington, D.C., 1984), p. 72.

early 1980s was distributed among *all* major sources, not just the Soviet Union. West Germany's imports of Soviet gas declined less than its imports of gas from other sources; consequently, Soviet gas grew from 24.9 percent to 30.1 percent of total gas imports. French and Italian imports of Soviet gas increased while imports from most other sources declined. By 1982 the Soviet share of their gas import markets had increased from 23.3 to 26.5 percent and from 46.2 to 64.2 percent, respectively.

Price and volume were being renegotiated with all suppliers, not with the Soviet Union alone. And contrary to the warnings of the Reagan administration and the editorial page of the *Wall Street Journal*,[66] the Soviets proved quite flexible in the renegotiations with France and West Germany and in revising the terms of the preliminary agreement with Italy. They obviously had tried to get the best

[66]The Siberian pipeline and its associated gas contracts were a bête noire for the editors of the *Wall Street Journal*. Highly critical editorials and columns appeared with great regularity; see, for example, December 13, 1983, p. 26; December 16, 1983, p. 30; January 12, 1984, p. 24; and May 29, 1984, p. 26. See also the response to the December 13 article by two Ruhrgas executives in a letter to the editor, January 12, 1984, p. 25.

deal possible and still hoped to do so. But as Jonathan Stern aptly puts it,

> irrespective of the fine print in the contract, the spirit of the agreement . . . appears to be that neither side shall be unduly penalized by applying contract terms which are grossly out of line with the current competitive position of the fuel in the market. The partners, as is the case of Ruhrgas for example, have usually been trading for more than a decade and are intending to be in a similar relationship for at least another three decades. It is in neither partner's interest to hold the other to unrealistic conditions which might gravely weaken its trading position.[67]

These points—that the drop in current and planned European imports of Soviet gas had more to do with economics than with politics and that it did not reflect a turning away from Soviet gas in particular—provide a context for interpreting the ambiguities of the IEA communiqué "Energy Requirements and Security," issued in May 1983.[68] This communiqué was the result of the study agreed to in November 1982 when American countersanctions were lifted. The Reagan administration had hoped to use this process to legitimize and institutionalize strict limits on imports of Soviet gas. Its goal was to set a *binding* maximum ceiling at 30 percent of total gas consumption.[69] But the Europeans refused to go along. They did acknowledge "the potential risks associated with high levels of dependence on single supplier countries." They agreed "to ensure that no one producer is in a position to exercise monopoly control." They stressed "diversification of sources of energy imports." They gave priority to "indigenous gas resources" (i.e., intra-OECD). And they pledged to develop "appropriate cost-effective measures suited to each country's situation to strengthen their ability to deal with supply disruption."

But nowhere was Soviet gas singled out as more threatening than that of other non-OECD suppliers. The Europeans offered no binding policy strictures, only policy guidelines. Then again, they never had disagreed about the principles they now expressed. The whole point of increasing Soviet gas imports in the first place had been to avoid the risks of high levels of dependence on single supplier countries, to ensure that no one producer would gain monopoly control, to

[67]Stern, *International Gas Trade in Europe*, p. 151; a similar position is taken by Hewett, *Energy, Economics, and Foreign Policy*, p. 190.

[68]International Energy Agency, "Meeting of Governing Board at Ministerial Level," Communiqué and Annex 1, May 8, 1983 (mimeo).

[69]Based on a series of interviews (see n. 64). See also the reports in *Christian Science Monitor*, May 9, 1983, p. 5, and *Wall Street Journal*, May 9, 1983, p. 37.

diversify. So agreement on these principles was no problem. To agree to an American-determined strict ceiling was an entirely different matter. In fact, according to some forecasts, France, West Germany, and Italy all might be at or over the 30 percent ceiling by 1990. For Italy the predictions have run as high as 40 percent.[70]

In sum, the United States made very little headway in getting its allies to be allies rather than alternative trade partners for the Soviet Union.

ROUGH SLEDDING AT HOME

Perhaps even more surprising to the Reagan administration than the imbroglio with the European allies was the domestic opposition aroused by the Siberian pipeline sanctions. Ronald Reagan and his hawkish foreign policy team had come to office with the clear expectation that a steadier, more inspirational hand at the helm would shake the American people out of the malaise that had set in as a result of the Vietnam complex and the Carter presidency. With effective leadership they would rally round the flag and meet the Soviet threat head on wherever, whenever, and however it reared its ugly head. Building up the American nuclear arsenal, containing communism in Central America, waging economic warfare so as to protest martial law in Poland and also squeeze the Soviet economy at a time of alleged maximum weakness—the guiding presumption was that as in the pre-1970s past, these and other Cold War–style policies had a basic ideological appeal that overrode more specific or substantive criticisms and thus could be counted on to minimize domestic constraints.

Quite to the contrary, however, the American public never embraced the pipeline sanctions. In fact, whereas even Jimmy Carter's grain embargo initially received 76 percent support in the Gallup poll, Reagan's pipeline sanctions garnered only a 48 percent approval rating.[71] In another poll only 47 percent responded that they favored anti-Soviet trade controls as a general foreign policy approach. To the question "Do you favor undertaking joint efforts with the Soviet Union to solve energy problems?" 64 percent responded affirma-

[70]Stern, *International Gas Trade in Europe*, p. 166. See also Jonathan B. Stein, "Prospects for Soviet Trade; Focus on Western Europe," *Geopolitics of Energy*, May 1984, p. 4.

[71]*Gallup Opinion Index*, Report no. 174 (January 1980), p. 8, and Report no. 203 (August 1982), p. 13.

tively.[72] The sanctions were especially unpopular among those groups that had to bear their major economic costs. They mounted a lobbying campaign against the sanctions that was reminiscent of the farmers' opposition to the 1980 grain embargo—and quite unlike the Friendship oil pipeline case, in which the key interest groups actively abetted the oil trade sanctions.

One of the companies hardest hit by the Siberian pipeline sanctions was Caterpillar Tractor. Caterpillar had been one of the first American corporations to enter the Soviet market in the early 1970s. In addition to agricultural equipment, one of its major exports was machinery for construction of Soviet pipelines. As of 1978, Caterpillar had outstripped its principal international competitor, Komatsu of Japan, in sales to the Soviet Union: 1,943 Caterpillar pipelayers to Komatsu's 341. Caterpillar's market position first began to slip after the 1978 Shcharansky sanctions (with which the Japanese were no more cooperative than the Europeans). The 1980 Afghanistan sanctions were a further hindrance. By 1981 the market shares had been almost exactly reversed: 1,998 pipelayers sold by Komatsu since 1978, 336 by Caterpillar.[73]

The Siberian pipeline presented an opportunity for Caterpillar to recover its position. In early 1981 it won contracts for $300 million in pipelayer equipment and $100 million in spare parts. It lacked only export licenses from the Reagan administration. As a firm with headquarters in Illinois, it was able to enlist the aid of Republican Senator Charles Percy, who was chairman of the Senate Foreign Relations Committee, and Republican Congressman Bob Michel, who was the House minority leader. Percy and Michel appealed directly to the president. Even with their influence the task was not easy, but on December 9, 1981, Caterpillar was granted an export license. Only four days later, however, martial law was declared in Poland. And when President Reagan announced the suspension of all licenses to export energy-related equipment and technology (as well as all other

[72]These percentages are for the sample drawn from the general public. Of the "leadership" sample, 78% responded affirmatively to the energy question. See John E. Rielly, ed., *American Public Opinion and U.S. Foreign Policy, 1983* (Chicago: Chicago Council on Foreign Relations, 1983), p. 15.

[73]Testimony of Robert H. Coyle, sales manager of Caterpillar Tractor Co., in U.S. Congress, House, Foreign Affairs Committee, Subcommittees on Europe and the Middle East and International Economic Policy and Trade, *Export Controls on Oil and Gas Equipment: Hearings*, 97th Cong., 1st and 2d sess., November 1981–August 1982, p. 83. Data are also based on interviews with other Caterpillar executives, November 8, 1983, and personal communications.

high technology), no exception was made for Caterpillar, not even with the Percy-Michel lobbying team working on its behalf.

In earlier times Caterpillar perhaps could have written off $400 million in lost export sales. It could not do so in 1981–82, in the midst of the most severe recession since the Great Depression. With the pipeline sanctions added to its woes, Caterpillar racked up a company record loss of $334 million in the first three quarters of 1983.[74] Other companies were equally vulnerable. Fiat Allis, another Illinois company that lost $500 million in sales to trade sanctions, already had seen employment at its Springfield plant plummet from 4,400 in mid-1979 to 2,300 in 1981.[75] The head of the Illinois Department of Commerce, a Republican, identified the pipeline sanctions as the principal cause of the state's economic problems.[76] This may have been an exaggeration, but it reflected the dominant perceptions and attitudes. As one company executive told a congressional committee, in the aggregate "the lost profits and jobs resulting from the sanctions may not seem very significant. . . . But if they are not, someone should tell that to the 15,000 Armco employees who have been laid off in the last 12 months due to the current recession."[77]

Another big economic loser was General Electric, whose $170 million in contracts for turbine rotor blades was the principal target of the sanctions. Because the export controls also prohibited GE from fulfilling non-Soviet contracts (e.g., from shipping rotors to Nuovo Pignone for compressors ordered by Abu Dhabi), one GE executive stressed that a true estimate of economic costs had to include such "ancillary consequences." Since 90 percent of GE's business in energy-related equipment and technology was international and only 10 percent domestic—a sharp reversal of the pattern of even ten years earlier, when domestic sales were dominant—these additional costs were far from negligible. "You've got to turn a lot of somersaults these days," remarked the GE executive, "just to get *any* sales."[78]

Another economically interested group consisted of some of the major oil multinationals. They faced the sanctions now not as the Soviets' competitors, as in 1962–63, but as their commercial partners.

[74]*Wall Street Journal*, October 19, 1983, p. 16.
[75]Testimony of Harry Wells, president, United Auto Workers Local no. 1027, in House Foreign Affairs Committee, *Export Controls on Oil and Gas Equipment*, p. 83.
[76]*Wall Street Journal*, November 3, 1982, p. 31.
[77]Testimony of Kempton B. Jenkins, vice-president of Armco, in U.S. Congress, Senate, Committee on Foreign Relations, *On the Effectiveness of U.S. Economic Pressures on Soviet Policy: Hearings*, 97th Cong., 2d sess., August 12, 1982, p. 115.
[78]Interview, November 7, 1983, Washington, D.C.

Over a quarter of Ruhrgas' stock was owned by major American oil companies: Exxon held 15.0 percent, Mobil 7.4 percent, and Texaco 3.5 percent.[79] They thus stood to profit from expanded trade. While their stake was not so great as to make them as active on this issue as on others, the fact that they were not leading the opposition as in 1962–63 was significant in itself.

The problem of fallout beyond the contracts specifically related to the Soviet pipeline prompted the peak associations broadly representative of business interests, the U.S. Chamber of Commerce and the National Association of Manufacturers (NAM), to join the opposition. In February 1982 Richard Lesher, president of the U.S. Chamber of Commerce, wrote Reagan that the sanctions were "not in the best interests of the country." Exporters stood to lose an estimated $1.2 billion directly, plus the inestimable costs that would ensue from "aggravating further our already poor international reputation for commercial reliability." By August Alexander Trowbridge, president of the NAM and a former secretary of commerce during the Johnson administration, used much stronger language, characterizing the administration's policy as "confusing, contradictory and counterproductive."[80]

A certain amount of pressure also came from Capitol Hill. The Office of Technology Assessment (OTA) released its extensive study, *Technology and Soviet Energy Availability*, in December 1981. This was a thoroughly documented analysis of the Soviets' energy capabilities and the role played in them by Western trade. The report's release made for the kind of media event that focuses attention on Congress. Congressmen and senators who had been involved in commissioning the study issued press releases and made the rounds of the more serious television talk shows. Various subcommittees held hearings at which OTA staff elaborated on the study's findings. The OTA study, which could not be faulted on its thoroughness and unbiased analysis, came down against the efficacy of energy trade sanctions. When the issue heated up in the summer of 1982, a special update was issued to reiterate this position even more strongly.

The summer and fall of 1982 also saw numerous hearings called by congressional committees to provide opportunities for affected interest groups, prominent critics, and Western European governments to present their arguments against the sanctions. Administration offi-

---

[79]*Journal of Commerce*, October 2, 1981, p. 23D.
[80]Lesher to Reagan, February 5, 1982, in House Foreign Affairs Committee, *Export Controls on Oil and Gas Equipment*, pp. 224–25; Trowbridge to Reagan, August 11, 1982, interview with NAM official, August 1982.

cials also were called to testify, for the most part under barrages of hostile questioning. At one point the House of Representatives came very close to repealing the sanctions. A bill was approved by the House Foreign Affairs Committee 22 to 12, with 7 of the 17 Republicans on the committee voting against their president. The bill lost on the floor, but by such a close vote (206 to 203) that it still sent a message to the other end of Pennsylvania Avenue.

Among the Republicans who voted to repeal the sanctions was Minority Leader Michel. His dilemma illustrated how much the domestic political economy of East-West energy trade had changed. Michel himself was a conservative. As minority leader he had worked hard in support of most if not all other issues on the president's legislative agenda. But the pipeline sanctions were costing one of the major constituents in his congressional district $500 million. One might have thought that having been reelected by healthy majorities twelve consecutive times, Michel was in a position to stay the course with his president. Not so in 1982. Local unions and Michel's Democratic opponent made the label "Reagan-Michel sanctions" stick and made the sanctions the symbol of the more general discontent stirred by the Republican recession. Even though Michel had voted for the bill to repeal the sanctions, he could not shed the label or the symbol. As a result, he barely squeaked through in the November 1982 elections, with only a 51 percent majority. This was by far his smallest margin ever—and its message was not lost on incumbents whose positions were less strong. Grain was not the only issue on which embargoes could be politically life-threatening.

When the Export Administration Act came up for renewal in 1983 and the Reagan administration proposed a number of more restrictive changes, business lobbyists and congressional opponents worked together to block many of these measures. A bill embodying many of the administration's proposals passed the Senate under the stewardship of conservative Senator Jake Garn (R-Utah). But with 52 of 157 Republicans crossing over, the House passed a more liberal measure, which set up the 98th Congress's longest running and least successful conference committee.[81] The issue had to be reintroduced in 1985, at which time a compromise measure finally was passed by

---

[81]Key differences between the original House and Senate bills concerned the licensing requirement for exports to COCOM countries (House eliminate, Senate expand); the role of the Defense Department in export control policy (House limit, Senate expand); the use of embargoes for foreign policy purposes (House limit, Senate maintain); extraterritoriality (House limit, Senate maintain); and the lead agency for enforcement (House keep Commerce, Senate shift to the more zealous Customs Service).

both House and Senate. While the Export Administration Act of 1985 did not give business everything it wanted, it did impose new constraints on executive authority which would make it more difficult for a president to wield the embargo stick in the future.[82]

Finally, and perhaps most significant, the Siberian pipeline sanctions had opened up major splits within the Reagan administration. The most gaping split came over the June 18 decision to extend the sanctions to Western Europe. The president took this action on the advice of National Security Adviser William Clark and Secretary of Defense Caspar Weinberger and over the vehement objections of Secretary of State Alexander Haig and the somewhat less vehement ones of Commerce Secretary Malcolm Baldridge. Throughout the previous six months of deliberations Haig had stressed the damage that such an action could cause to intra-alliance relations. The decision to go ahead anyway was taken at an NSC meeting that, according to Haig, Clark had intentionally scheduled on a date when Haig was out of town and with "little discussion of the issue, and virtually no participation by the President." Other issues had contributed to Haig's problems, in particular the Falklands War and the Israeli invasion of Lebanon. The Siberian pipeline sanctions were the final straw. Within a week he had resigned.[83]

George Shultz, who was appointed the new secretary of state, arrived with his own antisanctions reputation. In 1979 he had excoriated the "light-switch diplomacy" of the Carter administration. It was foolhardy, Shultz then wrote, to think "that individual trades can be turned on and off like a light switch to induce changes in the domestic and foreign policies of a host government. . . . It is hard to see that these manipulations have had any impact on the nature and operation of Soviet society."[84] One of Shultz's first moves was to circulate a study conducted by the State Department's Bureau of Intelligence and Research, questioning the potential efficacy of anti-Soviet sanctions generally. Even if the European allies cooperated and the sanctions were expanded to cover all manufactured goods, the State Department study concluded, Soviet economic growth would be slowed

---

[82]*Congressional Quarterly Weekly Report,* June 29, 1985, pp. 1302–3.

[83]Haig, *Caveat,* pp. 312, 314–16. The public story was that Haig had resigned. The president made this statement, and Haig reiterated it through a letter of resignation critical of the administration's foreign policy. But Haig also states in his memoirs that a few hours earlier the president actually had fired him (or, more diplomatically, handed him a letter accepting "a letter of resignation that I had not submitted").

[84]*Business Week,* May 28, 1979, pp. 24–26.

by only 0.2 percent annually, a total of $4.5 billion through 1983. Yet the costs incurred by the embargoes were estimated at $30 billion.[85]

The pro-sanctions forces within the administration sought to suppress the State Department study. They stressed instead a recent Census Bureau study that found "greater Soviet vulnerability to economic sanctions than has been understood up to now," and a Defense Intelligence Agency study that contended that "the Soviet leadership has acknowledged and is increasingly concerned that the current and growing heavy reliance on foreign inputs of technology has created a strong dependence on the West." In a speech at an international symposium in England, Assistant Commerce Secretary Brady went even further, asserting that "there is little question that if the West exercises its collective will to enforce these sanctions, the entire Soviet bloc will find itself in very difficult straits throughout the rest of the decade."[86]

A few months later, on November 13, the president decided to change course and lift the extraterritorial sanctions against Western Europe. Shultz, Commerce Secretary Baldridge, and Special Trade Representative Brock are generally credited with this victory. But in bureaucratic politics, a battle won seldom means the end of the war. The issue remained somewhat ambiguous: while the extraterritorial sanctions were rescinded, the licensing requirements for export of American energy-related equipment were left in place. Thus exports could still be embargoed case by case. This situation was causing problems for, among others, Caterpillar. When the Soviets decided to purchase 500 more pipelayers, they did not even invite Caterpillar to bid.[87] As long as the licensing requirement was still on the books, they argued, they could not be assured that Caterpillar would be a reliable supplier. Finally, six months later, the administration agreed to eliminate all licensing requirements for pipelayers. Even then, though, administration officials went to great lengths to stress that the liberalization of regulations governing pipelayers did not signify a more general relaxation of controls on exports of energy-related equipment.[88]

A few weeks later an interagency advisory group headed by Assistant Commerce Secretary Brady recommended denial of a license sought by a subsidiary of the Hughes Tool Company to export $40

---

[85]The study was leaked to the *Washington Post* and reported on the front page on July 24, 1982, p. A1.

[86]Ibid.

[87]*Congressional Quarterly Weekly Report*, March 26, 1983, p. 614.

[88]*Times of London*, August 21, 1983, p. 10.

million in submersible pumps for offshore oil development. The
Brady group also recommended that strict controls be enforced over
seventeen other products intended for use in oil and gas exploration.
This maneuver, coming only two weeks after the Soviets shot down
Korean Airlines flight 007, was shrewdly timed. National Security
Adviser Clark added his endorsement, as did Defense Secretary
Weinberger. Newspaper accounts held Secretary of State Shultz to be
"furious." William Root, director of the State Department's Office of
East-West Trade since 1965, tendered his resignation over the incident.[89] A combination of this counterpressure and a shift toward a
more moderate stance in general as the 1984 presidential campaign
approached (and, apparently, the wish to force Brady's resignation)
caused President Reagan to overrule the Brady panel's recommendations. The Hughes Tool Company was granted the license for the
submersible pumps. The seventeen types of oil and gas exploration
equipment still were kept under case-by-case licensing requirements,
but the threat of another embargo effort had been headed off.[90]

This disarray within the administration was also apparent in regard
to the more general issue of who should have what role in the formulation and implementation of export control policy. Commerce
and Defense vied openly, Commerce to maintain its dominance and
Defense to gain a greater role. The president appeared at times to
favor Defense, issuing an executive order in March 1984 granting it
new authority to review licenses for exports to fifteen noncommunist
countries suspected of being entrepôts for reexport to the Soviet
bloc.[91] But a few months later, when Defense Secretary Weinberger
urged Senator Garn to include in this legislation a provision to give
the Defense Department authority over exports to COCOM countries, the White House sent Garn a letter that the *Washington Post*
characterized as "a gentle rebuke" to Weinberger.[92] Commerce also
got its way on procedural reforms that have had the effect of making
the export control review process less burdensome and of putting

[89]*New York Times*, September 20, 1983, p. D1; *Wall Street Journal*, September 21,
1983, p. 3; Root, "Trade Controls That Work."
[90]*New York Times*, December 4, 1983, p. 1; *Journal of Commerce*, March 9, 1984, p.
11A.
[91]*New York Times*, March 21, 1984, pp. D1, D23. Previously Defense had authority
only to review licenses for exports to communist countries. Also of note was an internal
change within the Defense Department shifting export control authority from the
under secretary for research and engineering to the office of the assistant secretary for
defense policy, which was headed by Richard Perle.
[92]"Pentagon Loses Round in Export Controls Fight," *Washington Post*, July 21, 1984,
pp. D1, D9.

greater emphasis on foreign availability as a basis for eliminating unilateral American controls.[93]

As Reagan's second term began, the secretary of commerce headed the first official trade delegation to Moscow since 1978. While these meetings resulted in no major breakthroughs, the very fact that they occurred contrasted markedly with the economic warfare strategy with which the first Reagan administration had begun—and to which some top administration officials, perhaps even the president himself, still subscribed. Future policy was unclear, but there could be little doubt that the domestic politics of export controls had become more conflictual than ever before.

SUMMARY: CONSTRAINTS ON ECONOMIC COERCION

One of the ironies of the whole Siberian pipeline experience was that the Reagan administration's diagnosis of the Soviets' potential vulnerability to energy trade sanctions was basically accurate (albeit overstated), but its assessment of America's economic coercive power was wholly inaccurate. Any attempt by the Soviets to rely on their own industry for the gas turbines for the pipeline compressor stations would have been, in Ed Hewett's view, "unrealistic," and would have made it "virtually certain" that they would fall short of output targets.[94] Soviet technological capabilities at the time were limited to 6- to 10-megawatt turbines. A minimum of eight of these less powerful turbines would be required to substitute for the three 25-megawatt imported turbines to be installed in each compressor station. Even then construction costs would rise, construction would be delayed, and performance would probably be inferior. It also was questionable whether the necessary quantity would be available. The Eleventh Five-Year Plan (1981–85) had called for construction of a total of 40,000 kilometers of new pipeline. This figure represented an increase of almost one-third over the entire existing gas pipeline system. Yet even under the less ambitious Ninth (1971–75) and Tenth (1976–80) five-year plans, the highest rate of fulfillment for turbine production was 57.6 percent.[95]

[93]*Wall Street Journal*, September 11, 1984, p. 20, and September 13, 1984, p. 30; *New York Times*, March 15, 1985, pp. D1, D8.

[94]Hewett, *Energy, Economics, and Foreign Policy*, p. 81.

[95]Campbell, *Soviet Energy Technologies*, pp. 215–18. In fact, turbine production was down under the Eleventh Five-Year Plan. In 1980 production was 20.3 million kilowatts, while for 1981–83 the annual average was 16.1 million kilowatts (Economist

By early 1984 the Soviets were resorting to a propaganda campaign to cover up the problems they were encountering on the pipeline. On January 2 TASS announced that the new pipeline "has started functioning" and that the first shipments of newly contracted gas had arrived in France. A "crushing strike" had been achieved, TASS asserted, against the "notorious policy of sanctions which became an inseparable element of the U.S. aggressive imperialist policy."[96] Quite to the contrary, however, constuction of the new Siberian pipeline actually was running behind schedule. A fire had destroyed the main header compressor station, and only four of the forty-one other stations had been installed. Press, diplomatic, and intelligence reports confirmed that new gas was flowing to France, but found that it was coming through the preexisting pipeline system.[97] Construction problems were reported to have led to the firing of the director of development of the Urengoi field and to the fining or disciplining of some twenty-eight associate directors, deputy directors, and executives.[98]

This was hardly the stuff of crushing strikes. One of the lessons was that despite all their disclaimers and disinformation, the Soviets still relied heavily on Western energy equipment and technology. When the sanctions were imposed, they boasted that they would turn out 25-megawatt turbines "like blinis."[99] But even with the additional resources allocated and investments made, Soviet industry was unable to produce the turbines needed for the pipeline.[100]

In terms of actual impact, then, a degree of success could be claimed for the economic defense objective of limiting Soviet capabilities. The delays caused in the construction of the pipeline did carry some economic costs. These costs, however, fell well short of the Reagan administration's economic warfare objectives. As for the array of political instrumental objectives, here even less success could be claimed. The containment objective involved a reduction of Western

Intelligence Unit, *Quarterly Economic Report: USSR,* 1984 Annual Supplement, p. 11).
See also Robert Campbell's more recent article, "Technology Transfer in the Soviet Energy Sector," in *Trade, Technology and Soviet–American Relations,* ed. Bruce Parrott (Bloomington: Indiana University Press, 1985), pp. 141–68.

[96]*Washington Post,* national weekly ed., January 23, 1984, p. 15; *Wall Street Journal,* January 19, 1984, p. 32.

[97]The estimate of four out of forty-one is from *Washington Post,* national weekly ed., January 23, 1984, pp. 15–16. An Associated Press report put it at only two compressor stations (*Sacramento Bee,* January 12, 1984, p. AA8). See also *New York Times,* January 5, 1984, p. D1, and Campbell, "Technology Transfer," pp. 148–54.

[98]*Geopolitics of Energy,* May 1984, p. 5.

[99]*New York Times,* July 20, 1982, p. D1.

[100]Ed A. Hewett, "The Pipeline Connection: Issues for the Alliance," *Brookings Review* 1 (Fall 1982): 19.

European imports of Soviet gas. Gas imports were somewhat curtailed, but the reasons had more to do with changes in the marketplace than with American leverage. Yet even the lower levels were not considered low enough by the Reagan administration. It pushed for but did not get firm agreement on a 30 percent ceiling. Indeed, the levels of Soviet gas imported by all three major Western European allies were forecast to reach or surpass 30 percent.

Nor did American efforts to compel the Soviets to change their policy toward Poland have any significant impact. Time and again the compellence objective had been stressed. The initial proclamation of sanctions was cast as an effort "to speak for the people of Poland." The extraterritorial extension was justified as necessary "to advance reconciliation in Poland." And each time countersanctions were slapped on European firms, the official press release stressed that "little has changed concerning the situation in Poland."[101] Yet even though little had changed in Poland, the extraterritoriality claim was dropped in November 1982. In a further retreat a year later the president overruled his own domestic advisory committee and turned down the additional controls it recommended on oil and gas equipment and technology—yet little had changed in Poland.

Finally, there was the question of the effects of sanctions on the American deterrence posture. The original intent was to demonstrate both resolve and capability. But the actual effect was to reveal the intra-alliance and domestic divisions, and the concomitant lack of coercive power. Accordingly, Secretary of State Shultz was prompted to observe that East–West trade "can become a serious irritant in relations with our allies and thus even weaken the moral foundation of our common defense."[102] "Instead of punishing the Soviets," as one foreign correspondent caustically put it, "Reagan's policy has set Americans and Europeans to squabble . . . with Moscow left to enjoy the spectacle."[103] There has been some interesting and informed speculation that the very disarray demonstrated by the pipeline imbroglio prompted the Soviets to mount their propaganda campaign against the planned deployment of the Pershing and cruise intermediate-range nuclear missiles. Less speculative is William Root's con-

---

[101]Commerce Department press releases announcing countersanctions against Creusot Loire and Dresser France (August 26, 1982), Nuovo Pignone (September 14, 1982), John Brown Engineering (September 9, 1982), and AEG-Kanis (October 5, 1982).

[102]Speech to the South Carolina Bar Association, May 5, 1984, *Department of State Bulletin*, June 1984, p. 35.

[103]*Newsweek*, August 2, 1982, p. 39.

tention that conflict over East–West energy trade made agreement more difficult on the more critical issue of controls on militarily relevant high technologies.[104] Thus Reagan's energy trade sanctions did not merely fail to achieve their deterrence objective: their net effect was negative. The American deterrence posture was weaker, not stronger, on their account.

In sum, the American economic coercive strategy had achieved very little. And the reasons had important implications for the future.

[104]Root, "Trade Controls That Work."

CHAPTER SEVEN

The Complex Political Economy
of East–West Energy Trade

PIPELINE POLITICS: SUMMARY

In Chapter 1 I put forward two principal sets of arguments about the politics of East–West energy trade. The first concerned the consequences of the multilevel constraints on American economic coercive power over the Soviet Union. I argued that whatever symbolic functions anti-Soviet sanctions might have, their value in regard to instrumental coercive objectives (economic warfare, economic defense; political compellence, deterrence, containment) has been subject to the multilateral constraints of the Western allies' failure to collaborate and the domestic constraints of American domestic opposition. I argued further that these constraints have been particularly acute in regard to energy trade sanctions, and that they have become increasingly so over time.

The three cases of sanctions examined in Chapters 2 through 6 largely bore out this first set of arguments. In none of the cases did the sanctions register overwhelming success. In relative terms, however, the early Cold War sanctions were the most successful. They also were the ones least subject to multilateral and domestic constraints. The main constraint was at the unilateral level of Soviet capacity to counter the economic impact of the sanctions through regional integration (COMECON) and semi-autarkic industrialization. These counterstrategies kept the economic impact of the sanctions well short of the more extreme economic warfare objectives. To a degree, they also countered the capabilities-limiting economic defense objective. But as Chapter 2 noted, some of the key problems encountered by the

Soviets in the early 1950s, such as the negative growth rate of capital goods production, could be attributed to their limited access to Western alternative trade partners. Moreover, the very fact that the NATO allies came around to collaborating with the sanctions, and that the sanctions were backed by a strong consensus within the United States, strengthened both the credibility of the Western deterrence posture and the solidarity of Western containment at a time of high tensions and maximum threat.

In the case of the 1962–63 oil trade sanctions, the domestic constraints still were slight; with the major American oil companies supporting and actively abetting the sanctions, domestic support was greater than it had been in the early Cold War period. The multilateral constraints, however, began to increase when West Germany became the Soviets' alternative pipe supplier and Italy their principal oil customer. Both countries did respond to American leverage, decreasing their exports of pipe and imports of oil, respectively. These measures eliminated the threat to containment posed by the prospect of Italy's increasing dependence on Soviet oil, but in other respects they fell short of total success. They achieved some economic impact in terms of reduced hard-currency earnings, internal technological bottlenecks, and other economic inefficiencies. But Soviet oil production continued to increase. The sanctions also advanced the deterrence objective, given the tenuous military-strategic context of 1962–63, by delaying completion of the Friendship oil pipeline. At the same time, though, the Western posture was shaken by the intra-alliance conflict stirred up in the process of leveraging the allies. Chancellor Adenauer and the Christian Democrats paid a stiff domestic political price for being the loyal ally and joining the pipe embargo (especially for going so far as to nullify existing contracts). The lessons they drew were compounded by the embarrassment of Britain's unwillingness to support the embargo and the costliness of West Germany's exclusion from the later surge in Soviet–West European trade. Thus the very victory of American leverage sowed the seeds of even greater multilateral constraints in the future.

All of these trends culminated in the politics of the Siberian natural gas pipeline. Ironically, the unilateral constraints actually were weaker than ever before because the Soviets' need to trade with the West, both to earn hard currency by selling their natural gas and to acquire the equipment and technology for efficient operation and expansion, was greater than ever before. Yet any latent opportunities for American economic coercive power were undermined by the increase in the multilateral and domestic constraints. Whereas in the early 1960s the

Friendship oil pipeline controversy had strained the Western alliance, the United States was now engaged in an all-out imbroglio with a united Western Europe. American attempts at leverage did not change European policy in any significant way, as they had done in 1962–63. In addition, political constraints within the United States were much greater now. Congress was pushing for fewer, not more, trade controls. Interest groups were working against, not in tandem with, the export embargo. And the executive bureaucracy was so fragmented that this issue spurred more resignations than any other single issue that confronted the first Reagan administration.

As a result, the only claim that could be made for the sanctions was that they produced a limited economic impact by delaying completion of the Siberian gas pipeline. The volume of gas imported by Western Europe grew less rapidly than it had been forecast to do, but as we saw in Chapter 6, this was a function less of American leverage than of altered market conditions (lower projected economic growth rates, falling world oil prices). Moreover, the November 1982 "compromise" notwithstanding, European exporters went ahead and signed a large number of additional contracts for energy equipment and technology. On the political side the scorecard was even weaker. The Soviets were not compelled to lift martial law in Poland. The display of alliance disunity witnessed by Soviet leaders ran directly counter to the Reagan administration's efforts to strengthen the credibility of the Western deterrent in Soviet eyes. And the bitterness engendered toward the United States in Western Europe, coming on top of other sources of tension and mutual suspicion, did more to weaken containment than Soviet gas could possibly have hoped to achieve on its own. In this respect the sanctions not only did not succeed, they ended up having a net negative political effect.

We must now consider the second set of arguments introduced in Chapter 1 and developed in the ensuing chapters, concerning the *causes* of the increases observed in the multilateral and domestic constraints on American economic coercive power. My original argument was that at both levels the changing pictures of the politics of East–West energy trade were related to broader changes in the underlying political economy. The political economy of the Western alliance was cast in terms of three factors: the extent of disputes over foreign policy strategy, the degree of divergence of economic interests, and the sources of American leverage. The American domestic political economy was explained in terms of two factors, ideology and group economic interests. Each of these levels of pipeline politics needs to be considered separately.

THE WESTERN ALLIANCE AND EAST–WEST ENERGY TRADE

Again the cases are supportive. European collaboration was great-est in the early Cold War period because all three factors were positive. There then was little dispute over the basic foreign policy strategy that the Western alliance should pursue against the Soviet Union. To a greater extent than ever before (or since) the allies con-curred with the American assessment of the nature and severity of the Soviet threat. Any initial doubts had been dispelled by the series of events in 1948–50 (Czechoslovakian coup, Berlin blockade, Soviet A-bomb, Korean War), which raised fears about both the hostility of the Soviets and the formidableness of their capabilities. The full scope of trade controls still was debated, but only within the parameters set by the shared conviction that collective Western trade controls were a necessary part of a strong and credible deterrence posture.

Another contributing factor was the relative weakness of Europe's economic motives for trade with the Soviet Union in those years (i.e., minimal divergence). Even without Soviet bloc markets, European exports were enjoying rapid rates of growth. Nor was unemployment a particularly pressing problem. What Europe principally needed during this period of reconstruction was immediate emergency relief supplies and long-term investment capital. Both were being provided by the Marshall Plan and other American foreign economic policies. Not only could the Soviets not have provided these things, but under Stalin's economic policies they showed little interest in doing so.

Reinforcing these basic dispositions toward collaboration on trade controls were the extensive sources of leverage the United States then possessed. The still-fresh memories of World War II and the per-ceived beneficence of the Marshall Plan conferred on the United States a kind of political prestige that lent legitimacy to its leadership. American economic resources also provided both carrots and sticks. The carrots were not always directly linked to collaboration on trade controls (e.g., Investment Guaranty Program, Offshore Procurement Policy), although in some cases countries were directly compensated for the costs they incurred by forgoing trade with the Soviet Union. The sticks, however, were directly linked to collaboration, primarily through the provisions of the Battle Act which made violation of export controls a ground for cutting off Marshall Plan aid.

The principal difference between the early Cold War and Friend-ship oil pipeline cases was the increased divergence of economic in-terests. From the mid-1950s on, a combination of cyclical downturns, the need for new export markets, and gestures to the West by the post-Stalin leadership made trade with the Soviet Union generally more commercially attractive to Western Europe. The low prices and large volumes of oil the Soviets offered particularly fitted the needs and interests of such oil consumers as Italy and West Germany. In addition, their vigorous demand for wide-diameter pipe provided a major market at a time when the European steel sector was beginning to experience problems of overcapacity. There is even a within-case comparison here showing the influence on policy of economic interests. Neither France nor Great Britain imported Soviet oil or exported wide-diameter pipe to the Soviet Union. Both were increasing their trade with the Soviets in other sectors. But because of their foreign oil holdings, both viewed Soviet oil from the perspective of competing producers rather than interested consumers. Thus they collaborated with their fellow oil producer the United States.

Foreign policy strategy, on the other hand, was *not* a major motivation for either Italy's or West Germany's trade with the Soviet Union. There still was little dispute within the Western alliance over the basic deterrence and containment strategy. This was particularly the case in regard to West Germany, where the ruling Christian Democratic party and Chancellor Adenauer still drew on their close identification with the United States as a source of popular support. In fact, it was on this basis that the Kennedy administration was able to pressure the Adenauer government to reverse its policy and join the embargo of wide-diameter pipe.

American leverage against Italy was based more on economic compensation. The State Department and major American oil companies, whose interests were being threatened by the competition from Soviet oil, worked together to offer Italy a compensatory package of large quantities of oil at artificially low prices. In one sense both of these leverage strategies came too late, as the Soviet Union already had derived extensive benefits from the trade previously transacted. They also proved difficult to sustain for very long. Nevertheless, it was testimony to the still extensive resources of American power that they had the moderating effect on West German and Italian policy that they did.

The growth of European–Soviet natural gas trade in the 1970s was seen in Chapter 5 as a prelude to the Siberian pipeline case of the early 1980s, when the level of multilateral constraints reached unprecedented heights. By then the American–European relationship had changed along all three dimensions. The specifics of the case were detailed in Chapter 6: the fundamental foreign policy dispute over the political and strategic consequences of the Siberian pipeline and the associated gas contracts, the divergent economic interests at stake in both the energy equipment exports and the gas imports, and the failed American attempts at leverage. What needs to be done now is to explore the extent to which each of these specific points of contention in reality were manifestations of more fundamental, general, and continuing sources of intra-alliance tension.

Foreign Policy Strategy

Reduced to their most basic level, the specific disputes over the strategic significance of the Siberian pipeline's hard-currency earning power and of European dependence on Soviet gas reflected differences between the American and European perceptions of détente and defense as contradictory or complementary. The Reagan administration has espoused the former view, largely on the basis of what have been called the "Riga axioms" or the "essentialist" conception of the Soviet Union (or, more crudely, the "evil empire" view).[1] The disillusioning experiences of the 1970s détente are taken as substantiation of the charge that the Soviet Union is inherently bent on expansionism and totalitarianism. The United States is said to have done all the giving: trade, technology, credits, restraint on new weapons systems, nonintervention in the Third World. The Soviets received all these economic offerings while at the same time building up their nuclear arsenal and mounting operations in Angola, Ethiopia, Vietnam, Afghanistan, Central America, and elsewhere. People who do not perceive the world in these terms are implicitly if not explicitly tagged as naive, idealist, pacifist, and neutralist.

The Europeans, in contrast, tend to see détente and defense as complementary. Détente allows the inhabitants of a divided continent to live together in peace and holds open the prospect of a future without blocs in Europe. Defense ensures that such a future is not reached through the imposition of the Eastern system on the West. Herein lies the logic for deploying the Pershing and cruise missiles despite heavy domestic political criticism while at the same time refusing to go along with the sanctions against the Siberian pipeline. As the president of the European Parliament put it, Europeans reject "the

[1]Daniel Yergin, *Shattered Peace: The Origins of the Cold War and the National Security State* (Boston: Houghton Mifflin, 1977); Lawrence T. Caldwell and Alexander Dallin, "United States Policy toward the Soviet Union," in *Eagle Entangled: U.S. Foreign Policy in a Complex World*, ed. Kenneth A. Oye, Robert J. Lieber, and Donald Rothchild (New York: Longman, 1979), pp. 215–19. See also William Welch, *American Images of Soviet Foreign Policy* (New Haven: Yale University Press, 1970).

thesis prevalent in the [American] administration that the West is in a state of permanent conflict with the Soviet Union."[2] They do not dismiss the Soviet threat, but, as another official put it, they try to avoid "the American habit of overreacting."[3] In their view, it is not that they are pacifists but that the Americans tend to flirt too closely with escalation.

The agendas by which détente is evaluated differ as well. "The word 'détente,'" West German Foreign Minister Hans-Dietrich Genscher has written, "has different meanings for Americans and Europeans."[4] Such issues as nuclear arms control and the conventional military balance, of great concern to the United States, have also been on the European agenda. But such American priorities as the treatment of Soviet Jews and other dissidents and most cases of Third World interventionism have not been of comparable concern to Europeans. Instead they have put much greater weight on the repatriation of families, the opening up of visiting privileges, and other intracontinental matters. Especially for West Germany, détente in certain respects is a substitute for reunification, a way to increase contacts within the one German nation while living with two German states.[5] Or, as an aide to conservative Christian Democrat Chancellor Helmut Kohl explained the reason for continuing the *Ostpolitik* of the Social Democrats, "there is no other country that suffers more in times of tense U.S.–Soviet relations than us, and no leader more than the West German Chancellor."[6]

Finally, as both cause and effect of these overarching differences of foreign policy strategy, the Europeans also tend to see greater potential for trade to have a positive impact on overall East–West relations. The West German historical experience, as Angela Stent has summarized it, was that while "German–Soviet relations were not normalized because of economic factors . . . neither were they [i.e., the economic factors] irrelevant." The Soviets' interest in West German trade was not the sole or even the principal motivation for their will-

[2]Pieter Dankert, "Europe Together, America Apart," *Foreign Policy* 53 (Winter 1983–84): 22.

[3]Interview with British Embassy official, Washington, D.C., March 7, 1985. In the same vein, an opinion poll in late 1984 found that 50% of respondents in Great Britain and 38% in West Germany believed that Reagan's foreign policy had increased the risk of war (*New York Times*, October 31, 1984, p. 12).

[4]Hans-Dietrich Genscher, "Toward an Overall Western Strategy for Peace, Freedom, and Progress," *Foreign Affairs* 61 (Fall 1982); 43. See also Stanley Hoffmann, "The Western Alliance: Drift or Harmony?" *International Security* 6 (Fall 1981): 105–25.

[5]Hans-Adolf Jacobsen, director of the Political Science Institute, University of Bonn, lecture at the University of California–Davis, October 22, 1984.

[6]*Wall Street Journal*, October 19, 1983, p. 24.

ingness to normalize relations. It did, however, prove to be "a productive lever when judiciously used."[7] A similar point is made by a French government official, who, while warning against "illusions of the political windfall benefits of trade," with a touch of reverse logic also stresses that "the collapse of trade would have a negative political impact."[8] This is an interesting point because it introduces into the discussion a relative instead of absolute measure of prospective foreign policy gains. The absolute foreign policy gains to be made by East–West trade may not be particularly substantial. But in light of the likely negative impact of sanctions, they take on greater significance.

At the same time the Europeans worry less that gas imports may make them so dependent on the Soviet Union that their security may be endangered. In a sense the logic of this position expresses the more abstract conceptual distinction made by Robert Keohane and Joseph Nye between the "sensitivity" and "vulnerability" dimensions of international interdependence.[9] "Sensitivity" refers to the initial costs imposed on a nation by external events or actions taken by other states; in this case, the immediate economic disruption that would be caused in Western Europe by a Soviet cutoff of natural gas supplies. "Vulnerability" refers to the continuing costs that a nation suffers because of external events or actions. It takes into account the ability of a nation-state to "reduce its costs by altering its policy." Sensitivity may be high but vulnerability low if through autonomous actions or relations with other states initial exposure can be reduced. The Europeans, as we saw in Chapter 6, contend that the safety net measures they have been developing would limit their vulnerability sufficiently in the event of a politically motivated gas embargo by the Soviet Union.[10] Consequently, even if they accept the American worst case premise of the likelihood of a Soviet gas embargo during a moment of crisis or as coercive leverage in a diplomatic dispute, they feel secure in their ability to resist Soviet demands.

[7]Angela Stent, *From Embargo to Ostpolitik: The Political Economy of West German–Soviet Relations, 1955–1980* (New York: Cambridge University Press, 1981), p. 251.

[8]Jean-Marie Guillaume (pseud.), "A European View of East–West Trade in the 1980s," in *Economic Relations with the USSR: Issues for the Western Alliance*, ed. Abraham S. Becker (Lexington, Mass.: Heath, 1983), p. 144.

[9]Robert O. Keohane and Joseph S. Nye, Jr., *Power and Interdependence* (Boston: Little, Brown, 1977), pp. 11–19.

[10]Stefanie Lenway and Eric Paul Thompson, "Trading with the Adversary: Managed Interdependence in East–West Energy Trade," paper presented at the annual conference of the American Political Science Association, Washington D.C., August 30–September 2, 1984; Hans W. Maull, *Natural Gas and Economic Security* (Paris: Atlantic Institute for International Studies, 1981).

They also question the premise itself. They do not totally dismiss the possibility of Soviet economic coercion, but they question its probability. Here, too, the reasoning can be understood in terms of more general theories of the effects of economic interdependence on the exercise of power and influence in international relations. When the disruption of an economic relationship carries substantial costs for both sides, the strongest incentives are for continuation of the economic relationship. This is not to say that trade is in any way held to be a sufficient condition for stable political relations. It is, however, to bring into the analysis factors that are likely to affect the relative probabilities of different possible actions. In this case the severe economic costs that the Soviets would incur are a disincentive to a gas embargo. They would stand to lose their major source of hard-currency earnings; throughout the 1980s oil and gas exports have accounted for over 80 percent of total Soviet hard-currency earnings. Such a loss would in turn cut into the Soviets' ability to import the industrial technology and grain on which their economy increasingly has come to rely. And even if the embargo did not last long enough to cause major hard-currency losses, the Soviets would still have to face the damaging long-term effect of a ruined reputation for commercial reliability. A reputation for reliability is perhaps the Soviets' greatest asset in its commercial dealings with the West.[11] Without it they would be much less likely to secure the credits, loans, and long-term barter arrangements that they need to trade outside their own bloc.

Finally, Americans and Europeans have developed fundamental differences in their conceptions of security. Ellen Frost and Angela Stent make the point that "the American concept of security is overwhelmingly *military* in nature, whereas that espoused by the Europeans is *as economic as it is military.*"[12] This distinction has a number of bases but most especially reflects two differences in the American and European structural positions in the international system. One is that as the only country with military capabilities comparable to the Soviet Union's, the United States sees itself and is seen by most other countries as having principal responsibility for deterring Soviet military aggression. The other difference is in the American and European

[11]One is reminded of some of the reactions of relief in the international banking community when martial law was proclaimed in Poland. The *Wall Street Journal* (December 21, 1981) quoted a Citicorp executive as saying, "Who knows which political system works? The only test we care about is: can they pay their bills?" Such responses caused the reporter to conclude that "most bankers think authoritarian governments are good because they impose discipline."

[12]Ellen L. Frost and Angela E. Stent, "NATO's Troubles with East–West Trade," *International Security* 8 (Summer 1983): 180 (emphasis added).

economic positions, particularly the Europeans' great need for expanding export markets and secure supplies of imported energy. In the United States, such terms as "economic security" and "energy security" crop up in times of crisis but then fade away (until the next crisis). In Europe they have had to be taken much more seriously. Economies in which exports account for as much as 26 percent of GNP and in which 81 percent of energy supplies are imported have a much more compelling need to conceptualize security in economic and energy as well as military terms than a country that exports only 7 percent of its GNP and imports only 15 percent of its energy supply.[13] These differences of course also bear on the question of divergence of economic interests. But their significance in making for distinct conceptions of security and therefore differing and at times conflicting foreign policy strategies also must be recognized.

Divergent Economic Interests

Simply put, in the Siberian pipeline case the United States had less to gain from the trade than Europe and therefore less to lose from sanctions. The one sector in which its economic interests were strong, the grain trade, was neatly exempted from the otherwise economic warfare–like scope of the economic sanctions pushed by the Reagan administration. For the Europeans, recession-ridden and, by virtue of their structural position in the world economy, energy consumers, much more was at stake. In the wake of the second OPEC shock, diversification of energy import portfolios was an understandably high priority. Amidst double-digit unemployment and the worst wave of bankruptcies of the postwar era, so were the jobs and profits expected to be created by the pipeline exports.

Recent developments and trends make it seem likely that this basic divergence of American and Western European economic interests as they pertain to East–West energy trade will continue in the future. Even with the growth rates of future consumption predicted to decline in line with slower GNP growth rates and the drop in world oil prices, natural gas still is expected to increase from the 20 to 22

---

[13]The economies in which exports account for 26% and 7% of GNP are West Germany and the United States, respectively. Other ratios are 21% for Italy, 21% for Britain, and 18% for France (all cited from the Bundesbank in *Wall Street Journal*, October 23, 1984, p. 34). The figure of 81% for foreign sources of energy is the 1980 aggregate average for Western Europe (International Energy Agency, *World Energy Outlook* [Paris, 1982], p. 444). The U.S. energy import figure is for 1983 (IEA/OECD, *Energy Balances of OECD Countries, 1982/83* [Paris, 1983], p. 118).

percent of European energy consumption by the end of the century.[14] Some of this increase can be met by European gas production. Dutch reserves have been revalued upward by 25 percent and, in a reversal of the trend from 1977 to 1982, exports rose 4 percent in 1983.[15] Over the long term, however, this only means a slower rate of decline, not an increase, in Dutch gas exports. Additional discoveries of gas in the British North Sea, adding 6 trillion cubic feet to Britain's proved and probable reserves, led the British to pull out of plans to begin importing large volumes of gas from the Norwegian Sleipner fields in the 1990s. It is possible that the Sleipner fields still may be developed and that the gas may become available to France and West Germany. But government and utility officials in both countries have expressed serious doubts about both the timeliness of Sleipner supplies and their price competitiveness.[16]

Consequently, the demand for gas from non-European sources is expected to continue to increase. Imports of gas from non-European suppliers are predicted to increase from a third of total imports in 1980 to roughly half by 1990.[17] With respect to Algeria, the same concern that arose in 1981–82 remains relevant: the peril of relying heavily for gas on a country that is a member of OPEC and that in the past has resorted to embargoes and has failed to fulfill contracts during commercial disputes. Soviet gas, in contrast, is not likely to have the volume problems of Dutch gas, the price problems of Norwegian gas, or the reliability problems of Algerian gas.[18] There has been some lingering concern over the negotiating tactics used by the Soviets in the 1981–82 import agreements, but their later willingness to renegotiate the floor price and to stretch out the minimum volume

[14]*Journal of Commerce*, February 12, 1985, p. 13A. This figure is based in part on the IEA estimate of 7.4% average annual increase in gas consumption in the 1990s.

[15]*Journal of Commerce*, March 19, 1984, p. 13A. See also Jonathan P. Stern, *International Gas Trade in Europe: The Policies of Exporting and Importing Countries* (London: Heinemann, 1984), pp. 105–20, 184.

[16]Personal interviews, March 1985 (Washington, D.C.) and July 1985 (Britain, France, West Germany, Belgium). See also *Oil and Gas Journal*, February 18, 1985, pp. 59, 68–69; *Wall Street Journal*, February 12, 1985, p. 35. The same questions surround the Troll fields, Norway's other major new prospect. Future production estimates for these fields alone run as high as 30 bcm. But production costs have tended to exceed estimates and so have made the gas less commercially competitive. Jonathan Stern comments that "the question of whether Troll gas can compete in the market is already exercising the minds of all the relevant decision makers in Norway" (*International Gas Trade*, pp. 14–15, 25).

[17]Stern, *International Gas Trade*, p. viii.

[18]A recent example of how the mere presence of the Soviets in the gas market helps consumer countries was the Dutch Gasunie's decision to cut prices 15% to counter a low Soviet offer to Belgium (*Wall Street Journal*, July 13, 1984, p. 18).

appears to have alleviated much of this concern.[19] In late 1984 Turkey, another NATO member, signed on for its first imports of Soviet gas.[20] Talks on a possible pipeline between the Soviet Union and Greece were under way in 1985, as were negotiations for new or additional gas with West Germany, Belgium, the Netherlands, Spain, and Switzerland.[21]

It is reasonable to conclude that Soviet gas will continue to be attractive to European consumer nations. The 1981 OTA study was on the mark analytically in concluding that "in Western Europe, growing energy interdependence with the Council for Mutual Economic Assistance . . . is a fact of life."[22] The Soviets by no means will have a lock on European markets. That would only recreate the energy security problem that was a major reason for Western Europe to turn to the Soviets in the first place. Technical difficulties that caused oil deliveries to be scaled back during the winter of 1985 raised additional nonpolitical reasons for prudence.[23] All in all, though, predictions that Soviet gas will have 30 percent shares of European markets appear conservative. The 35–40 percent range is more likely.

Future trends also point to continued incentives for Europe to export energy equipment and technology to the Soviet Union. The surge in new contracts for such exports immediately following the lifting of the American extraterritorial sanctions in November 1982 was noted in Chapter 6. It continued through the rest of the Eleventh Five-Year Plan as the Soviets ordered the additional equipment, wide-diameter pipe, and spare parts needed to complete their pipeline systems.[24] The draft guidelines for the Twelfth Five-Year Plan, is-

---

[19]On the agreement to renegotiate the Gaz de France contracts, see *Journal of Commerce,* May 4, 1984, p. 11A; *Financial Times,* May 4, 1984, p. 5.; *Wall Street Journal,* June 7, 1985, p. 29. On the Ruhrgas renegotiation see *East European Markets,* August 20, 1984, p. 4. I also have drawn on my interviews and communications with company officials, July–October 1985.

[20]The Soviet–Turkish agreement, calling for gas imports of 6 bcm a year for 25 years beginning in 1987, was signed in October 1984 (*Journal of Commerce,* October 11, 1984, p. 11A).

[21]*Financial Times,* June 27, 1985, p. 2; *Journal of Commerce,* October 11, 1984, p. 11A.

[22]U.S. Congress, Office of Technology Assessment (OTA), *Technology and Soviet Energy Availability* (Washington, D.C.: Government Printing Office, 1981), p. 351.

[23]*Christian Science Monitor,* February 11, 1985, p. 12; *Foreign Broadcast Information Service,* February 6, 1985, G1. This was not the first time that winter deliveries had fallen short. In the first three months of 1981, oil deliveries to Western Europe had to be cut one-third because of production problems (Stern, *International Gas Trade,* p. 54).

[24]Some of the contracts reported in the press were new contracts with Mannesmann for 245,000 additional tons of wide-diameter pipe and $45 million for pipeline laying engineering (*Financial Times,* March 20, 1984, p. 7; *Wall Street Journal,* February 8, 1984, p. 37); with Finsider for 800,000 tons of wide-diameter pipe (*American Metal*

sued in November 1985, indicated that development of energy resources would continue to be among the Soviet Union's highest priorities. The Plan guidelines called for the downward trend in oil
production not just to be slowed, but to be reversed. The goal set for
1990 was 12.8 million barrels per day, an 8 percent increase over the
11.8 million barrels per day estimated for 1985. As for natural gas,
the goal of a 31 percent increase, from 645 bcm to 845 bcm, may be
ambitious even in view of the Soviets' past successes in this sector.
What is certain, though, given these goals, is that the Soviets' demand
for imports of energy equipment and technology will continue to
grow.[25] In 1985 they had already begun to let some contracts and
take bids on new energy projects for the southwest Asian natural gas
fields, an eastern Siberian pipeline system, offshore oil exploration in
the Barents Sea, and a potentially multibillion-dollar coal slurry
pipeline.[26]

To be sure, obstacles still remain in the way of any rapid expansion
of trade. In particular, as Thane Gustafson puts it, "now as always,
the governing constraint on Soviet foreign trade is the scarcity of
things to export."[27] With world oil prices having fallen even further

---

Market, January 16, 1984, p. 19); with Vallourec (France) for 200,000 tons of pipe
(*Ecotass,* April 1, 1985, p. 14); with Lurgi (France) for $150 million in spare parts for oil
equipment (*Ecotass,* February 18, 1985, p. 18); with Kesting (West Germany) for a $12
million concrete plant for construction of housing along the pipeline (*Financial Times,*
July 20, 1984, p. 4). In addition, the new French–Soviet five-year trade agreement calls
for the Soviets to increase their imports of French industrial equipment by 500%. Most
analysts expect that energy equipment will be a major component of these purchases
(*New York Times,* February 4, 1984, p. 26; *Journal of Commerce,* February 6, 1984, p.
23B).

[25]The plan guidelines were reported in the *New York Times,* November 17, 1985, p.
12, and the *Oil and Gas Journal* December 2, 1985, pp. 48–49. When the future general
secretary Mikhail Gorbachev toured Great Britain and spoke of a possible 500% increase in British–Soviet trade, one of the industries he stressed was oil and gas equipment (*Foreign Broadcast Information Service,* December 21, 1984, G1). Western firms
appear to be thinking in similar terms; 366 were represented at the December 1984
Moscow oil and gas exhibition (*Ecotass,* December 24, 1984, p. 7). One more concrete
advance indicator of Soviet plans was Finsider's $2 billion contract to supply 6
million metric tons of steel products between 1986 and 1990—an amount equal to
Finsider's total steel exports to the Soviets over the last ten years (*Journal of Commerce,*
April 25, 1985, p. 2A; *Financial Times,* April 25, 1985, p. 1).

[26]Technip (France) got a $260 million contract to build a gas processing and de-
sulfurization plant at Astrakhan, and Lurgi (France) got a $135 million contract for a
natural gas condensate plant at Tengiz (*Wall Street Journal,* April 3, 1985, p. 35; *Journal
of Commerce,* April 29, 1985, p. 23A). Both ENI (Italy) and Armand Hammer's Occidental Petroleum were negotiating on the coal slurry pipeline (*Ecotass,* February 25, 1985,
p. 8.) And by one estimate, inquiries were being made for over $600 million in equip-
ment to explore for oil beneath the Barents Sea (*Business Week,* March 11, 1985, p. 2).

[27]Thane Gustafson, *Soviet Negotiating Strategy: The East–West Gas Pipeline Deal, 1980–
1984,* R-3220-FF (Santa Monica: Rand, 1985), p. vii.

and the recession having slowed the rate of increase in the West's consumption of energy, Soviet hard-currency earnings have been further pinched. At least, though, by 1984–85 commercial lending windows had begun to reopen. New loans to all of CMEA were up almost 300 percent, from $1 billion in 1983 to $2.9 billion in 1984. The Soviet Union itself received over $800 million in new loans. By early 1985 the *Wall Street Journal* was moved to comment (somewhat grudgingly) on "the growing market appetite for Eastern European loans."[28] Few economists were predicting growth along the lines of the early 1970s. But it also was clear that the market was much more favorable than it had been in the early 1980s.

Finally, there is the pressure generated by continued high unemployment. European jobless rates were *higher* in 1985 than in 1982.[29] Exports to the Soviet Union still may not amount to a great deal in the aggregate; even West Germany's sales to the Soviet Union accounted for only 2.7 percent of its total exports.[30] But their relative importance is far greater than their absolute value because they are concentrated in sectors that have severe problems of overcapacity, such as steel and engineering. The point made in Chapter 6 bears repeating, that at a time when world energy markets are plagued by low prices and limited growth, there are few large customers for wide-diameter pipe, gas pipeline compressors, and other energy industry equipment other than the Soviet Union.[31] Unless a government or opposition party is prepared to write off the economic welfare and political power of firms and unions in these sectors, it cannot help giving serious consideration to their interests.

American Leverage

Pitted against this scenario of strong and deep Western European political and economic interests in the Soviet trade is the evidence of

---

[28]*Wall Street Journal,* November 20, 1984, p. 35; September 28, 1984, p. 31; February 12, 1985, p. 34. Two months later the *Journal* reported that a $90 million loan for Vnestorgbank, the Soviet foreign trade bank, was oversubscribed and thus was doubled to $180 million (April 3, 1985, p. 35). See also *New York Times,* November 26, 1985, pp. D1, D7, on the first loan in five years involving American banks.

[29]West Germany: 9.7% compared to 7.7%; France: 11.2% compared to 9.9%; Italy: 13.7% compared to 9.2%. British unemployment was down slightly, from 13.0% to 12.6%. The 1985 figures are from the European Community, as reported in the *Christian Science Monitor,* March 25, 1985, pp. 36; the 1982 figures are from United Nations, *Monthly Bulletin of Statistics,* March 1983.

[30]The figure from *Journal of Commerce,* January 11, 1984, p. 7, is for 1983.

[31]Frost and Stent state that about 60% of Mannesmann's exports of wide-diameter pipe go to the Soviet Union. The firm constructed an entire factory at Muelheim just to produce pipe for the Soviet market ("NATO's Troubles with East-West Trade." p.188).

declining American leverage. The contrast with the leverage brought to bear in the earlier cases is quite striking. In the early 1980s, what Europe most needed economically, export markets and energy supplies, the United States would not or could not offer. The "would not" was made clear in March 1985, when the Reagan administration turned down a proposal to import from the EC 320,000 tons of steel pipe and tube products in excess of the amount set by the existing voluntary export restraint agreement.[32] This action was not explicitly linked to East–West trade issues, but in rejecting the European bid the Reagan administration passed up an opportunity for compensatory leverage. The "could not" applied more to the issue of substitute energy supplies. The proposals taken to Europe in 1981–82 by Reagan administration officials for compensation with American coal and other supplies were too plagued with uncertainties to be accepted as a realistic substitute for Soviet natural gas. There was a sense that the climatic conditions and topography of Siberia presented a lesser obstacle to production than American bureaucratic barriers to coal production. The suggestion for increased use of nuclear power flew in the face of political realities, especially in West Germany, where the Greens were mounting their offensive. And the Norwegian gas option was not something the United States could deliver on.[33]

Far from being sweetened by any offer of substitute export markets, the pipeline dispute was exacerbated by its intersection with other West–West trade and economic policy conflicts. At the same time that the Reagan administration was pushing the pipeline extraterritorial countersanctions, the United States and Western Europe were at loggerheads over such key issues as the effects of the EC's Common Agricultural Policy on American agricultural exports and the consequences for European "domestic" macroeconomic policies of high American interest rates and the overvalued dollar. A top Reagan administration trade official conceded in congressional testimony that "our economic relations with Europe are as turbulent as I can remember them in the nearly thirty years that I have been associated with European affairs."[34] In the past, economic interdependence generally was counted on as a tie that bound amidst other

[32]*Wall Street Journal*, March 25, 1985, p. 31. The pipe would have been used for a new 1,783-mile crude oil pipeline being constructed between Santa Barbara, California, and Freeport, Texas.

[33]Stern concludes that this "badgering" of the Norwegian government "was a great mistake. . . . This kind of overt pressure may give rise to a more restricted and rigid timetable, as politicians may feel themselves forced to demonstrate [Norway's] sovereignty over its resources" (*International Gas Trade in Europe*, p. 30).

[34]*National Journal*, November 19, 1983, p. 2004.

Table 7.1. Percentage of respondents in four European COCOM countries indicating degrees of respect for and confidence in the United States, 1972 and 1981

	Year	Great Britain	France	West Germany	Italy
Respect for United States	1972				
Great/considerable		70%	81%	82%	80%
Little/very little		19	16	14	17
Don't know/no opinion		11	3	4	3
All responses		100%	100%	100%	100%
Respect for United States	1981				
Great/considerable		54	62	56	75
Little/very little		42	23	28	22
Don't know/no opinion		4	15	16	3
All responses		100%	100%	100%	100%
Confidence in United States' ability to deal responsibly with world problems	1981				
Great deal/fair amount		47	46	43	61
Not very much/none		49	41	42	35
Don't know/no opinion		4	13	15	4
All responses		100%	100%	100%	100%

SOURCES: William Schneider, "Europeans Have Their Doubts about Reliability of U.S. Political Leadership," *National Journal,* July 23, 1983, pp. 1566–67, citing U.S. International Communications Agency.

disputes. Now, however, fewer benefits were being manifested as counterweights to other disputes.

The final aspect of the transformation of the alliance politics of East–West energy trade was the depletion of America's political prestige, what Robert Gilpin has called "the everyday currency of international relations."[35] As elusive a concept as political prestige is, at least some possible indicators can be cited. One such indicator is the opinion poll data presented in Table 7.1. In 1972 overwhelming majorities of Europeans, from 70 to 82 percent, responded that they had great or considerable respect for the United States. By 1981, however, the favorable responses were down rather substantially. Even less positive were the responses to a question about confidence in American leadership. In Great Britain the people who expressed little or no confidence in American leadership outnumbered those who expressed a fair amount or a great deal of confidence.

The same point can be made more forcefully, albeit more impressionistically, by the juxtaposition of the images of John Kennedy's reception in Berlin in 1963 and Ronald Reagan's reception in Bonn in

[35]Robert Gilpin, *War and Change in International Politics* (New York: Cambridge University Press, 1981), p. 3.

1982. One was greeted by cheering crowds, the other by tomato-throwing and placard-waving protesters. In 1962–63 the United States could draw upon a store of goodwill and its position as alliance leader and security provider to persuade Chancellor Adenauer to cooperate with the embargo. Adenauer in turn could draw on America's reputation and status among the German people to legitimize his action. Over the ensuing twenty years, however, America's foreign policy failures and domestic political scandals have been even more deleterious to its prestige than to its power. The contrast was put in appropriately stark terms by a foreign correspondent who remarked, with reference to West Germany but with implications for all of Western Europe, that "whoever becomes Chancellor from the successor generation will know little of the Marshall Plan, won't have seen a CARE package, but will be well-versed in Watergate, McDonald's and Haiphong harbor."[36] Moreover, with the pipeline issue coming on the heels of the recent succession of American urgings for sanctions against Iran, sanctions against the Soviet Union following the Afghanistan invasion, and the boycott of the Moscow Olympics, the political capital account was somewhat overdrawn. Threats and punishments only compounded the problem because divergent interests and punitive measures interacted synergistically to infuse alliance relations with what Josef Joffee has called a "politics of resentment".[37]

It is for all of these reasons that the pipeline dispute fueled so much speculation on the possibility of a lasting rupture in alliance relations. Robert Tucker, a scholar noted for the unsentimentality of his foreign policy analysis, concluded that "the critics are largely justified in their vision of a dark future. . . . The alliance is visibly unravelling today, and the rising tempo of its disintegration can fail to impress only the most determined of optimists."[38] A study by the nonpartisan Congressional Research Service agreed that the Atlantic alliance was "without question in the midst of the most severe crisis it has faced for many years."[39] And the London-based International Institute for

[36]*Wall Street Journal,* October 19, 1983, p. 24. For scholarly analyses of the generational issue, see Stephen F. Szabo, ed., *The Successor Generation: International Perspectives of Postwar Europeans* (London: Butterworths, 1983), and Ronald Inglehart, "Generational Change and the Future of the Atlantic Alliance," *PS* 17 (Summer 1984): 525–35.

[37]Josef Joffe, "Europe and America: The Politics of Resentment," *Foreign Affairs* 61 (1982): 569–90.

[38]Robert Tucker, *The Atlantic Alliance and Its Critics* (New York: Praeger, 1983), p. 188.

[39]Library of Congress, Congressional Research Service, *Crisis in the Atlantic Alliance: Origins and Implications* (Washington, D.C.: Government Printing Office, 1982), p. 1.

Strategic Studies warned that "collapse was not out of the question."[40]

In the ensuing years the Western alliance has managed to avoid the worst of these predictions. It has not unraveled, the crisis has been managed, there has been no collapse. The principal reason for this resilience was captured by the French journalist André Fontaine, who, while strongly critical of the pipeline sanctions, nevertheless concluded that "the Western alliance still works because it is essential."[41] As long as there is a Soviet threat there will be a Western alliance. For whatever the centrifugal forces pulling the allies apart, shared security interests against a common adversary act as a centripetal force pushing them back together. This is particularly true when Soviet rhetoric, actions, and policies are as provocative and antagonistic as they were in the late 1970s and early 1980s.[42]

Three conclusions can be drawn. First, the deterioration of Western collaboration on East–West energy trade controls both reflects and is an effect of broader changes in the political economy of intra-alliance relations. The disputes over foreign policy strategy encompass much more than just the energy trade issue. The divergent economic interests are rooted in structural differences between the American and Western European economies. And the diminution of American prestige has been a function of changes in relative power that are secular and complex, and therefore not specific to the East–West energy trade issue.

The second conclusion is that while the Siberian pipeline conflict was originally an effect of the deterioration of alliance relations, as it developed it caused those relations to deteriorate further. The worst case "end is nigh" scenarios have not materialized, and the issues have been pushed to the back burner. But as soon as one looks beneath the surface, it is quite apparent that these issues continue to play a more important and more divisive role than ever before.[43] Nor do the

---

[40]Cited in *New York Times,* May 19, 1983, p. A5.

[41]Testimony in U.S. Congress, Joint Economic Committee, *Soviet Pipeline Sanctions: The European Perspective: Hearings,* 97th Cong., 2d sess., 1982, p. 10.

[42]Thus, while American political prestige has declined as Table 7.1 indicates, Western European attitudes toward the Soviet Union have soured even more. In West Germany the percentage of respondents who characterized the Soviet Union as a threat to their country rose from 28% in 1971 to 44% in 1982. In 1975, only 19% of French respondents believed that the Soviets were not sincerely committed to peace; in 1980, 46% believed that they were not. Italians' attitudes toward the Soviet Union were still slightly more positive than negative as late as 1978; by 1982, negative responses outnumbered positive ones by 55%. (William Schneider, "Europeans Have Their Doubts about Reliability of U.S. Political Leadership," *National Journal,* July 23, 1983, p. 1566).

[43]Frost and Stent, "NATO's Troubles with East-West Trade," p. 179 and passim; Beverly Crawford and Stefanie Lenway, "Decision Modes and International Regime

conflicts manifested and resentments engendered stay confined to the energy trade issue. They spill over and affect other issues of East–West trade on which collaboration is especially necessary, such as high-technology controls. They also have a negative impact on alliance relations generally.

Finally, there are the constraining consequences for American economic coercive power. Unilateral American sanctions cannot block Soviet energy projects because "with few exceptions, adequate quantities of the energy equipment sought by the USSR are produced and available outside the United States, and the quality of these foreign goods is generally comparable to that of their U.S. counterparts."[44] Moreover, as the Siberian pipeline case has so aptly shown, the Soviet Union is not about to be compelled by actions that reveal the West's lack of solidarity. Such actions do not strengthen the overall Western deterrence posture; they weaken it. As a result, not only do the multilateral constraints of allies turned alternative trade partners make coercive success impossible, they also have a net negative effect. The pursued gains are not made, and those who pursue them inflict losses on themselves in the process. This is a very different and far more damaging matter than the mere failure of the sanctions to achieve their objectives. The United States and the Western alliance are left worse off than they would have been if they had done nothing. Thus, far from being a solution, energy trade sanctions are part of the problem.

AMERICAN DOMESTIC POLITICS AND EAST–WEST ENERGY TRADE

Similar albeit less pronounced patterns and developments marked the American domestic politics of East–West energy trade. The level of constraints between the early Cold War and the Friendship oil pipeline cases, unlike the politics of the Western alliance, did not change. Nor were the domestic constraints in the Siberian gas pipeline case as high as the multilateral ones. Nevertheless, the very fact that change did occur after such a long period of consensus has important implications and requires explanation.

For the first twenty to twenty-five years of the post–World War II

Change: Western Collaboration on East–West Trade," *World Politics* 37 (April 1985): 375–402; Gary Bertsch, *East-West Strategic Trade, COCOM, and the Atlantic Alliance* (Paris: Atlantic Institute for International Affairs, 1983). This assessment also was confirmed in my interviews with European government officials, June–July 1985.

[44]OTA, *Technology and Soviet Energy Availability*, p. 392; see also pp. 225–45.

era, the Cold War ideology prevailed as the basis for foreign policy consensus. Export controls were entirely consistent with both the "moral equivalent of war" sentiment of its anticommunist ethic and the "functional equivalent of war" strategy of its national security imperative. Consequently, the kinds of legitimacy problems that Alexander George has stressed as a principal source of domestic constraints on American foreign policy did not affect anti-Soviet sanctions. To the contrary, it was the option of permitting trade with the Soviet Union that was constrained by not being "consistent with fundamental national values and [not] contributing to their enhancement."[45] As Chapter 2 showed, the only political conflicts were spurred by congressional concerns that the Truman administration was not doing enough to pressure the Western European allies to wage economic warfare more energetically.

Even had there been groups with substantial economic interests at stake in the late 1940s and early 1950s, it is doubtful that they would have risked the wrath of Senator McCarthy by pressuring against export controls. More important are the reasons why exports to the Soviet Union were not economically significant in this period. Essentially American exporters were prospering quite nicely without the Soviet market. The annual export growth rate between 1949 and 1953 was 17.4 percent; in fact, the real problem was that foreign demand was so high as to create periodic inflationary shortages of supply in the domestic market. In addition, with some exceptions the American business community feared both the commercial risks of dealing with the Soviets and the precedents that might be set by the introduction of a nonmarket economy into the liberal international economic order.

In the Friendship oil pipeline case it was not that business was disinterested but rather that trade controls were functional to the economic interests of a particularly powerful pressure group, the major multinational oil companies. The situation may have been anomalous in terms of classical trade theory but it was perfectly logical for an oligopolistic market. For the Kennedy administration, the issue was that it was *Soviet* oil that Italy was buying in such large quantities. For SONJ and other majors, the issue was that it was anybody's oil other than their own (and at market-depressing cut-rate prices). The state and the corporations could and did serve their mutual interests

<hr>

[45]Alexander L. George, "Domestic Constraints on Regime Change in U.S. Foreign Policy: The Need for Policy Legitimacy," in *Change in the International System*, ed. Ole R. Holsti, Randolph M. Siverson, and Alexander L. George (Boulder: Westview Press, 1980), p. 235.

by working together to gain leverage against Italy. At the same time, ideology was still contributing to consensus, as evidenced by the images conjured up in Congress of being "drowned in a sea of oil" and the passage of the Export Control Act of 1962.

The 1970s were a period of transition, both for export controls policy and for the underlying politics. As we saw in Chapter 5, the Nixon administration broke sharply with the past and began to promote trade in energy and other sectors (e.g., grain) with the Soviet Union as part of its overall détente strategy. From the very beginning, though, this new policy encountered almost as many difficulties at home as it did along the superpower axis. One problem was the ideological ambiguity both of the policy itself and of the times. The old Cold War ideology may not have been so widely held as in the past, but nonsupport for the old had not translated into strong support for the new. There were many reasons for this situation, not the least of which were antipathy toward Richard Nixon and Henry Kissinger and the tendency of many of the people most inclined to favor trade to link it with the issue of the emigration of Soviet Jews. Another factor was the intensity and political astuteness of the conservative opposition, who mounted a concerted effort to block this abandonment of what it considered to be first principles.

A second problem was the alignment of economic interest groups on both sides of the issue. Such groups as energy equipment exporters, commercial banks, natural gas companies, and engineering firms exerted significant pressure for energy trade; labor, consumer, and other groups opposed expanded trade with the Soviet Union in general and the North Star and Yakutsk natural gas projects in particular.

The Nixon-Kissinger strategy for promoting American–Soviet energy trade as an inducement for superpower détente could not escape the constraints imposed by the highly conflictual domestic politics. Similar constraints were encountered by the Carter administration with its economic diplomacy variant. Thus, whether economic inducement was or was not an offer that could not be refused, it proved to be an offer that could not be delivered.

In a sense, then, the domestic constraints on economic inducement reflected the continuity in the American domestic politics of East–West trade. But the constraints seen in the case of the Siberian gas pipeline sanctions of the early 1980s, and the reasons for them, revealed the extent of the changes that the domestic political economy had undergone. The Reagan administration's original calculation was that the issue of martial law in Poland was tailor-made for remobilizing the Cold War consensus. After all, it was in Poland that East–West conflict had started almost forty years earlier. Events now seemed to be fulfilling the most dire predictions of the earliest critics of Yalta. And the charismatic figure of Lech Walesa had become a veritable folk hero to the American public. Surely the combination of historical parallels and heroic struggle would create the drama that would re-confirm and thus reactivate the old Cold War ideology. Moreover, the economic impact of the energy sanctions would be less concentrated than that of the grain embargo on a specific group and specific geo-graphical regions; and to the extent that specific groups were hit hard, the damage would be on a much smaller scale. Therefore, and especially amidst the presumed ideological upswell, the pressure ex-erted by economic interest groups was expected to be minimal.

The actual domestic political reaction, as we saw in Chapter 6, was quite the opposite. Instead of rallying round the flag and behind the cause, the public responded skeptically. Interest groups lobbied hard and long against the sanctions, and then against administration pro-posals for a more restrictive Export Administration Act. In Congress the administration could not even consistently hold its own party members in line on key votes. And within the executive branch itself, there was fragmentation rather than unity as two successive secre-taries of state, in alliance with the secretary of commerce, pushed for a more pragmatic, less restrictive approach while the secretary of defense, national security adviser, and other administration officials pressed for all-out economic warfare.

Political Ideology

The fact that the anticipated ideological upswell was not forthcom-ing indicated how far ideological ambiguity had deteriorated into ideological anomie. To be sure, for some groups within the general public and for the influential neoconservative segment of the foreign policy elite, the Cold War ideology now had more meaning than ever before.[46] But despite the best efforts and deft articulation of Ronald Reagan, the breadth of appeal that in past decades had given the Cold War ideology its virtual unchallengeability could not be restored. Various studies showed both a pervasive sense of disorientation

[46]One prominent neoconservative, Norman Podhoretz, even took President Reagan to task for showing signs of becoming too much the pragmatist and too little the purist ("The Reagan Road to Détente," *Foreign Affairs* 63 [America and the World, 1984]: 447–64).

among the general public and deep divisions within the foreign policy elite.

"As far as the public is concerned," one analyst aptly concluded, "we are neither in a period of détente nor in a cold war like the 1950s."[47] Other studies confirmed and elaborated on this assessment. The data from one of these studies, conducted by Daniel Yankelovich and the Public Agenda Foundation, are particularly instructive. They showed a renewed antipathy toward and distrust of the Soviet Union, yet without the old crusade-like sense of moral equivalence to war which had marked American anticommunism/anti-Sovietism in the Cold War decades. Yankelovich characterizes this prevalent attitude as "'a live-and-let-live pragmatism,' not an anticommunist crusade." Some 61 percent of respondents agreed that "the Soviets lie, cheat and steal—do anything to further the cause of communism." Yet 67 percent of the same sample asserted that "we should let the communists have their system while we have ours, that 'there's room in the world for both.'" And the so-called new patriotism notwithstanding, 76 percent felt that "America has been less than forthcoming in working things out with the Russians than it might be and that we have to share some of the blame for the deterioration of the relationship."[48]

The old functional equivalence to war also was lacking. Sixty-one percent of respondents were "convinced that the Soviets will seize every possible advantage they can" and that they "have cheated on just about every treaty and agreement they've ever signed." But they also felt that "it is time for negotiations, not confrontations." One reason was increased unwillingness to subordinate other priorities, especially economic ones, to the national security imperative. A second and even more compelling reason was a greater fear of nuclear war than the American public had ever experienced before. Scenarios of limited or winnable nuclear war were rejected (89 to 9 percent and 83 to 14 percent on the most relevant questions). At the same time, concern was rising that the escalation of the arms race and the deterioration of overall relations were making the prospect of nuclear war

[47]Tom W. Smith, "The Polls: American Attitudes toward the Soviet Union and Communism," *Public Opinion Quarterly* 47 (Summer 1983): 279.

[48]Daniel Yankelovich and John Doble, "The Public Mood," *Foreign Affairs* 63 (Fall 1984): 33–46. See also William Schneider, "Conservatism, Not Interventionism: Trends in Foreign Policy Opinion, 1974–1982," in *Eagle Defiant: United States Foreign Policy in the 1980s*, ed. Kenneth A. Oye, Robert J. Lieber, and Donald Rothchild (Boston: Little, Brown, 1983), pp. 33–64; and John E. Rielly, ed., *American Public Opinion and U.S. Foreign Policy, 1983* (Chicago: Chicago Council on Foreign Relations, 1983).

Table 7.2. Percentage of U.S. respondents who approved President Reagan's overall job performance and handling of foreign policy, February 1981–September 1984

Month and years	Overall job performance[a]	Handling of foreign policy[b]
February 1981	55%	—
August 1981	60	52%
March 1982	46	36
July 1982	46	36
December 1982	41	38
April 1983	41	32
October 1983[c]	53	61
November 1983	53	46
February 1984	55	40
July 1984	53	43
September 1984	55	49

NOTE: All responses are from Gallup polls with the exception of those to the questions regarding Reagan's handling of foreign policy in October 1983 (ABC-*Washington Post* poll) and September 1984 (Harris poll).

[a]Standard Gallup question: "Do you approve or disapprove of the way Ronald Reagan is handling his job as president?"

[b]Standard Gallup question: "Do you approve or disapprove of the way President Reagan is handling foreign policy?"

[c]The polls conducted in October 1983 followed the bombing of the American Marine barracks in Beirut and the invasion of Grenada.

more likely. Over two-thirds of the respondents felt that if the nuclear arms race continued, "it's only a matter of time before they are used." And an overwhelming 96 percent felt that "picking a fight with the Soviet Union is too dangerous in a nuclear world."[49]

Ronald Reagan's enormous election victories in 1980 and 1984 obscured somewhat the extent of the American public's foreign policy disorientation. As many studies have shown, however, the Reagan landslides reflected more enthusiasm for his persona than for his policies. And to the extent that votes were issue-based, they had more to do with Reagan's economic policies than with his foreign policies. Reagan's handling of foreign policy received consistently lower ratings than his overall job performance (see Table 7.2). Only in October 1983, in the wake of the bombing of the American Marine barracks in Beirut and the invasion of Grenada, did the president receive a higher rating for his foreign policy performance. The Grenada invasion was hailed as a success, and while the Beirut bombing manifested a policy failure, it nevertheless set off the rally effect common to foreign policy crises. More telling is the 15-point decline in Reagan's

[49]Yankelovich and Doble, "Public Mood."

foreign policy rating within a month. The rally effect did not last, and the Grenada invasion did not cause Americans to reassess in any general way their reluctance to accept Reagan's approach to foreign policy.

At the level of elite opinion, Ole Holsti and James Rosenau's characterization of a "three-headed eagle" still seems to apply.[50] These authors trace the cracking of the old consensus to the Vietnam War. Since then, while there has been "broad agreement in deploring" such actions as the Soviet invasion of Afghanistan, the divisions over the implications for American–Soviet relations have persisted and even deepened. They found "near unanimity about the expansionist character of Soviet foreign policy goals," but "a far greater diversity of view . . . on the question of how best to deal with the USSR." Criticism of the failings of détente was widespread, but fewer than 1 in 3 respondents agreed with the sweeping critique of détente as "a dangerous form of appeasement." Similarly, concern over a military imbalance led a majority of respondents to support increased defense spending, but a majority also cited arms control as a "very important" foreign policy goal. On the basis of these and other findings, they conclude that "efforts by the Reagan administration to create a foreign policy consensus" even within the elite have met with "only modest success."[51]

Thus, while the détente strategy pursued in the 1970s remained largely discredited, the Cold War ideology had not recaptured its old legitimacy. The general feeling was that while the reality of the Soviet threat may have been underemphasized in the détente era, the exigencies of Cold War now seemed to be overemphasized. Anticommunism still was a powerful ethic but fell short of the moral equivalent of war. National security still was an obvious imperative but its pursuit failed to attain the status of the functional equivalent of war. This paradox engendered the sense of ideological anomie that contributed to the domestic constraints that were seen in the Siberian pipeline case and, more broadly, has colored the continuing search for a new foreign policy identity. Until this search somehow is re-

---

[50]Ole R. Holsti and James N. Rosenau, *American Leadership in World Affairs: Vietnam and the Breakdown of Consensus* (Boston: Allen & Unwin, 1984). The "three heads" of the American eagle are identified as the Cold War Internationalists, the Post–Cold War Internationalists, and the Semi-Isolationists.

[51]Ibid., pp. 233–34, 228. The study by the Chicago Council on Foreign Relations supports this conclusion. On a number of key issues the dominant opinion in its leadership sample opposed key Reagan policies: e.g., 69% opposed restricting U.S.–Soviet trade and 79% favored a freeze on nuclear weapons "right now if the Soviets would agree" (*American Public Opinion and U.S. Foreign Policy, 1983*, p. 37).

solved, there is likely to continue to be more conflict than consensus not only on East–West energy trade but on most other foreign policy issues as well.

Group Economic Interests

Further complicating this search is the complexity introduced by the increased salience of economic interests. Here, too, the Siberian pipeline case reflects broader trends and transformations. Instead of exhibiting the complementarity of private economic and state political interests seen in the Friendship oil pipeline case, or even the ambivalence of the early 1970s, economic interests lined up squarely against the sanctions. In part this was a result of timing: the 1982 recession made it excessively difficult for groups to absorb any additional economic costs. The $180 million that the Caterpillar Tractor Company lost to the sanctions contributed rather substantially to the $264 million loss (a company record) posted for the first half of 1983. But the problem ran deeper than inauspicious timing. The overall production pattern of companies that manufactured energy equipment and technology had become highly export-oriented. In 1982, for example, 55 percent of the total output of drilling and other field machinery was exported. There simply was not much new oil and gas development going on in the United States. Profitability therefore depended on the ability to expand exports. Yet it was difficult to do so without the Soviet market. General Electric's $171 million sale of compressor stations for the Siberian pipeline represented 19 percent of the total exports by compressor manufacturers in 1982. Had the GE sale gone through, the dollar value of the total U.S. compressor exports would have increased 11 percent in 1982; with the embargo, it declined 10 percent.[52]

In the future the relative importance of the Soviet market for energy equipment and technology exports is likely to increase. With the OPEC countries enforcing production quotas upon themselves, the Soviet Union is one of the few countries in the world that is planning major increases in oil and gas production. At the preliminary American–Soviet trade talks held in Moscow in January 1985, Soviet officials reportedly expressed strong interest in American equipment and technology for a number of their energy projects, in particular the $600 million Barents Sea project, citing the similarities with Alaskan oil

[52]U.S. Department of Commerce, *1983 Industrial Outlook* (Washington, D.C.: Government Printing Office, 1983), pp. 23–7, 22–9.

projects. At the same time, though, they stressed that "energy development plans would proceed with or without the United States."[53]

Another project reportedly under discussion with American firms was the 2,500-mile Siberia-to-Moscow coal slurry pipeline. According to one commentator, such an undertaking "would be quite simply the biggest technological project in human history, and among the most technologically challenging."[54] It could involve substantial amounts of imported equipment (wide-diameter pipe, pipelaying equipment, processing plants, compressor stations) as well as technology licensing agreements, engineering contracts, and barter deals. Needless to say, Western European firms are known to be quite interested. In late 1982 the ubiquitous Armand Hammer told a press conference in Moscow that his Occidental Petroleum Company and Bechtel Engineering were interested. Even if Soviet planners decide to go ahead with the project, however, American firms cannot be certain that American regulators will permit the exports. In addition, for reasons of both retaliation and pragmatism, following the Siberian gas pipeline sanctions the Soviets began to discriminate against American firms and their foreign subsidiaries in their requests for bids and letting of contracts. In early 1985 there even were reports that the Twelfth Five-Year Plan would exclude American firms as much as possible.[55]

Of course, even given the possibility that some or all of these contracts might go to American firms, the trade directly at stake still would not be extensive. It would amount to much less, for example, than either the energy equipment exported by Western Europe or the grain exported by the United States. But it is precisely for this reason that the arousal of American manufacturers by and since the pipeline sanctions has been so significant. Such groups as the National Association of Manufacturers (NAM) and the U.S. Chamber of Commerce have been concerned not just about the direct costs of the sanctions but especially about delays that result from the cumbersome licensing process, which, because of apprehension over illegal transshipment, also affects many exports to noncommunist destinations. According to the President's Commission on Industrial Competitiveness, a blue-ribbon group appointed by President Reagan, as much as $12 billion of the 1984 trade deficit could be traced to the delays and denials of the export control licensing process.[56]

[53]*New York Times*, February 3, 1985, p. 7.

[54]*Journal of Commerce*, December 6, 1982, p. 1C.

[55]*Washington Post*, March 1, 1985, p. A1, and April 4, 1985, p. E4.

[56]Figure cited by Rep. Don Bonker (D-Wash.), in "Guest Column," *Europe* (March/April 1985), p. 56.

American industry could ill afford these broader costs. Exports, which as recently as 1972 amounted to only 12 percent of total manufacturing production, now accounted for 23 percent. For key sectors the export share of output was even greater: 62 percent for aerospace, 49 percent for oil field machinery, 43 percent for construction machinery, 30 percent for farm machinery, 30 percent for computers.[57] Yet trends in the early 1980s were not particularly reassuring. The trade deficit hit a record $148.5 billion in 1985, in part because of rising imports and in part because of the overvaluation of the dollar. But in more fundamental ways the problem was the deterioration in the competitiveness of American manufactured and technological exports. As an NAM report stated in 1985, "the problem of competitiveness is real, is pervasive across all sectors of industry, is deep-rooted and is well exemplified by the trade crisis."[58]

Another measure of the increased importance of exports to the overall American economy was the fact that between 1977 and 1980 manufactured exports accounted for nearly 30 percent of the net increase in total private-sector employment, for a growth rate of 47 percent at a time when the aggregate unemployment rate was going up. Again, while the direct effect of the anti-Soviet energy trade sanctions was not particularly great, its marginal value was made far greater by existing conditions of high unemployment. While hard statistics are lacking, there also has been speculation on the indirect unemployment effects of encouraging U.S.-based multinationals to relocate their production with their foreign affiliates, out of the reach of unilateral American sanctions.

Quite simply, then, the economic burdens to be borne and the price to be paid for anti-Soviet energy trade sanctions, or for that matter for other parts of the struggle against the Soviet Union, had become much less affordable than they once were.[59] Back in 1961, when John Kennedy made this clarion call, the American economy was enjoying an era of unprecedented prosperity. Since then, however, it has been

[57]Data from Stephen L. Cooney, Jr., *U.S. Trade: Record of the 1970s, Challenge of the 1980s* (Washington, D.C.: National Association of Manufacturers, 1983).

[58]Stephen L. Cooney, Jr., *U.S. Trade, Industrial Competitiveness, and Economic Growth* (Washington, D.C.: National Association of Manufacturers, 1985), p. 5.

[59]On military spending, for example, public support fell off almost as rapidly as it had risen. Respondents who believe that the United States was spending "too little" on defense increased from about 35% in January 1979 to 42% in January 1980 to 57% in January 1981. By January 1982 the percentage had dropped back to 32%, and by January 1983 to about 12% (William Schneider, "Military Spending: The Public Seems to Say, 'We've Gone Far Enough,'" *National Journal*, April 23, 1983, pp. 866–67).

plagued by recurring recessions, declining international competitiveness, and mounting trade deficits. Such a weakened economy, like the eroded ideology, is not a particularly strong base on which to build foreign policy consensus. And because the root sources involve secular changes even more than just the temporalities of the business cycle, the prospect of restoring the kind of consensus that precludes domestic constraints on economically costly foreign policies appears to be slight.

CONCLUSIONS: THE LIMITS OF AMERICAN ECONOMIC COERCIVE POWER

The United States thus finds its economic coercive power against the Soviet Union severely constrained by the combined effects of the multilateral alternative trade partner dilemma and the domestic bluffer's dilemma. When we reach this conclusion, though, it is important to bear in mind three points about the scope and the limits of its implications.

First, at the broad theoretical level, I am *not* making a sweeping claim against the efficacy of economic coercion in international relations. In some respects the difficulties encountered by attempts to limit East–West energy trade are to be expected in all efforts to wield economic coercive power. This is especially the case, for example, in respect to the alternative trade partner dilemma. With industrial production having become so internationalized, and with so many channels for technology transfer, the possibilities for any target state to find alternative trade partners seem almost endless. Nevertheless, each particular case must be analyzed within its particular structural and relational context. The essence of my critique of American sanctions against the Soviet Union has been based on the particular complex political economy in which this particular coercer state has attempted to exercise its economic power against this particular target state. Other cases involving other coercer and target states (or, for that matter, the same coercer but a different target state) will have their own particular political economies. Therefore, while the theoretical thrust of this analysis does reinforce the general contention that sanctions don't work, any generalizations must be kept at the level of patterns and probabilities.

A second qualification goes back to the original distinction made in Chapter 1 between the symbolic-expressive objectives and the instrumental objectives of economic sanctions. The evidence I have presented and the explanation I have offered concerning the constraints on American instrumental economic coercive power do not refute the Wilsonian-style arguments in favor of anti-Soviet sanctions as symbolic-expressive action. They do, however, imply that whatever value symbolic action may be deemed to have must neither be mistaken for instrumental success nor presumed automatically to override the political and economic costs entailed by the imposition of sanctions. Moreover, as Chapter 1 also stressed and as the Siberian gas pipeline case especially brought out, symbolic value should not be confused with the more instrumental signal-sending deterrent function that sanctions also usually are intended to have. It is only in the symbolic sense that success comes with the taking of the action in and of itself. Because deterrence requires that the signal be received as it was intended, it is more subject to constraints at both the multilateral and domestic levels.

Third, the energy sanctions have implications for other sectors of East–West trade. Here the high-technology sector is the exception that proves the rule. As I first noted in Chapter 1 and discussed in more detail in Chapter 6, at the same time that the intra-alliance imbroglio erupted over the Siberian gas pipeline, the COCOM nations forged a new agreement for tighter controls on militarily relevant high technologies. This sector is set apart by the many direct connections between the exports being controlled and Soviet military capabilities. The Western allies debate where the line of military relevance should be drawn, but this subject does not arouse the same kind of disagreement as energy trade over whether multilateral controls serve mutual foreign policy interests. Nor is there as much contention within American politics over export opportunities lost to controls on militarily relevant high technology.

In virtually all other sectors of trade, however, multilateral and domestic constraints are substantial. Grain is the most salient other example. The multilateral constraints that surrounded the sale of grain in 1980 included an even wider range of alternative trade partners than the energy case encountered.[60] The domestic constraints also were perhaps among the most blatant examples ever of interest group pressure in American politics. Even more important, the constraints that American economic coercive power now faces in the grain sector and in most others are deeply rooted in the contemporary international and domestic political economy. They involve not

---

[60]See, for example, Robert L. Paarlberg, *Food Trade and Foreign Policy: India, the Soviet Union, and the United States* (Ithaca: Cornell University Press, 1985).

just policy-specific disagreements or situational disputes but broader changes in the definition of interests and the distribution of power in world politics. These trends and transformations may be somewhat malleable under certain conditions, such as an extraordinarily severe East–West political crisis. Short of such a drastic development, they are not likely to be reversed or abated.

In sum, the prospect that any anti-Soviet sanctions may produce significant gains for American foreign policy in terms of any of its long-standing economic and political-instrumental objectives is exceedingly slight. The first Reagan administration's rhetoric about the imminent collapse of the Soviet economy if only the United States and its allies would continue to wage economic warfare against it was somewhat lacking in realism. It seemed to be shaped far more by ideological conceptions than by hard analysis. At minimum, as Ed Hewett has noted, the Soviets have a capacity "to muddle through in conditions that would not be tolerated in the West."[61] We may have reason to doubt whether the Soviet system will be capable of overcoming its own inherent obstacles to economic progress. But we have far greater reason to doubt the claims and visions of recent American proponents of economic warfare.

Prospects for the economic defense objective of limiting the Soviet Union's most militarily relevant economic capabilities may be better, but only if a sound policy is pursued in energy and other less strategic sectors of trade. Experience shows that the more vehemently the United States pushes its allies for everything, the less likely it is to get anything.[62] It also bears noting that even if sanctions were to have a significant effect on the Soviet economy, their impact would be less likely to be translated into curtailment of Soviet military spending than the simplistic resource-freeing model suggests. It might be costly for the Soviets to keep military spending up, but, as Marshall Shulman writes, "no one who knows the Russians can doubt that this is what they will do."[63] As for the objective of political influence, economic sanctions are unlikely to have even limited success. There has yet to be a major issue, foreign or domestic, on which economic sanctions have compelled the Soviets to change their policies. The war in Afghanistan goes on, martial law continues in Poland, Soviet dissi-

---

[61]Ed A. Hewett, *Energy, Economics and Foreign Policy in the Soviet Union* (Washington, D.C.: Brookings Institution, 1984), p. 81.

[62]William Root, "Trade Controls That Work," *Foreign Policy* 56 (Fall 1984): 61–80; Frost and Stent, "NATO's Troubles with East–West Trade."

[63]Marshall Shulman, "A Coming Tornado in U.S.–Soviet Relations," *New York Times*, June 2, 1985, p. E23.

dents continue to be repressed. As for the containment objective, which really is as much about reinforcing Western solidarity as about stopping Soviet influence, future sanctions run the risk of being not just unsuccessful but counterproductive. The essential reason is stated in more general terms by Stanley Hoffmann, in whose view "the biggest threat to the alliance today is not the Soviet menace . . . the gravest threat lies in the centrifugal potential of the present situation."[64] The American objective in the Siberian pipeline case may have been to stop the threat of dependence on Soviet gas. But the actual effects did more harm than good to alliance solidarity.

Finally, there is the issue of the deterrent effect of sanctions. The accepted wisdom has been that to go about business as usual would be to undermine the credibility of the overall American deterrence posture, that the United States had to do something to demonstrate its will and resolve as well as its capabilities. But when alliance solidarity and domestic consensus give way to alternative trade partners and domestic conflict, Moscow receives a very different signal from the one that Washington intended to send. Economic sanctions become evidence of American weakness rather than strength and thus sap rather than buttress the credibility of deterrence.

What, then, is to be done? The author often faces a dilemma: it is wrong to ignore the prescriptive implications of one's arguments yet difficult to develop them as fully as an intensive analysis requires. Let me therefore simply refer to my detailed discussion elsewhere of the logic of a renewed attempt at economic inducement.[65] My arguments there are based in part on positive reasoning, on the possibilities held out by an economic inducement strategy as a source of American bargaining influence in the initial stages of a renewed détente and as a necessary (but not sufficient) condition for longer term stabilization of the superpower relationship. They also are based in part on negative reasoning, on the limits that the complexities of the contemporary international and domestic political economy have imposed on American economic coercive power. This point has been at the center of this study and needs to be emphasized at its close. For in respect to East–West trade as well as other foreign policy issues, policies predicated on yesterday's realities stand little chance of succeeding in tomorrow's world.

[64]Hoffman, "Western Alliance," p. 124.
[65]Bruce W. Jentleson, "The Political Basis for Trade in U.S.–Soviet Relations," *Millennium: Journal of International Studies* 15 (Spring 1986): 27–47.

Bibliography

BOOKS, ARTICLES, PAPERS, AND PUBLIC DOCUMENTS

Acheson, Dean. *Present at the Creation.* New York: Norton, 1969.

Adelman, M. A. *The World Petroleum Market.* Baltimore: Johns Hopkins University Press, 1972.

Adler-Karlsson, Gunnar. *Western Economic Warfare, 1947–1967.* Stockholm: Almquist & Wiksell, 1968.

Agnelli, Giovanni. "East–West Trade: A European View." *Foreign Affairs* 58 (Summer 1980): 1016–33.

Baer, George W. "Sanctions and Security: The League of Nations and the Italian–Ethiopian War, 1935–1936." *International Organization* 27 (Spring 1973): 165–79.

Baldwin, David A. *Economic Statecraft.* Princeton: Princeton University Press, 1985.

Barber, James. "Economic Sanctions as a Policy Instrument." *International Affairs* (London) 55 (July 1979): 367–84.

Becker, Abraham S., ed. *Economic Relations with the USSR.* Lexington, Mass.: Heath, 1983.

Bergson, Abram, and Herbert S. Levine, eds. *The Soviet Economy toward the Year 2000.* London: George Allen & Unwin, 1983.

Berkowitz, Morton, and P. G. Bock. "National Security." In *International Encyclopedia of the Social Sciences,* vol. 11. New York: Free Press, 1968.

Berman, Harold J., and John R. Garson. "United States Export Controls: Past, Present, and Future." *Columbia Law Review* 67 (May 1967): 791–890.

Bertsch, Gary K. *East–West Strategic Trade, COCOM, and the Atlantic Alliance.* Paris: Atlantic Institute, 1983.

⸻ and John S. McIntyre, eds. *National Security and Technology Transfer: The Strategic Dimensions of East–West Trade.* Boulder, Colo.: Westview Press, 1983.

Bingham, Jonathan, and Victor Johnson. "A Rational Approach to Export Controls." *Foreign Affairs* 57 (Spring 1979): 894–920.

Blau, Peter M. *Exchange and Power in Social Life.* New York: Wiley, 1964.

247

Brzezinski, Zbigniew. *Power and Principle: Memoirs of the National Security Advisor.* New York: Farrar, Straus, Giroux, 1983.

Bucy, J. Fred. "Technology Transfer and East–West Trade: A Reappraisal." *International Security* 5 (Winter 1980–81): 132–51.

Caldwell, Dan. *American–Soviet Relations from 1947 to the Nixon-Kissinger Grand Design.* Westport, Conn.: Greenwood Press, 1981.

Caldwell, Lawrence T., and William Diebold, Jr. *Soviet–American Relations in the 1980s: Superpower Politics and East–West Trade.* New York: McGraw-Hill, 1981.

Campbell, Robert W. *Soviet Energy Technologies.* Bloomington: Indiana University Press, 1981.

_____. *The Economics of Soviet Oil and Gas.* Baltimore: Johns Hopkins University Press, 1968.

Chapman, John W. "Coercion in Politics and Strategy." In *Coercion,* ed. J. Roland Pennock and John W. Chapman, pp. 289–321. Chicago: Aldine-Atherton, 1972.

Chuthasmit, Suchati. "The Experience of the United States and Its Allies in Controlling Trade with the Red Bloc." Ph.D. dissertation, Fletcher School of Law and Diplomacy, Tufts University, 1961.

Crawford, Beverly, and Stefanie Lenway. "Decision Modes and International Regime Change: Western Collaboration on East–West Trade." *World Politics* 37 (April 1985): 375–407.

Dahl, Robert A. "Power." In *International Encyclopedia of the Social Sciences.* Vol. 12, New York: Free Press, 1968.

_____. "The Concept of Power." *Behavioral Science* 2 (July 1957): 201–15.

Dean, Robert W. *West German Trade with the East: The Political Dimension.* New York: Praeger, 1974.

De Porte, A. W. *Europe between the Superpowers: The Enduring Balance.* New Haven: Yale University Press, 1979.

Destler, I. M. *Making Foreign Economic Policy.* Washington, D.C.: Brookings Institution, 1980.

Dienes, Leslie, and Theodore Shabad. *The Soviet Energy System: Resource Use and Policies.* New York: Wiley, 1979.

Doxey, Margaret P. *Economic Sanctions and International Enforcement.* New York: Oxford University Press, 1980.

_____. "International Sanctions: A Framework for Analysis with Special Reference to the U.N. and Southern Africa." *International Organization* 26 (Summer 1972): 525–50.

Frankel, P. H. *Mattei: Oil and Power Politics.* New York: Praeger, 1966.

Freedman, Robert Owen. *Economic Warfare in the Communist Bloc.* New York: Praeger, 1970.

Frost, Ellen L., and Angela E. Stent. "NATO's Troubles with East–West Trade." *International Security* 8 (Summer 1983): 179–200.

Gaddis, John Lewis. *Strategies of Containment.* New York: Oxford University Press, 1982.

_____. *The United States and the Origins of the Cold War.* New York: Columbia University Press, 1972.

Galtung, Johan. "On the Effects of International Sanctions, with Examples from the Case of Rhodesia." *World Politics* 19 (April 1967): 378–416.

Garthoff, Raymond L. *Détente and Confrontation: American–Soviet Relations from Nixon to Reagan.* Washington, D.C.: Brookings Institution, 1985.

Gelman, Harry. *The Brezhnev Politburo and the Decline of Détente.* Ithaca: Cornell University Press, 1984.

George, Alexander L. "Domestic Constraints on Regime Change in U.S. Foreign Policy: The Need for Policy Legitimacy." In *Change in the International System,* ed. Ole R. Holsti, Randolph M. Siverson, and Alexander L. George, pp. 233–62. Boulder, Colo.: Westview Press, 1980.

_____. "Case Studies and Theory Development: The Method of Structured, Focused Comparison." In *Diplomatic History: New Approaches,* ed. Paul Gordon Laurer, pp. 43–68. New York: Free Press, 1979.

_____ and Richard Smoke. *Deterrence in American Foreign Policy: Theory and Practice.* New York: Columbia University Press, 1974.

Gershman, Carl. "Selling Them the Rope: Business and the Soviets." *Commentary* 67 (April 1979): 35–45.

Gilmore, Richard. *A Poor Harvest: The Clash of Policies and Interests in the Grain Trade.* New York: Longmans, 1982.

Gilpin, Robert. *War and Change in International Politics.* New York: Cambridge University Press, 1981.

Golan, Jeffrey W. "U.S. Technology Transfers to the Soviet Union and the Protection of National Security." *Law and Policy in International Business* 11 (1979): 1037–1107.

Goldman, Marshall I. *The Enigma of Soviet Petroleum.* London: George Allen & Unwin, 1980.

_____. *Détente and Dollars.* New York: Basic Books, 1975.

Goldstein, Donald J., ed. *Energy and National Security: Proceedings of a Special Conference.* Washington, D.C.: National Defense University Press, 1981.

Gustafson, Thane. *Soviet Negotiating Strategy: The East–West Gas Pipeline Deal, 1980–1984.* R-3220-FF. Santa Monica: Rand, 1985.

_____. *Selling Them the Rope: Soviet Technology Policy and U.S. Export Controls.* R-2649-ARPA. Santa Monica: Rand, 1981.

Haig, Alexander M. *Caveat: Realism, Reagan, and Foreign Policy.* New York: Macmillan, 1984.

Hanson, Philip. *Trade and Technology in Soviet–Western Relations.* New York: Columbia University Press, 1981.

Hardt, John P., and George D. Holliday. *U.S.–Soviet Commercial Relations: The Interplay of Economics, Technology Transfer, and Diplomacy.* Washington, D.C.: Government Printing Office, 1973.

_____, _____, and Young C. Kim. *Western Investment in Communist Economies.* Washington, D.C.: Government Printing Office, 1974.

Hart, Jeffrey. "Three Approaches to the Measurement of Power in International Relations." *International Organization* 30 (Spring 1976): 289–305.

Hartshorn, J. E. *Politics and World Oil Economics.* New York: Praeger, 1967.

Hartz, Louis. *The Liberal Tradition in America.* New York: Harcourt Brace Jovanovich, 1955.

Hassmann, Heinrich. *Oil in the Soviet Union.* Princeton: Princeton University Press, 1953.

Hersh, Seymour M. *The Price of Power: Kissinger in the Nixon White House.* New York: Summit, 1983.

Hewett, Ed A. *Energy, Economics, and Foreign Policy in the Soviet Union*. Washington, D.C.: Brookings Institution, 1984.

Hirschman, Albert O. *National Power and the Structure of Foreign Trade*. Rev. ed. Berkeley: University of California Press, 1980.

Hoffman, Michael L. "Problems of East–West Trade." *International Conciliation*, no. 511, January 1957.

Hoffmann, Stanley. "The Western Alliance: Drift or Harmony?" *International Security* 6 (Fall 1981): 105–25.

Holsti, Ole R., and James N. Rosenau. *American Leadership in World Affairs: Vietnam and the Breakdown of Consensus*. Boston: Allen & Unwin, 1984.

Holzman, Franklyn D., and Robert Legvold. "The Economics and Politics of East–West Relations." *International Organization* 29 (Winter 1975): 275–320.

Hufbauer, Gary C., and Jeffery J. Schott. *Economic Sanctions Reconsidered: History and Current Policy*. Washington, D.C.: Institute for International Economics, 1985.

Huntington, Samuel P. "Trade, Technology, and Leverage: Economic Diplomacy." *Foreign Policy* 32 (Fall 1978): 63–80.

International Energy Agency. *Energy Policies and Programmes of IEA Countries, 1984*. Paris: IEA/OECD, 1984.

Jensen, Robert G., Theodore Shabad, and Arthur W. Wright, eds. *Soviet Natural Resources in the World Economy*. Chicago: University of Chicago Press, 1983.

Jentleson, Bruce W. "The Political Basis for Trade in U.S.–Soviet Relations." *Millennium: Journal of International Studies*, 15 (Spring 1986): 27–47.

———. "From Consensus to Conflict: The Domestic Political Economy of East–West Energy Trade." *International Organization* 38 (Autumn 1984): 625–60.

———. "Khrushchev's Oil and Brezhnev's Natural Gas Pipelines." In *Will Europe Fight for Oil? Energy Relations in the Atlantic Area*, ed. Robert J. Lieber, pp. 33–69. New York: Praeger, 1983.

Karr, Miriam, and Roger W. Robinson, Jr. "Soviet Gas: Risk or Reward?" *Washington Quarterly* 4 (Autumn 1981): 3–11.

Katzenstein, Peter J., ed. *Between Power and Plenty: Foreign Economic Policies of Advanced Industrial States*. Madison: University of Wisconsin Press, 1978.

———. "International Relations and Domestic Structures: Foreign Economic Policies of Advanced Industrial States." *International Organization* 30 (Winter 1976): 1–45.

Kennan, George F. *Memoirs, 1925–1950*. Boston: Little, Brown, 1967.

———. [Mr. X] "The Sources of Soviet Conduct." *Foreign Affairs* 25 (July 1947): 566–82.

Keohane, Robert O. "Theory of World Politics: Structural Realism and Beyond." Paper presented at the 1982 Annual Meeting of the American Political Science Association, Denver, September 2–5, 1982.

——— and Joseph S. Nye, Jr. *Power and Interdependence*. Boston: Little, Brown, 1977.

Khrushchev, Nikita S. "On Peaceful Coexistence." *Foreign Affairs* 38 (October 1959): 1–18.

Kissinger, Henry. *Years of Upheaval*. Boston: Little, Brown, 1982.

———. *White House Years*. Boston: Little, Brown, 1982.

———. *American Foreign Policy*. New York: Norton, 1977.

Klinghoffer, Arthur Jay. *The Soviet Union and International Oil Politics.* New York: Columbia University Press, 1977.

Knorr, Klaus. *The Power of Nations: The Political Economy of International Relations.* New York: Basic Books, 1975.

_____ and Frank N. Trager, eds. *Economic Issues and National Security.* Lawrence, Kans.: Allen Press, 1977.

Kogan, Norman. *The Politics of Italian Foreign Policy.* New York: Praeger, 1963.

Kolodziej, Edward A. *French International Policy under de Gaulle and Pompidou.* Ithaca: Cornell University Press, 1974.

Krasner, Stephen. "Structural Causes and Regime Consequences: Regimes as Intervening Variables." *International Organization* 36 (Spring 1982): 185–206.

_____. *Defending the National Interest: Raw Materials Investments and U.S. Foreign Policy.* Princeton: Princeton University Press, 1978.

LaFeber, Walter. *America, Russia, and the Cold War, 1945–1984.* 5th ed. New York: Knopf, 1985.

Lebahn, Axel. "The Yamal Gas Pipeline from the USSR to Western Europe in the East–West Conflict." *Aussenpolitik* 3 (1983) 257–81.

Levine, Herbert S. "Soviet Economic Development, Technology Transfer, and Foreign Policy." In *The Domestic Context of Soviet Foreign Policy,* ed. Seweryn Bialer, pp. 177–201. Boulder, Colo.: Westview Press, 1981.

Lindblom, Charles E. *Politics and Markets.* New York: Basic Books, 1977.

Lowi, Theodore J. *The End of Liberalism.* 2d ed. New York: Norton, 1979.

_____. "American Business, Public Policy, Case Studies and Political Theory." *World Politics* 16 (July 1964): 677–715.

McIntosh, Donald. "Coercion and International Politics: A Theoretical Analysis." In *Coercion,* ed. J. Roland Pennock and John W. Chapman, pp. 243–71. Chicago: Aldine-Atherton, 1972.

Marer, Paul, ed. *U.S. Financing of East–West Trade: The Political Economy of Government Credits and the National Interest.* Bloomington, Ind.: International Development Research Center, 1975.

Mastanduno, Michael. "Strategies of Economic Containment: U.S. Trade Relations with the Soviet Union." *World Politics* 37 (July 1985): 503–31.

Maull, Hanns. *Europe and World Energy.* London: Butterworths, 1980.

_____. *Oil and Influence: The Oil Weapon Examined.* Adelphi Paper no. 117. London: International Institute for Strategic Studies, 1975.

Mikesell, Raymond F., and Jack N. Behrman. *Financing Free World Trade with the Sino-Soviet Bloc.* Princeton: Princeton University Press, 1958.

Mill, John Stuart. *Principles of Political Economy.* 7th ed. London, 1929.

Morgan, Dan. *Merchants of Grain.* New York: Viking, 1979.

Morse, Edward. "The Transformation of Foreign Policies: Modernization, Interdependence, and Externalization." *World Politics* 22 (April 1970: 371–93.

National Petroleum Council. *Impact of Oil Exports from the Soviet Bloc.* 2 vols. Washington, D.C., 1962.

Nincic, Miroslav, and Peter Wallensteen, eds. *Dilemmas of Economic Coercion: Sanctions in World Politics.* New York: Praeger, 1983.

Olson, Richard Stuart. "Economic Coercion in World Politics: With a Focus on North–South Relations." *World Politics* 31 (July 1979): 471–94.

Organization for Economic Cooperation and Development. *East–West Technology Transfer*. Paris, 1984.

Organization for European Economic Cooperation. *Europe's Need for Oil: Implications and Lessons of the Suez Crisis*. Paris, 1958.

——. *Private United States Investment in Europe and the Overseas Territories*. Paris, 1955.

Osgood, Theodore K. "East–West Trade Controls and Economic Warfare." Ph.D. thesis, Faculty of Economics, Yale University, 1957.

Ozergene, N. I. *Lessons of the Pipeline Negotiations*. CISA Working Paper no. 40. Los Angeles: Center for International and Strategic Affairs, UCLA, 1983.

Paarlberg, Robert L. *Food Trade and Foreign Policy: India, the Soviet Union, and the United States*. Ithaca: Cornell University Press, 1985.

Parenti, Michael. *The Anti-Communist Impulse*. New York: Random House, 1969.

Parrott, Bruce. *Politics and Technology in the Soviet Union*. Cambridge: MIT Press, 1983.

——, ed. *Trade, Technology, and Soviet–American Relations*. Bloomington: Indiana University Press, 1985.

Perle, Richard. "The Strategic Implications of West–East Technology Transfer." In *The Conduct of East–West Relations in the 1980s*, pt. 2, Adelphi Paper no. 190, pp. 20–27. London: International Institute for Strategic Studies, 1984.

Peterson, Peter G. *U.S.–Soviet Commercial Relations in a New Era*. Washington, D.C.: Government Printing Office, 1972.

Pisar, Samuel. *Coexistence and Commerce*. New York: McGraw-Hill, 1972.

Root, William. "Trade Controls That Work." *Foreign Policy* 56 (Fall 1984): 61–80.

Rosecrance, Richard N. *International Relations: Peace or War?* New York: McGraw-Hill, 1973.

Russell, Jeremy. *Geopolitics of Natural Gas*. Cambridge, Mass.: Ballinger, 1983.

——. *Energy as a Factor in Soviet Foreign Policy*. Lexington, Mass.: Heath, 1976.

Schelling, Thomas C. *International Economics*. Boston: Allyn & Bacon, 1958.

Schlesinger, Arthur M., Jr. *The Imperial Presidency*. Boston: Houghton Mifflin, 1973.

Schreiber, Anna P. "Economic Coercion as an Instrument of Foreign Policy: U.S. Economic Measures against Cuba and the Dominican Republic." *World Politics* 25 (April 1973): 387–413.

Shonfield, Andrew. *Modern Capitalism: The Changing Balance of Public and Private Power*. New York: Oxford University Press, 1965.

Smith, Gordon B., ed. *The Politics of East–West Trade*. Boulder, Colo.: Westview Press, 1984.

Spero, Joan Edelman. *The Politics of International Economic Relations*. New York: St. Martin's Press, 1977.

Stent, Angela. *From Embargo to Ostpolitik: The Political Economy of West German–Soviet Relations, 1955–1980*. New York: Cambridge University Press, 1981.

——. *East–West Technology Transfer: European Perspectives*. Beverly Hills, Calif.: Sage, 1980.

Stern, Jonathan P. *International Gas Trade in Europe: The Policies of Exporting and Importing Countries.* London: Heinemann, 1984.
____. "Specters and Pipe Dreams." *Foreign Policy* 48 (Fall 1982): 21–36.
____. *Soviet Natural Gas Development to 1990.* Lexington, Mass.: Heath, 1980.
Stern, Paula. *Water's Edge: Domestic Politics and the Making of American Foreign Policy.* Westport, Conn.: Greenwood Press, 1979.
Stowell, Christopher E. *Oil and Gas Development in the U.S.S.R.* Tulsa: Petroleum Publishing Company, 1974.
Strack, Harry R. *Sanctions: The Case of Rhodesia.* Syracuse, N.Y.: Syracuse University Press, 1978.
Sutton, Antony C. *Western Technology and Soviet Economic Development, 1945 to 1965.* Stanford: Hoover Institution Press, 1973.
Trilateral Commission. *East–West Trade at a Crossroads: Economic Relations with the Soviet Union and Eastern Europe.* New York: New York University Press, 1982.
Tugendhat, Christopher. *Oil: The Biggest Business.* New York: Putnam, 1968.
Ulam, Adam B. *Expansion and Coexistence: The History of Soviet Foreign Policy, 1917–67.* New York: Praeger, 1968.
United Nations, Economic Commission for Europe. *Economic Survey of Europe since the War.* Geneva, 1953.
____. *Economic Survey for Europe, 1953.* New York, 1954.
United States. Central Intelligence Agency. "Prospects for Soviet Oil Production: A Supplemental Analysis." ER 77-10425. July 1977.
____. "Prospects for Soviet Oil Production." ER 77-10270. April 1977.
____. "U.S.S.R. Hard Currency Trade and Payments, 1977–78." ER 77-10035 U. March 1977.
____. "U.S.S.R.: Long-Range Prospects for Hard Currency Trade." A (ER) 75–61. January 1975.
U.S. Congress. Senate. Committee on Banking, Housing, and Urban Affairs. *Proposed Trans-Siberian Natural Gas Pipeline: Hearings.* 97th Cong., 1st sess., 1981.
____. *U.S. Export Control Policy and Extension of the Export Administration Act: Hearings.* 96th Cong., 1st sess., 1979.
____. Subcommittee on International Finance. *Reauthorization of the Export Administration Act: Hearings.* 98th Cong., 1st sess., 1983.
____. *U.S. Embargo of Food and Technology to the Soviet Union: Hearings.* 96th Cong., 2d sess., 1980.
____. *U.S. Export Policy.* 96th Cong., 1st sess., 1979.
____. *Trade and Technology: Hearings.* 96th Cong., 1st sess., 1979.
____. *Export Expansion and Regulation: Hearings.* 91st Cong. 1st sess., 1969.
____. Committee on Foreign Relations. *NATO Today: The Alliance in Evolution.* Washington, D.C.: Government Printing Office, 1982.
____. *East–West Trade: Hearings.* 89th Cong., 1st sess., 1965.
____. *East–West Trade: Hearings.* 88th Cong., 2d sess., 1964.
____. *East–West Trade: Hearings.* 83d Cong., 2d sess., 1954.
____. Subcommittee on Multinational Corporations. *Multinational Corporations and United States Foreign Policy: Hearings.* 94th Cong., 1st sess., 1975.
____. *U.S. Trade and Investment in the Soviet Union and Eastern Europe: The Role of Multinational Corporations.* 93d Cong., 2d sess., 1974.

———. *Control of Trade with the Soviet Bloc: Hearings.* 83d Cong., 1st sess., 1953.
———. Committee on the Judiciary, Subcommittee to Investigate the Administration of the Internal Security Act and Other Internal Security Laws. *Problems Raised by the Soviet Oil Offensive.* Committee Print. 87th Cong., 2d sess., 1962.
———. *Soviet Oil in East–West Trade: Hearings.* 87th Cong., 2d sess., 1962.
———. Committee on Science and Technology, Subcommittee on Investigation and Oversight. *American Technology Transfer and Soviet Energy Planning: Hearings.* 97th Cong., 1st and 2d sess., 1981–82.
———. Select Committee on Intelligence. *The Soviet Oil Situation: An Evaluation of CIA Analyses of Soviet Oil Production.* Staff Report. 95th Cong., 2d sess., 1978.
———. Joint Economic Committee. *East–West Commercial Policy: A Congressional Dialogue with the Reagan Administration.* 97th Cong., 2d sess., 1982.
———. *Soviet Economy in the 1980s: Problems and Prospects.* Joint Committee Print. 97th Cong., 2d sess., 1982.
———. *Issues in East–West Commercial Relations.* 95th Cong., 2d sess., 1979.
———. *Soviet Economic Prospects for the Seventies.* 93d Cong., 1st sess., 1973.
———. *A New Look at Trade Policy toward the Communist Bloc.* 87th Cong., 1st sess., 1961.
U.S. Congress. House. Committee on Banking, Housing, and Urban Affairs, Subcommittee on International Finance. *The Role of the Export-Import Bank and Export Controls in U.S. International Economic Policy: Hearings.* 93rd Cong., 2d sess., 1974.
———. Subcommittee on International Trade. *To Extend and Amend the Export Control Act of 1949: Hearings.* 91st Cong., 1st sess., 1969.
———. Committee on International Relations, Subcommittee on International Economic Policy and Trade. *Export Licensing: COCOM List Review Proposals of the United States: Hearings.* 95th Cong., 2d sess., 1978.
———. *Export Licensing of Advanced Technology: A Review: Hearings.* 94th Cong., 2d sess., 1976.
———. Select Committee on Export Control. *Investigation and Study of the Administration, Operation, and Enforcement of the Export Control Act of 1949, and Related Acts: Hearings.* 87th Cong., 1st and 2d sess., 1961–62.
———. Select Committee on Foreign Aid. *Final Report on Foreign Aid.* H. Rpt. 1845. 80th Cong., 2d sess., 1948.
———. Congressional Research Service. *Crisis in the Atlantic Alliance: Origins and Implications.* Washington, D.C.: Government Printing Office, 1982.
———. Office of Technology Assessment. *Technology and East–West Trade: An Update.* 98th Cong., 1st sess., 1983.
———. *Technology and Soviet Energy Availability.* 97th Cong., 1st sess., 1981.
———. *Technology and East–West Trade.* 96th Cong., 1st sess., 1977.
U.S. Department of Commerce. Bureau of Foreign Commerce. Office of Export Control. *Quarterly Reports under the Export Control and Export Administration Acts.* Washington, D.C.: Government Printing Office, 1947–74.
U.S. Department of Defense. *Soviet Acquisition of Militarily Significant Western Technology: An Update.* Washington, D.C.: Government Printing Office, 1985.
———. *Soviet Acquisition of Western Technology.* Washington, D.C.: Government Printing Office, 1982.

_____. *An Analysis of Export Control of U.S. Technology: A DOD Perspective.* Report of the Defense Science Board Task Force, 1976.

U.S. Department of the Interior. Bureau of Mines. Division of Foreign Activities. *The Soviet Seven-Year Plan (1959–65) for Oil.* Washington, D.C.: Government Printing Office, 1960.

U.S. Department of State. *The Battle Act Reports, 1952–1973.* Washington, D.C.: Government Printing Office, 1952–73.

_____. "Report of the Special Committee on U.S. Trade with East European Countries and the Soviet Union [Miller Committee]." *Department of State Bulletin* 54 (May 30, 1966).

_____. *Foreign Relations of the United States, 1948–1951.* Washington, D.C.: Government Printing Office, 1974–85.

_____. *A Report on Recovery Progress and United States Aid.* Washington, D.C.: Government Printing Office, 1949.

U.S. East–West Foreign Trade Board. *Quarterly Reports on Trade between the United States and Non-Market Economy Countries to the President and the Congress.* Washington, D.C.: Government Printing Office, 1975–78.

U.S. International Trade Commission. *Quarterly Reports to the Congress and the East–West Foreign Trade Board on Trade between the United States and the Non-Market Economy Countries.* Washington, D.C.: Government Printing Office, 1975–85.

Vernon, Raymond. "The Fragile Foundations of East–West Trade." *Foreign Affairs* 57 (Summer 1979): 1035–51.

_____. "Apparatchiks and Entrepreneurs: U.S.–Soviet Economic Relations." *Foreign Affairs* 52 (January 1974): 249–62.

Viner, Jacob. "Power vs. Plenty as Objectives of Foreign Policy in the 17th and 18th Centuries." *World Politics* 1 (October 1948): 1–29.

Votaw, Dow. *The Six-Legged Dog.* Berkeley: University of California Press, 1964.

Wadekin, Karl-Eugen. "Soviet Agriculture's Dependence on the West." *Foreign Affairs* 60 (Spring 1982): 882–903.

Wallensteen, Peter. "Characteristics of Economic Sanctions." *Journal of Peace Research* 3 (1968): 248–67.

Weintraub, Sidney, ed. *Economic Coercion and U.S. Foreign Policy: Implications of Case Studies from the Johnson Administration.* Boulder, Colo.: Westview Press, 1982.

Yankelovich, Daniel, and John Doble. "The Public Mood." *Foreign Affairs* 63 (Fall 1984): 33–46.

Yergin, Daniel. *Shattered Peace: The Origins of the Cold War and the National Security State.* Boston: Houghton Mifflin, 1978.

MAJOR NEWSPAPER AND NEWS MAGAZINE SOURCES

Aviation Week and Space Technology
British Board of Trade Journal
Business Week
Christian Science Monitor
Congressional Quarterly Weekly Report
Current Digest of the Soviet Press

Economic Bulletin, German Institute for Economic Research
Economist
Financial Times of London
Geopolitics of Energy
Interflo: An East-West Trade News Monitor
Journal of Commerce
National Journal
Newsweek
New York Times
Oil and Gas Journal
Petroleum Press Service/Petroleum Economist
San Jose Mercury-News
Time
Times of London
Wall Street Journal
Washington Post
World Petroleum

ARCHIVES

Harry S Truman Presidential Library, Independence, Missouri
Dwight D. Eisenhower Presidential Library, Abilene, Kansas
John F. Kennedy Presidential Library, Boston, Massachusetts
Lyndon B. Johnson Presidential Library, Austin, Texas
Gerald R. Ford Presidential Library, Ann Arbor, Michigan
National Archives, Washington, D.C.
Declassified Documents Quarterly Catalog, published by Carrollton Press, Inc.,
    and available on microfiche, Olin Library, Cornell University, and Shields
    Library, University of California, Davis

Index

257

Library of Congress Cataloging-in-Publication Data

Jentleson, Bruce W., 1951–
    Pipeline politics.

    (Cornell studies in political economy)
    Bibliography: p.
    Includes index.
    1. Energy industries—Political aspects—Soviet Union. 2. Energy
industries—Political aspects—Europe. 3. Europe—Foreign relations—
Soviet Union. 4. Soviet Union—Foreign relations—Europe. 5. Europe—
Foreign relations—United States. 6. United States—Foreign relations—
Europe. I. Title. II. Series.
HD9502.S652J46   1986   382'.45621042'0947   86-47643
ISBN 0-8014-1923-9 (alk. paper)